Bordering intimacy

MANCHESTER
1824

Manchester University Press

THEORY FOR A GLOBAL AGE

Series Editor: Gurminder K. Bhambra, Professor of Postcolonial and Decolonial Studies in the School of Global Studies, University of Sussex

Globalization is widely viewed as a current condition of the world, but there is little engagement with how this changes the way we understand it. The Theory for a Global Age series addresses the impact of globalization on the social sciences and humanities. Each title will focus on a particular theoretical issue or topic of empirical controversy and debate, addressing theory in a more global and interconnected manner. With contributions from scholars across the globe, the series will explore different perspectives to examine globalization from a global viewpoint. True to its global character, the Theory for a Global Age series will be available for online access worldwide via Creative Commons licensing, aiming to stimulate wide debate within academia and beyond.

Bordering intimacy

Postcolonial governance and the policing of family

Joe Turner

Manchester University Press

Published by Manchester University Press
Oxford Road, Manchester M13 9PL
www.manchesteruniversitypress.co.uk

British Library Cataloguing-in-Publication Data is available

ISBN 978 1 5261 4696 0 hardback
ISBN 978 1 5261 4694 6 open access
ISBN 978 1 5261 6374 5 paperback

First published by Manchester University Press in hardback 2020

This edition published 2022

The publisher has no responsibility for the persistence or accuracy of URLs for any external
or third-party internet websites referred to in this book, and does not guarantee that any
content on such websites is, or will remain, accurate or appropriate.

Typeset by Toppan Best-set Premedia Limited

For William-Cem

Contents

Figures

Series editor's foreword

Recent years have seen borders and bordering practices gain ever-greater visibility and political purchase in a variety of locations across the globe. In *Bordering intimacy: Postcolonial governance and the policing of family*, Joe Turner powerfully examines how borders work to manage intimacy in the present. He explores how intimacy, manifest in particular ideas of the family, is constructed historically through the racial categories and processes of governance that were central to imperial and colonial formations. He does this through an exploration of ideas and practices of domestication and the deprivation of rights and of the creation of monsters and the contrast with notions of the good migrant. In particular, he suggests that ideas of family were not only used to create hierarchies of development, but that such notions were a key aspect in the processes by way of which colonised peoples were dispossessed and disinherited.

Whilst Turner's substantive focus is on Britain and the British Empire, his analysis has a much broader resonance in terms of setting out how the co-constitution of intimacy and borders has been a central feature, more generally, of modes of postcolonial governance. He traces the continuity to the present of colonial-era ideas of who is understood to be fully human or not-quite-human and therefore who has even the possibility of being able to belong. Turner expertly contextualises this in relation to the making and remaking of racialised violence in the periphery and its perpetuation in the metropole. In bringing together scholarship on coloniality, race, borders, intimacy and family, Turner extends the boundaries of the fields within which he works and marks a distinctive position for his arguments within them.

The Theory for a Global Age series, of which this book is a part, seeks to transform the standard understandings which shape our disciplines and academic fields by starting from other places. Turner brilliantly demonstrates how work that situates Britain itself as post-colonial, that recognises Britain's contemporary political landscape as configured by its historical colonial conditions, opens up new vistas and new questions which have the potential to startle us out of our complacent renditions and understandings. This book is a powerful recontextualisation of contemporary Britain as postcolonial Britain understood in terms of its discourses and practices around borders and bordering, intimacy and family, governance and domestication. In the process, it also provokes us to rethink our understandings of borders, of intimacy, of family and of governance. It is a superb, and timely, addition to the series.

Gurminder K. Bhambra
University of Sussex

Acknowledgements

I always like reading acknowledgements. Academic labour is too often individualised so it is good to be reminded of the collaborative character of knowledge production. Books so often have communal origins and the writing of them is shaped by complex intimacies. This one is no different.

The groundwork for this book began in 2015 and I would like to thank all of those who provided initial support and an intellectual environment where the idea could develop. Robbie Shilliam saw potential in the project from the start and for that I am grateful. The germination of this work was helped by two years of involvement in the Postcolonial Governmentality workshops organised by Terri-Anne Teo and Elisa Wynne-Hughes. Likewise, the creation of the Colonial, Decolonial and Postcolonial BISA working group by Meera Sabaratnam, Mustapha Pasha and Robbie (and continued by Lisa Tilley, Kerem Nisancioglu, Nivi Manchanda and Gargi Bhattacharya) provided a vital and inspiring intellectual space for the type of research which does not always fit in British politics departments. Books start with an idea (or in this case an encounter) but they are pursued through an orientation and drive. For me this was to recognise the importance of (and yet absence of) the colonial to my work and the reasons for that. For this I am indebted to Inanna Hamati-Ataya's questioning of Eurocentric positionality throughout my research.

During my time at the University of Sheffield I was lucky enough to find a group of supportive colleagues. Particular thanks go out to those involved in the International Politics Research Group, as well as to the IR and Decolonial reading group members for interesting discussions and solidarity. In our regular book club, I found colleagues who were willing not only to share ideas, read drafts and give constructive feedback but also to support the emotional labour of booking writing. To Joanna Tidy, Liam Stanley and Jonna Nyman – a big thank you!

Remember, it all starts with 'bodies and borders'. Numerous colleagues read drafts and sections of this book and for this I am indebted, particularly to Jonathan Joseph, Joanna Tidy, Lucy Mayblin, Amna Kaleem, Dan Bailey, Matt Wood, Luke de Noronha and Cemal Burak Tansel. Spike Peterson was a constant source of support and encouragement throughout the writing process and for this I am forever grateful.

Sections of this book were presented at several seminars, workshops and conferences – the University of Manchester, Universitat Pompeu Fabra, Barcelona, Queen Mary University of London, and BISA Brighton, ISA Toronto, ECPG Amsterdam – and I would like to thank all of the fellow panel members and organisers for their ideas and feedback.

I am so pleased that the book has a home in the wonderful Theory for a Global Age series. Gurminder Bhambra was an exemplary editor and the book's inclusion in the series feels particularly right given that so much of her research has inspired my own work. I would also like to thank Caroline Wintersgill and Alun Richards from Manchester University Press for their patience and support through the editing process and Joe Haining for his diligent copy-editing of the manuscript.

This book was only made possible by the hidden labour and support of my friends-family, in Sheffield, Manchester, Leeds, Toronto and Istanbul. Thank you for constantly reminding me of the often-narrow confines of academia. Unintentionally or not, many a late-night discussion concerning inequality, immigration, child care, colonialism (sometimes all at the same time) has shaped the course of this book. I also want to thank Jill Turner for her courage and commitment to creativity in both her life and work; to Matt and Caroline Turner for their constant emotional support and wisdom; Gülşen and Kemal Aridici, who constantly remind me of the sacrifice demanded to resist domination and to stand for something you believe in. This book would not have been finished without the love and support of Nuray. For her patience whilst I worked through difficult parts of the book with her and for her kindness and optimism that can clear the darkest of northern skies. Lastly, to Willie-Cem who would far rather I ran around with him outside than try and read him this book.

Introduction: bordering intimacy

This book began on an EasyJet flight. Or to be more specific, it began when my partner and I were stopped from getting on an EasyJet flight. In the early hours of the morning we had arrived at the airport to board a flight to Sicily for fieldwork and to attend a conference. As we queued to board the plane with our young son, the airline staff made a further inspection of my partner's visa documents and her recently acquired family migration visa and marriage certificate. Unsure of the rules that applied to non-EU citizens travelling with family members to the Schengen Area, the airline staff had to contact immigration advisers for their approval for us to fly. Since 2000, as so many of us have become accustomed to, airline carriers bear the responsibility for checking the documentation of anyone boarding a plane. And in doing so they enact the (inter)national border. Whilst the plane waited on the tarmac, it became increasingly clear that the airline staff were not going to risk allowing us to board before they had received an official response from their head office. Whilst having a legal right to travel with myself as an EU citizen to an EU country, my partner needed to confirm this right with the UK Permanent Resident card, which she had yet to acquire. 'You'll probably just be deported as soon as you land in Catania', was the response of the ground staff as they finally confirmed that the plane would leave without us.

As we watched the plane fly away, we ruminated on the inequality of border practices that made my partner constantly experience precarity, not only in terms of increasingly limited rights in the UK but also access to mobility as a non-EU national. Whilst many of our colleagues' access to the plane was seamless, barriers were raised for her, just as they were in everyday life in Britain. Years of legislative change have rendered the family route to settlement and rights into a precarious and uncertain process, with non-EU nationals finding themselves blocked from welfare support, subject to language, intimacy tests and high salary thresholds. This was merely another reminder of such precarity, brought into stark relief.

At the same time as we sat in the dour terminal building waiting to be formally led back 'across the UK border', our minds turned to other points of transit and (im)mobility that had recently been in the news. Throughout the summer of 2015, EU states and border agencies had intensified the policing of people fleeing war in the Middle East and structural inequality throughout much of Africa who found themselves contained in camps, forced behind barbed wire, left stranded at sea, managed through infrastructural blockings such as closing down railways, road checkpoints and of course air travel. Newspapers were still full of images of the scores of refugees drowned off the Sicilian coast where we were due to travel. Our situation was an administrative nightmare, a financial and professional inconvenience, stuck in a terminal for hours, unable to attend an academic conference. But it served as a further reminder that if some borders work to violently dismantle bodies, relations, kinships, others work through more mundane means of confinement. We would walk out of the airport with each other. My partner would continue to enact her limited rights to settlement under the guise of our romantic connection to each other, and in turn the privilege of my settled citizenship and whiteness. Others would not be afforded this right.

As we were led sternly by a member of the airline staff 'back through' the UK border (a border we had perhaps never crossed because we were never allowed to leave) the border agent again demanded to see our passports and visa documentation. Grumbling at this bizarre, Kafka-like process, the border agent angrily replied to us that 'this is what it takes if you want a secure border!' To which my partner replied: 'That assumes that we want a secure border.' More than the content of this exchange, what was significant was the intimate connections this opened up.

Walking away from the desk, the member of staff escorting us turned to my partner and began to discuss, initially in hushed tones, her own experience of 'borders'. Something, it seemed, connected her to the experience of being stopped from boarding the plane and being forced to prove formal status again and again. As a self-identified British Asian she quite candidly began describing the everyday racism she experienced as a member of the airline crew. Her experience of customer service was saturated with derogatory references to her skin colour by passengers, racist language, even incidents of spitting, claims that she was not 'properly British' and often vile forms of Islamophobia, even though she was not in fact a Muslim. She then went on to describe how, as a part of her job, she was forced to monitor and regulate who could board flights, turn people away, question people's identity documents. She was torn, she said, and it caused her great discomfort; whilst experiencing solidarity with those she was policing, the economic realities of her life made the job, and following the prescribed rules, a necessity.

The intimate policing of where my partner could move to/from – in administrative errors, barriers to flying and the threat of deportation – meets here with everyday structures of race/racism in the UK, which in turn connect with the globally orientated management of mobility. Untangling these connections, which initially were merely *felt* and *sensed*, and to document them in a more 'analytical' manner has inspired the trajectory of this book and the further research and questions it poses. On reflection, the airline staff member's orientation towards my partner's exclusion, and sense of solidarity with those she was forced to police, reveal, I propose, a series of connections that are at the heart of the way that government, and with that bordering, functions in postcolonial Britain.

We might consider in this encounter how borders worked to manage intimacy, just as dominant ideas of intimacy, linked to love and family, organised (im)mobility. Not being 'family' enough to travel was a source of exclusion and precarity. At the same time being 'family' enough to continue to live in the UK was also a source of limited rights and temporal settlement (especially read against the violence done to those seeking to cross into Europe from the Global South). We might suggest here that (not) looking familial (or looking familial for the state and related authorities) is a source of power but also abandonment (Povinelli 2011). Abandonment here relates to both the propensity for violence, social and biological death but also more cruddy and everyday acts of forgetting and neglect (in camps, detention centres, on boats lost in the Mediterranean). We are reminded here that the history of being excluded for not looking like, being recognised as, deemed a 'proper family' has multiple histories which relate to the intersections of gender, sexuality, class, but also race. Perhaps it is the power of race that brings these different acts of bordering together.

The airline staff member's experience of structural/everyday racism is a stark reminder that colonial ideas of who belongs or who is properly human are alive and well in Britain today. However, it should also remind us that race has never solely been about biological markers or skin colour. Colonial racism was equally arranged by characterising kinships, affective relations, intimacies as improper and 'undomesticated' (McClintock 1995). So, the weight of race flows through these border encounters, just as it charges and energises the policing of borders more widely. Borders, we are reminded here, are not merely document inspections in the airport space but are instead materialised long before in bureaucratic complexity, visa regimes, barriers to citizenship and infrastructural blockages, and are performed in the everyday racism and structural violence that the airline crew member was subjected to and was forced (through economic survival and labour market pressure) to enact. Bordering can be performed and policed by legal categories of the state, by international organisations and private companies, just as it is enacted in spit from the mouth of the racist.

In revealing a series of circulations that tie together questions of intimacy, family, race, empire, borders, this event opens up a series of questions that drive this book: what ties the policing of family at the border to the structures of race? What role does family play in the management of mobility? How might we understand the coming together of questions over family, bordering and race as part of broader patterns of government and the distribution of violence in liberal states such as Britain? The purpose of this book is to explore how intimacy, manifest in dominant and authorised forms of 'family', is inextricably bound with the racial categories and governance of empire. And in turn how empire and colonial power is continually expressed, relived and resuscitated in practices of borders/bordering in contemporary Britain.

What this book does

This book traces the role that intimacy and 'family' plays in the contemporary government of mobility; specifically, how borders function to control certain people and populations as part of the ongoing legacies of European (and more specifically British) empire. As the title of this book suggests, it explores how intimacy and borders relate to each other as a conduit for postcolonial governance – that is, how borders make intimacy but equally how intimacy makes borders and how this remains bound up with the remaking of racialised violence. This is what is meant by 'bordering intimacy'.

It is perhaps easier to consider how intimacy and family are made and policed through borders. For example, we can think about who is allowed to move across a state border or claim rights based on 'family' or 'dependency'. This concerns who is allowed to be intimate with whom and have this intimacy sanctioned, recognised and managed by the state. But this book also explores how dominant modes of intimacy *make* borders. This views intimacy and, more specifically, family as having political power. In light of this I explore how dominant modes of socio-sexual intimacy known as 'family' have been central to the organisation of personhood and violence in modernity, including questions of who can/cannot move.

European ideas of normative sexuality and domesticity (i.e. 'family') emerged within the ideologies and practices of colonial violence, accumulation and dispossession, of which policing mobility through bordering was a vital tool. The global management of mobility began as an imperial project, relying on racial demarcations between 'civilised' (European) and 'backwards' (colonised) peoples. Central to such racial demarcations were ideas about which populations were capable of 'proper family life' and which were bereft and perverse. This book examines how shifting normative claims to family continue to shape how states restrict mobility, settlement and citizenship through bordering today. Whilst postcolonial states such as Britain now pledge to be 'postracial', ideas of who does family properly, who is capable of 'real love' and 'real family life', arguably continue to structure racial demarcations around who can belong, who must be controlled, who can be excluded. This raises further questions as to why we view colonial rule as a thing of the past rather than a present.

Britain (and with it other European postmetropoles) is still rarely analysed as a postcolonial state. That label instead conjures up images of the Global South, as mapped out in development studies and international relations; spaces of 'illegitimate' and often 'authoritarian' violence, detached from the legitimacy, freedom and democracy which supposedly defines the Global North. Despite the healthy upsurge in postcolonial and decolonial theory in studies of international politics (Anievas *et al.* 2015; Agathangelou and Killian 2016; Sabaratnam 2017; Rutazibwa and Shilliam 2018; Howell and Richter-Montpetit 2019), there is still a hesitance in bringing these analyses to bear on questions of government in spaces like Britain (although see Virdee 2014; Kapoor 2018; Shilliam 2018; Innes 2019). Whilst there is much historical scholarship on the British Empire, far less is said about how postmetropoles were and *remain* a site for ongoing forms of colonial rule (Barder 2015; Stoler 2016; Davies and Isakjee 2018). And, most importantly, how populations, communities and subjects both within and moving to these states are subject to the workings of colonial power and racial governance today. This of course reflects the contradictory place of empire in the wider social landscape of postcolonial northern states such as Britain. Colonial amnesia is rife in public discourse. And yet, as events such as the EU referendum in Britain show, empire both continues to be a source of nostalgia and to shape political possibilities, imaginations and institutions (El-Enany 2016, 2017; Bhambra 2017a; Andrews 2018).

Despite a huge body of evidence demonstrating how the British state functions as the racial state par excellence (see Andrews and Palmer 2016; Institute of Race Relations 2018; Kapoor 2018), studies of international politics have still rarely ventured to trace and tease out these connections and tie them to more global histories of empire. That in 2018 the UK incarcerated more black men as a percentage of the population than the United States still raises little attention among international politics scholars (Elliot-Cooper 2016; Sturge 2018). Nor how the life chances of many, in terms of education, health, labour market access or immigration status are most powerfully stratified by race (Shilliam 2018; Danewid 2019). Nor how the UK continually polices racialised groups through counter-insurgency tactics born out of colonial war (Sabir 2017; Turner 2018).

Where race is studied in Britain it often remains disconnected from questions of intimacy, love or family. Putting these terms together still occasions blank stares. Despite an extensive body of postcolonial, decolonial and black feminist scholarship on family, sexuality and race (Spillers 1987; Roberts 1997, 2015; Ferguson 2003; Povinelli 2006; Lugones 2008; Sharpe 2010; Arvin *et al.* 2013; Scott 2013), such studies have made little impact on how government, rule and power is analysed. Burgeoning feminist and queer work on intimacy and geopolitics have provided nuanced and startling insights into how issues of the intimate and domestic relate to governmental power (Mountz and Hyndman 2006; Oswin and Olund 2010; Pain and Staeheli 2014; Peterson 2014a). And yet these studies still rarely connect with the continuity of empire (for an overview see Peterson 2017; although see also Burton 2009; Lowe 2015; Mendoza 2016). Equally, scholars of family, sexuality and race still have relatively little to say about borders (although see Agathangelou 2004; Luibhéid and Cantú 2005; Lewis 2014).

Perhaps more surprisingly, given the modern function of borders, empire, race and family remain just as underanalysed in migration studies. Despite claims throughout the 1990s that we were increasingly living in a 'borderless' world, late liberal capitalism has instead produced a proliferation of borders (Mezzadra and Neilson 2013). We now have a complex understanding of how mobility is policed and governed in northern states (Walters 2006; Tazzioli 2014; Vaughan-Williams 2015; Jones 2016) but studies still struggle to draw upon postcolonial, decolonial and critical race theory to understand such trajectories (although see Bhambra 2017b; Mayblin 2017; Moffette and Walters 2018; de Noronha 2019). Despite the fact that migration patterns are almost invariably embedded within imperial histories (materialised through kinship, labour patterns, wealth inequalities and linguistic ties), it is surprising how the study of migration and the governance of mobility and borders often overlook or downplay the role of empire, either as historical or contemporary experience (although see Lake and Reynolds 2008; Saucier and Woods 2014; Walia 2014; Danewid 2017). Prem Kumar Rajaram (2018: 627) argues instead that migration studies 'tends to study refugees and migrants as groups with no relation to the racial and class structures and hierarchies of the societies in which they reside. They are strangers, governed through "integration" policy and border management.' Against this trend, recent studies have begun to push a postcolonial analysis of race onto the agenda (Grosfoguel *et al.* 2015; Danewid 2017; Mayblin 2017; De Genova 2018; El- Tudor 2018; El-Enany 2020). As yet though, this work has rarely connected up with questions of intimacy, love or family.

An emergent body of work within migration studies and international politics has begun to explore the role of 'family migration' in wider patterns of control and bordering (Kilkey and Palenga-Möllenbeck 2016). The best of this work historicises and challenges how intimacy and family are defined and managed in northern immigration regimes (Bonjour and Hart 2013; D'Aoust 2014, 2018) by tracing the particular relationship between family and exclusion. Such studies have sought to understand how 'family unification' is policed (Bonjour and Block

2016; Carver 2016; Wray 2016), the relationship between family, love, heteronormativity and citizenship (White 2014; D'Aoust 2018), and the treatment of family in detention/deportation regimes (Martin 2011, 2012; Gupta 2014; Beattie 2016). This book deepens and broadens this work, and in doing so speaks to the enduring silence regarding post-colonial rule in modern Britain. It does this in three ways:

1) It traces how government in Britain remains bound to empire. Here Britain is not only treated as a postcolonial state but a space for the ongoing *remaking* and *reworking* of colonial rule. This provides an opportunity to recontextualise contemporary processes such as the control of mobility, the architecture of the hostile environment or security practices of the War on Terror as part of the fabric of colonial rule and imperial formations.

2) It provides an alternative account of the politics of love and family. By taking seriously the work of postcolonial, decolonial and black feminists, the role that 'family' played in the making of empire is revealed – that is, in the making and unmaking of personhood through race – *and* how this is continued into the present day.

3) It explores how borders/bordering provide a particular transit point for reworking colonial rule and regimes of the family. Here borders/bordering are treated as more than immigration policy (as they so often are in migration studies). It examines borders/bordering functions across numerous sites of government, from policing, welfare, education and housing to counter-terrorism (to name but a few).

Whilst there is fascinating work on coloniality, race, borders and family, these are almost always dealt with as discrete categories and processes. This book brings this work together by examining the circulations between borders and family, both historically and in the contemporary political landscape in Britain. This, I argue, opens up further insights into the international/global circulations of liberal empire and its relationship to violence.

Bordering intimacy

In stating that this book is about bordering intimacy and the policing of family, what I want to emphasise is the political work that intimacy and family do. What it produces and brings together and equally silences and excludes. As I have begun to tease out, I am not only interested in how family is *policed* but also how dominant claims to family and intimacy also *police*. In the example I started with, 'family' is shown to make rights and mobility possible; just as these possibilities are closed down through acts of bordering (i.e. not appearing familial enough to travel). This opens up vital questions about the historical contingency of *who* gets to be a family. Or, more precisely, who is accorded the social and political power that comes from being recognised as sharing 'real love' and being a 'real family' (D'Aoust 2018). Being recognised (legally and culturally) as a real family opens doors (and borders) and possibilities; just as not being a real family closes them. To add to this, 'family' can also work as a rationale for creating borders, that is to say in the name of protecting family and with this the familial nation and 'civilisation'. Just as borders make and unmake families (through deportation, containment or the offer of rights), claims to protect, sustain and foster real family also make borders appear possible, necessary and naturalised.

As feminist international politics scholars have long demonstrated, the power of family is not only enacted by states but also remakes states and (inter)national order (Enloe 1990; Peterson 1992, 1999; Stevens 1999; Parashar *et al.* 2018). States, lest we forget, constantly *make* families. Whilst this takes place within a wider historical and cultural milieu, states continue to relay the power to authorise and privilege certain affective relations over others, in the codification and performance of marriage law, inheritance rights, the organisation of private property and so forth (Yuval-Davis 1997; Cott 2000; Neti 2014). Nowhere is this more starkly revealed than in immigration and citizenship law and practice (Shah 2012). We might consider, for instance, how citizenship is often inherited through legal definitions of parentage, or 'earnt' through evidencing intimate and romantic relations as a partner or spouse.

Intimacy codified as 'family', regulated by the state, is bound up with more than the organisation of movement; it also structures access to resources, wealth, property and exposure to spectacular and cruddy forms of violence and abandonment.

But states, and, with this, the liberal order, also rely upon 'family' as a site of reproduction, bound as this often is to heteronormative futurism (Edelman 2004). The family is the site for the continuity of labour, the nation and imperial civilisation (until the mid-twentieth century this would have been explicitly referenced as 'race'). As the unit of biopolitical intervention par excellence, the family promises continuity of capitalist heteronormative order (Foucault 1991). So, whilst appeals to 'family values' show that 'family' holds symbolic power, it is also bound into the material regeneration of biological, economic and cultural resources. States do not just intervene in family but family energises and propels a broader heteronormative order and with it practices of borders/bordering.

Investigations into the politics of family have often centred on questions of gender and sexuality, justifiably as sites of oppression and social reproduction (Federici 2004; Enloe 2018). Despite powerful interventions (McClintock 1995; Collins 1998; Feder 2007; Thomas 2007; Puar 2008; Rifkin 2015) far less is still said of how family is also deeply racialised. This is why tracing the history of family, borders *and* empire together is of such importance. Despite the privileging of European and internal national histories of domesticity and family (McKeon 2005), imperial encounters and colonial experiments in creating hierarchies of humanity were central to the history of the family. Without comprehending the formative history of where ideas about family come from, and the role they had in European empire, we are unable to grapple with the contemporary work that appeals to family organise and produce (see Scott 2013). If 'family' continues to wield social and political power, who is left inside/outside this story matters.

'Family' has a distinctly colonial/imperial history. This is relevant to whether we are examining the role of family in European society or in the (previously) colonised world. The family was viewed throughout the nineteenth century as the site for the reproduction not only of the nation but also of the empire (Davin 1978). Whilst states are vital in relation to the power of family, love and domesticity, as I noted above, we must remember that European states emerged as colonial and imperial before becoming national states (Bhambra 2016). So, the role of the modern state in making family is always/already imperial in orientation (and only later national).

In light of this, we should consider how claims to family, and with it, heteronormativity, are always bound to the making and unmaking of people within what Roderick Ferguson (2003: 78) calls 'taxonomies of perversion'. Taxonomies of perversion were part of the spatial and temporal markers of empire. Imperial mapping of the world into spaces of civilisation and spaces of savagery was frequently premised on accounts and imaginaries of perversions from European ideals of family and domesticity (McClintock 1995; Ghosh 2006) – that is, consumptive domesticity, Christian marriage, heterosexuality and patriarchal gendered relations. Whilst this casts perversions of sexuality as a form of arrested development (Hoad 2000; Weber 2016), these distinctions were already racialised in terms of who could be properly human/modern and with it not-quite/non-human (Spillers 1987; Weheliye 2014). This was used in colonies to justify and shore up colonial dispossession, violence and subjugation (Trexler 1995). But it was also networked into metropoles with regard to who was identified as civilised and how people were incorporated into capitalist political economy. In light of this, family must be understood to play a vital role in claims to modernity and with it the capitalist heteropatriarchy central to the spread of empire (Wynter 2003; Quijano 2007). These are not histories that are behind us; they are instead alive in the fabric of how family functions today.

Family and government

To speak of family in relation to race-making, empire and borders, as I do here, is to demonstrate that such an analysis goes beyond the production of *symbolic* hierarchies. It is about material processes and social organisation. In saying that intimacy and family *make*, I explore how claims to family were central to the ideology of empire and *practices* of colonial rule, of which I suggest borders and bordering are one important dimension. Claims to European domesticity and the bourgeois home not only placed people in a hierarchy of cultural inferiority, but this was also central to how they were governed, for example as bereft of humanity proper, as primed for labour, or conducive to genocide or slavery, as subjects of pacification and domestication. To Rifkin (2015: 11):

> Populations are racialised through their insertion into a political economy shaped around a foundational distinction between public and private sphere, with the latter defined by a naturalised, nuclear ideal against which other modes of sociality appear as lack/aberrance.

It is not just that 'difference' was constituted through measuring people's 'progress' towards European modernity/domesticity but that who was viewed as with/without family structured both the rationale and practice of dispossession and violence. 'Family' was not just an ideology of empire, it was part of the raw materials through which people were governed. And with this, how mobility was governed. It became an anthropological, sociological and governmental category for discovering, including/ assimilating and expunging different forms of intimacy and sociality which were different to the emerging European family (Amadiume 1987; Thomas 2007).

The point I make in this book is that we need to situate contemporary borders/bordering with these histories. Because, despite widespread forgetting and ignorance to the contrary, the management of mobility is shaped by these colonial histories of the family and empire. Borders/ bordering play an active part in the push to contain, manage, expel and include/exclude people through modern citizenship. This is not separate from but historically conditioned by empire (including categories and laws of citizenship itself). Not only do the structures of imperialism underpin how and why people move to postmetropoles like Britain, but the practices that border people and work to exclude them are directly related to the management of populations across European empires. This is not just about keeping certain people 'out' of places like Britain but also how the wish to exclude through colonial racism is also linked to internal forms of control.

To sum this up we might say that the role that family played in making empire is retold in border practices today. This is a broader point than merely suggesting that those who move for 'family life' are discriminated against. I go further than only looking at how people categorised as 'family migrants' are racialised and treated in places like Britain. Instead I examine how the imperial control of mobility was in part reliant upon different claims to protect or harness the family and that this structured the modern regulation of mobility. Further to this, I show how family does wider work in border regimes and in ongoing forms of internal colonisation in postmetropoles like Britain. External colonialism (in colonies) was always attached to internal colonialism (within the metropole) and this relationship intensifies through the practice of borders/bordering today.

To recognise the continuity and changes in the way colonial and imperial constructions of family work in contemporary government, Povinelli (2006) argues that whilst liberal claims to humanity often rely on the idea that 'love is universal', such apparently neutral claims remain bound to claims of superior civilisation and empire. Whether propelled through Hollywood romance or the legal apparatus of the state, 'liberal adult love depends on instantiating its opposite, a particular kind of illiberal, tribal, customary and ancestral love' (Povinelli 2006: 226). Properly romantic love is bound to white hetero- (and increasingly homo)normative coupledom, against which other intimacy and relations are viewed as (relatively) perverse.

Immigration law relies on sanctioning who can move on the basis of 'family life', just as citizenship law demarcates who can inherit property and rights through kinship. This has led to detailed practices of border officials attempting to document, evidence and decipher who can claim to be properly 'in love' – just as immigration law is a site for struggle over who is deemed properly familial – for example in the writing out and exclusion of polygamy from immigration law, or the writing in of same-sex marriage (D'Aoust 2018). We can trace the colonial orientation of questions of family in the way that ideas of 'sham' and forced marriage dominate debates surrounding family unification in the UK. Or how the Home Office's Operation Equal disrupts wedding ceremonies involving foreign nationals on the basis that the marriage may be one of 'convenience'. Appeals to the cultural neutrality of love work to constantly resurrect the unmarked colonial history of the European family and domesticity.

To consider the durability of colonial rule, it is useful to consider Stoler's (2016) approach to duress. Imperial and colonial rule does not so much continue from formal empire but is readapted and repurposed. To speak of duress then is to consider reinscriptions, modified displacements and amplified recuperations of colonial rule (Stoler 2016: 27). However, colonial duress is about more than immigration law. As this book contends, border/bordering practices and the regulation of movement around intimacy and family is found in more than just immigration law, and in the policing of people with migrant status. Immigration policy provides just one tool that connects up with a myriad of other practices which attempt to confine, contain, expel and domesticate racialised movement. This is why I distinguish between the concepts of 'bordering' and 'the border'.

Throughout the book, I trace out how 'family' works as an ideological rationale and site of intervention that circulates through numerous areas of government – social work, counter-terrorism, citizenship policy, policing – for example in the joining up of the UK counter-terrorism strategy, Prevent, with social work and the policing of 'failed' Muslim families; or in the way that criminals prosecuted for grooming have been deprived of their citizenship; or in how ideas of childhood structure who is allowed to be a 'real' refugee. It is this broader form of racialised governance that I refer to as 'bordering'. In showing how these sites are forms of bordering, I connect the treatment of people moving as migrants to that of settled black and South Asian communities within Britain who are frequently policed as 'internal colonies' (Turner 2018). The emphasis here is on the interconnection between the racialised governance and bordering of both 'migrants' and 'citizens'. But at the same time, there is a need to be sensitive to specific immigration practices that are focused on creating hierarchies of mobility and rights through sovereign power. Thus, when I speak of 'borders', I refer to practices which have a specific connection to immigration policy – that is, the sovereign law of a particular state with regard to migration, settlement and citizenship. When I speak of 'bordering', I refer to the broader process through which people are made 'out of place' (Ahmed 2000). This speaks to how bordering was/is constitutive of the broader push to manage populations through colonisation and the shifting dynamics of imperial/racialised capitalism, which borders play one distinct part in.

Violence and normalisation

In exploring the connection between borders/bordering and family, I am interested in how they are bound to the distribution of violence – that is, biophysical force and harm, as well more cruddy and everyday forms of structural inequality and abandonment (Povinelli 2011; Sharpe 2016). In the example I began with, my partner appeared to briefly lose her right to be counted as familial, or familial enough to travel, and this points at the wider issues of this book – how dominant notions of who is family/who is not sustains certain bodies and relationships as more or less perverse and more or less human. Whilst the dominant appeal to family is of warmth, closeness and familiarity, we also need to turn some of these affective, common-sense attachments on their head. The ongoing power of heteronormativity furnishes particular bodies and affective relations but it also excludes others who are deemed not only unfamilial but in turn unworthy/without value. This is more than organising who can *feel at home*, or who can *belong* (although this might be important). What I am interested here is how being familial – that is, with or without value – organises violence. Or, more specifically, how it energises, targets and normalises the violence of borders.

Take, for example, the dominant construction of the 'refugee crisis' in Europe which reached a peak in the summers of 2015 and 2016. A common-sense refrain to justify the exclusion of refugees has been a focus on single men on the move. These men, we are told, are not 'real refugees' and neither are they real men. During the UK's 2016 referendum on EU membership, one of the dominant images of the 'Leave' campaign was Nigel Farage (at the time leader of the far-right anti-immigration party UKIP, and subsequently leader of the Brexit Party) standing in front of a poster of predominantly male asylum seekers walking through Slovenia. The words 'breaking point', plastered over the image, further revealed the threat of race instilled in this moment. When asked in 2018 if he regretted the use of such imagery, Farage questioned where 'all the women and children' were in the picture. To Farage, these were just men: 'Where were the old people?' he remonstrated. 'Where were the disabled people? *These were not refugees in any classic sense*' (BBC 2018a, my emphasis). The unmarked appeal to family here does vital political work to dismantle and make the (inter)national rights of refuge/ asylum. We learn that 'real refugees' are not single brown men. Real refugees are 'victims' and 'families' (and, we assume here, whiter, heterosexual families). Single brown men are 'migrants', calculating economic migrants. If they were real refugees and real men, as the refrain goes, why did they not stay and fight in Syria, or Eritrea, or Libya (see Elshtain 1987)? For 'stay and fight', read protect their women folk, motherland and children as a real father would. Here the 'unreal' refugee/migrant is first presented as devoid of family – as a 'failed father' – and then presented as a racialised-sexualised threat to Europe (the danger of the single, male migrant).

This only makes sense once we are able to excavate how colonised populations were already posed as being unable to do family properly, and how family was tied to claims of modernity, humanness and civilisation. Moments such as this replay key imaginaries of empire, such as the threat of the 'black peril' (McCulloch 2000), the hypersexuality of the Orient (Said 1978) and the need to protect and foster the white family at all costs from savage hordes. Such demarcations and imaginaries are of central importance because they organise not just the abandonment of bodies and people (to camps, indefinite waiting, deportation or death) but normalise and hide the function of race through an appeal to family values.

In light of this, this book is engaged in both examining how borders and claims to family are brought together to violently exclude, but also investigating the work that family does to normalise and build the conditions of this violence – that is, to (re)produce sensibilities and orientations through which empire is both remade and hidden from view. We should remember, as I stated above, that love and family *make*. They were central to the building of empire and with it connected to acquisition of territories, dispossession, accumulation, the regulation of mobility, processes of civilisation and domestication. Equally, they continue to make today in ongoing distributions of violence and government in Britain and beyond. Here this making must be understood in terms of how borders work to delimit, refuse, expel and exclude people as unfamilial, but also how appeals to protect 'proper family' (often heteronormative and white) energise and rationalise borders both within and beyond the state. As feminists have long demonstrated, appeals to family are so powerful because they are *naturalised* and deemed 'outside of politics', this is why it is so vital to challenge and monitor the political work that claims to family enact.

Whilst one of the central claims I make is that family makes borders (and vice versa), family can also work as a site of powerful contestation and struggle. Because it has social and political power, claims to protect family can be used to make rights claims, to contest imperial repression and dehumanising violence (for 'home' and resistance see hooks 1999; Beckles-Raymond 2019; and also Turner 2016). In such struggles, a claim to family may rehumanise subjects by appealing to the dominant frame that 'family matters'. An example of this might be campaigns to stop the incarceration of irregularised migrant families and in particular children in British detention centres such as Yarl's Wood, or the separation of families through deportation regimes in Europe and North America. Appeals that families should not suffer can often work to contest (however momentarily) the racialised practices of detention, deportation and exclusion. On the one hand, we need to stay attuned to how appeals to family can be unruly and work to contest violence; on the other, we also need to investigate the limits of this type of contestation. At what and at whose expense does the protection and inclusion of some as 'family' come?

It may be the case that the 'inclusion' of subjects or the extension of rights through appeals to family work to 'reify the contours of legitimacy' (Puar 2008: 126) of existing practices of exclusion and violence, such as citizenship and the colonial-racial state. But struggles might also leave traces and possibilities of more radical alternatives and less racially charged, colonial and heteropatriarchal capitalist futures. Throughout this book I try to demonstrate what a colonial reading of 'family' does to reveal the limits of such contestation, whilst recognising the way in which intimacies, dependencies and kinships sustain communities and often give rise to practices of survival within colonial rule (see, for example, hooks 1999, 2008; Rifkin 2015).

Researching bordering intimacy

In exploring both the continuity and reworking of imperial sensibilities and colonial practices of rule into contemporary Britain, this book is dedicated to a particular approach to history. This is in many ways a 'history of the present' (Foucault 1984). I am interested in tracing where ideas, knowledges, practices, discourses and structures that shape the present emerged from and how their orientation and function may change or stay relatively continuous. For example, how knowledge of 'family' was produced by elites, from anthropologists to colonial administrators in the nineteenth century and how this (dis)connects with ideas of the family today, such as in border agents' monitoring of family visas, or the monitoring and safeguarding practices of social workers. This is broadly about how certain ways of doing, thinking and being became entrenched within modes of power and rendered *normal* (Walters 2012: 120; on colonial archives see Arondekar 2005). One way of exploring such a history is through law, and the way the law builds and collapses subjectivities, relations and bodies across time and space (Dayan 2011). An example of this is examining how colonial ordinances and acts of parliaments circulate across imperial space and how the law today builds and resurrects this architecture. Such an approach underpins much of the archival work in this book.

This is not solely a history of knowledge but also of practice. I trace where practices (which can also be legal practice) emerged from and what this tells us. For instance, in examining the history of borders/ bordering, I look at both the historical context through which the regulation of movement emerged (as a logic of government) but also where the specific practices that are used to govern people today – such as photo IDs, deportation and port inspections – came from (Ballantyne and Burton 2009). This reveals important material histories which in turn help us understand the orientation and functions of these practices today. It matters that we can trace the history of the passport and photo surveillance to the containment and ownership of slaves or the policing of indentured labourers (Browne 2015). This connects with how the exclusion of certain bodies and not others is organised through these practices today.

Revealing both the will to govern and the practices used to govern teases out in detail the shaping of modernity through colonialism in ways that are not always adequately addressed by work that focuses solely on issues of representation. Tracing where representative practices regarding race, gender, sexuality, class came from is of vital importance. These practices include orientalist imaginaries and inferior representation of body, mind, culture and so on (such as I sketched out above with regard to male asylum seekers). But I also want to supplement these histories by showing how tools, strategies and practices of rule and law emerged under imperial and colonial governance and how they are reused and resuscitated in Britain today, for example in the deprivation of citizenship or the use of marriage law to ratify legitimacy.

The analytical approach that I take throughout this book is equally indebted to feminist historiography (Stoler 2002, 2006) and feminist and queer geopolitical approaches to intimacy (Gopinath 2005; Lowe

2015; Pain 2015; Peterson 2017). There is an obvious connection to the intimate that runs through these pages: that intimacy and with that love, family, proximities and the innermost are always sites for the (re)production of power, and for the control and management of order. This follows from the most searing challenge of feminists to acknowledge that the personal is political.

Whilst this work is inspired by key debates in feminist and queer approaches to intimacy and family (Barrett and McIntosh 1991; Bell and Binnie 2000; Peterson 2014a), I put this into conversation with postcolonial and black feminists such as Elizabeth Povinelli, Christina Sharpe and Hortense Spillers, as well as scholars working in international politics on questions of international order and violence (Kaplan 2005; Owens 2015). Bringing this work together means better understanding the role of family with regard to the reproduction of government and the liberal international order (i.e. the intimate, the biopolitical and the geopolitical), and the very colonial and imperial and racialised roots of this role.

Drawing inspiration from Lisa Lowe (2015), I treat intimacy as an approach to historical and contemporary enquiry. Intimacy can work as a method that helps to collapse commonsensical approaches to space and time. Intimacy can help us explore and think in terms of circulations, for example the circulations of ways of doing, thinking, logics and rationalities that bind seemingly disparate and distant places, bodies and practices together. Intimate connections can make the past appear into the present. Thinking through the intimate in terms of time also helps us make geographical connections, from the globally distant to the proximate (Lowe 2015: 18). This helps us to recognise how processes such as slavery in the Caribbean, or the organisation of indentured labour in Tamil Nadu or South Africa, were not somehow separate but integrally bound to social, economic and domestic life in Britain and other spaces of the Empire. Intimate markers and connections remain – they remain in relations, ruins, and in structural connections, economies and modes of thought (Stoler 2016). These remains are important because they challenge the liberal push to divide time and history into the nation state (Lowe 2015: 19; also see Ballantyne and Burton 2009). Equally, by following the circulations of ideas, logics and practices, we are able to explore connections that work across areas of government – welfare, policing, counter-terrorism, immigration – that share familiar characteristics and would otherwise be obscured.

One element of using intimacies is connecting what are often termed 'macro' processes of state formation, colonialism and geopolitics with processes of the everyday and the mundane (Legg 2010; Guillaume 2011; Smith 2012). Once we start exploring the joining up of processes and exploring what is connected up in the meeting of family and borders, we can explore the different social and political sites in which power is reproduced. Here I am interested in examining how seemingly disparate processes, such as popular culture, exhibitions, images, narratives, novels and emotions, work to reform and energise dominant ideas about family, race, borders, and thus play a powerful role in mobilising and normalising forms of rule, practices of the state and legal apparatus. Thinking in this joined-up, circulatory way is useful for exploring where borders go and what they do, as well as how 'family' emerges to condition and propel these forms of rule. For instance, I examine how photography exhibitions connect to the global/humanitarian response to mobility, or how drone strikes in Syria connect to the criminals tried for child sexual exploitation offences in Rotherham, how popular 'confessional' novels are linked to white nationalist appeals to protect the 'real' white family, or how the policing of sham marriage connects to the UK counter-terrorism strategy Prevent. This matters, because studying law, policy and institutional arrangements only gets us so far. We miss out on the broader cultural landscape in which these processes operate and certain ways of doing and thinking become normalised and connected. Equally, only studying the everyday, representational or mundane fails to show how rule operates with regard to the apparatus of states and global/international order. We thus need both. Thinking through intimacy and circulations gives us that.

Amidst these broad methodological commitments within each chapter I also develop and draw upon different research methods. Whilst archival

research of the sort I explored above underpins this work, this is supplemented with discourse analysis, intertextual reading of documents,
institutional analysis, visual analysis, ethnography and interviews. The
use of a range of methods is propelled by a desire to trace the multitude
of sites through which government occurs and with that the way that
ongoing modes of colonial violence are accepted and distributed. Rather
than spending time justifying and explaining the methods used in the
main text, I have offered endnotes, where relevant, to expand in more
detail on how the evidence was gathered and analysed.

Book structure

In order to take up this task, this book is arranged into two parts. The
first explores in more detail the conceptual and historical trajectories
that bring family and borders together through empire. The second
examines the relationship between family and borders in contemporary
Britain and with this, the duress of colonial rule. I first set out the
mutually entangled history of family and borders under formal empire
(chapters 1 and 2) before examining how different borders/bordering
operate in the UK. The second part of the book is organised around
tracing three different forms of borders/bordering and their colonial
orientations, what I call 'intimate borders' (chapter 3); 'sticky borders'
(chapters 4 and 5); and 'visual borders' (chapter 6). The final chapter
(chapter 7) examines strategies and forms of resistance that have worked
to contest colonial bordering, in social movements but also in creative
activist projects.

Chapter 1, 'Domestication', further asks how we can understand the
relationship between family, borders and empire. I argue that turning
towards an analysis of domestication helps us understand how 'family'
is situated in relation to state formation, the organisation of violence
and the control of movement. Whilst the modern state has always been
orientated towards domestication (pacification and producing [dis]
order), this has always been a colonial and imperial project. It has a

colonial/global rather than national history. Domestication here relates
to the order of the domus – the household, home and family – just as
it relates to the means of dominating the unruly and the uncivilised
(McClintock 1995; Owens 2015).

To fully flesh out my approach to domestication and its colonial/
imperial orientation, I turn to an analysis of the figure of Bertha Mason in
Charlotte Bronte's *Jane Eyre* (Amadiume 1846). This nineteenth-century
novel provides a rich site to both study the material traces of Victorian
Empire and to theorise the role of family and borders. I do this by
examining the treatment of Bertha, who is confined within the attic of
Mr Rochester's English manor house. I ask how might we understand
Bertha to be domesticated. Through drawing together a literature on
government, domesticity and coloniality, I show how she is 'bordered'
within the attic (and later abandoned to die) because she is both bereft
of and a threat to 'proper family'. Here I develop a clearer connection to
the work of postcolonial, decolonial and black feminists and the role that
family had in empire-making (Amadiume 1987; Spillers 1987; Povinelli
2006; Lugones 2008). I propose that we should understand the role that
family has in terms of organising *development, dispossession* and *control*.

Drawing upon the theory of domestication I outline in the first chapter,
chapter 2, 'Making love, making empire', takes up a history of family and
borders across the British Empire from the early nineteenth century. It
traces how family was central to the development, dispossession and
control of colonised populations. This chapter shows that whilst family
was fostered and promoted for the coloniser, the destruction of kinships
through territorial acquisition, imposition of labour markets and colonial
war was constantly justified because non-European/colonised people
were deemed 'undomesticated'. In contributing to a history of borders/
bordering, this shows how nascent practices of borders/bordering formed
around the management of undomesticated movement – that which either
ran counter to the expansion of the state, emergent imperial capitalism or
the racialised-sexualised order of the colonial administration. Here we can
understand how family connected up with the management of mobility.
Notions of family could rationalise containment and sedentarism, just

as practices of expulsion and restriction were justified on the basis of the threat of interracial intimacies and the dangers to (white) family life. In this chapter, I begin to demonstrate that what we have come to know as immigration policy/law was experimented with in the control of movement across imperial space (particularly in settler colonies), before being entrenched in the metropole from 1905. I then show how immigration law worked to arrange intimacies of those moving to Britain around different taxonomies of family/perversion throughout the mid-to-late twentieth century.

After teasing out the conceptual framework the book rests upon in chapter 1 and the more traditional historical background in chapter 2, chapter 3, titled 'Shams', evidences how colonial logics and hierarchies are adapted and resuscitated in the present. It analyses the discourse of 'sham marriage' in the UK as a site of colonial duress. Sham marriage became an increasingly prominent issue in immigration policy throughout the 2000s, with elites and immigration 'experts' attempting to limit the number of people able to claim a right to settle in the UK as a 'family member'. This chapter first traces the racialised-sexualised coordinates of debates around sham marriage, debates which I show mirror discussions about the evolutionary hierarchy of marriage and family forms under the British Empire (who could be family/who was perverse). I thus ask: what is it to be a 'sham'? And what does the sham *do*? In the UK what has driven family migration restrictions has been a dual anxiety surrounding marriages of 'convenience' (i.e. for the benefit of immigration status) with concerns about deviant kinship practices such as polygamy, forced marriage and so-called honour killings, which are predominantly tied to Muslim communities.

I show how debates around shams link up with the wider history of bordering across empire, which I call 'intimate borders'. What has propelled this 'intimate bordering' has been a particular figuration of the 'unintegrated woman'. Intimate bordering tries to capture and govern the unintegrated woman, who is both at risk and risky. The last part of the chapter investigates how concerns about shams (sham marriages, intimacies or families) have increasingly been cast as both a national and civilisational threat by their inclusion in counter-terrorism strategies prompted by the War on Terror. Since 2010, Muslim families have been increasingly subject to intimate bordering through the UK Prevent strategy, such as in the intervention of social workers into 'radicalised homes'. What this tells us is that imperial and colonial categories of 'modern' or 'backwards' forms of family life are reinscribed into the present day through often mundane practices of government – from family migration visas and integration strategies, to safeguarding in social work.

Following on from this, chapters 4 and 5 focus on how claims to protect 'real family' can create borders and in doing so rationalise and justify certain types of violence. In chapter 4, 'Monsters', I examine the commitment made by the Home Office in 2016 to deprive of their citizenship subjects convicted of 'street grooming'. Deprivation of citizenship has increased in use since 2002 and intensified from 2010, often targeting 'suspected terrorists'. In this chapter I use the threat of deprivation to explore how borders 'stick' to certain bodies and populations (and not others). Borders appear to stick to some people even when they have settled/formal rights of citizenship. The effect of this is turning 'citizens' into 'migrants' who can be deported and killed with impunity. I explore what conditioned the move to deprive criminals of their citizenship and explore how street grooming has been made into a particular type of monstrous act. The chapter traces how the monstrousness of this crime relates to the way this violence was posed as a racialised-sexualised threat against 'white girls' by 'Asian men'. If chapter 3 examined the figure of the at risk/risky unintegrated woman, chapter 4 examines the politics of the deviant/hypersexualised black or Asian man. This familiar colonial figure animates numerous sticky bordering practices in the UK, from deprivation of citizenship, to the assassinations of 'terrorists' at the end of RAF drones, to the policing of gangs. I argue that in promising to violently deprive 'grooming' criminals of their citizenship, the British state is partaking in a white nationalist fantasy to secure and protect the 'real' (white) family against all odds. Borders do not just intervene in the intimacies of populations. Claims to protect, sustain and foster family also work to energise and animate borders.

Chapter 5, titled 'Deprivation', continues the discussion of sticky borders by examining what acts of deprivation tell us about postcolonial citizenship in places like Britain. The push by the British state to expand the terms of deprivation and denaturalisation has the effect of making large numbers of British citizens deportable. It makes populations who had settled rights subject to authoritarian immigration laws which target migrants. Whilst use of authoritarian security practices like deprivation of citizenship, detention and deportation has increased during the War on Terror and through anti-Muslim racism, I demonstrate in this chapter how deprivation must be understood as formative of modern citizenship crafted under empire. Deprivation of rights today is bound to the deprivation of personhood that structured imperial and colonial rule (organising people into racial categories of human/not-quite/non-human). Rather than an aberration of citizenship, sticky borders instead reveal the (im)possibility of citizenship after empire.

In chapter 6, 'The good migrant', I ask who can be 'included' in contemporary Britain. Or, more specifically, what the 'good' or domesticated migrant might look like. I argue that examining who can be imagined/imaged to be 'included' tells us about how exclusion is both organised and normalised. To do this, I first explore how visuals (looking, imaging, being seen) are central to borders/bordering. This means investigating the technical history of how visuals, and with this photography, have played a role in colonial government. It also means investigating the cultural history of who looks 'out of place' and who belongs – in other words, who looks like a 'real' refugee, a 'real' victim, a 'real' family, and so on. This history, I show, is bound up with photographic techniques such as the family portrait, something which is increasingly relied upon into border practices today (i.e. in visa regimes, cataloguing/judging settlement and right claims). So, if borders are intimate, and if they are sticky, we learn they are also visual.

In order to answer what the contemporary 'good' migrant looks like, I explore how humanitarian approaches to the 'refugee crisis' in Europe have sought to photograph migrants in order to 'humanise' them. I focus on an exhibition in Sheffield, England, called *Arrivals: Making Sheffield Home* as one example of such a liberal, inclusive strategy. Whilst different from more explicitly colonial ways of seeing migrants (as swarms, hordes, dangers, perverse) there are limits to this promise to 'include'. Not only do humanitarian and progressive nationalist promises to humanise migrants forget colonial/imperial histories, they equally risk forgetting day-to-day border violence through a celebration of progressive or tolerant 'whiteness'. This equally works to eviscerate and forget those that do not fit in and who can be violently excluded. Whilst appearing to be a family (heteronormative, domesticated) ameliorates migrants' troubling differences within this politics, migrants ultimately remain compared to the 'good' white host who is praised for welcoming and 'saving' them.

Chapter 7, 'Looking back', follows on from the discussion that concludes chapter 6 by exploring other ways of looking back and contesting borders. This poses the question: if humanitarianism and 'compassionate nationalism' can be co-opted and fail to challenge colonial power, then what other orientations, imaginaries and struggles can we turn to? Whilst the previous five chapters examine the duress of colonial rule in Britain, this chapter turns to practices of contestation and resistance. It draws from bell hooks's (1992) provocation that an oppositional gaze was always a central strategy against racist subjugation historically and continues today, even in the face of insurmountable violence. Whilst focused primarily on visual practices, this offers reflections on how various struggles contest the colonial politics of mobility, family, borders more broadly and how we can think this relationship differently. I offer three different ways of looking back: resistance, escape and decolonial aesthesis. Whilst all offer powerful challenges, I argue that decolonial aesthesis, linked to a broader decolonial politics, offers lessons for how we might think family and love otherwise than with empire.

In the short conclusion I reflect on the main conclusions that I draw across these chapters and explore why such a study is important. I then offer a few provocations on the absences and silences that echo through the book.

1

Domestication

Bertha Mason is mad, and she came of a mad family; – idiots and maniacs through three generations! Her mother, the Creole, was both a mad woman and a drunkard!...

He lifted the hangings from the wall, uncovering the second door: this, too, he opened. In a room without a window, there burnt a fire guarded by a high and strong fender, and a lamp suspended from the ceiling by a chain. ... In the deep shade, at the farther end of the room, a figure ran backwards and forwards. What it was, whether beast or human being, one could not, at first sight, tell: it grovelled, seemingly, on all fours; it snatched and growled like some strange wild animal: but it was covered with clothing, and a quantity of dark, grizzled hair, wild as a mane, hid its head and face.

> (Charlotte Bronte's initial introduction and description
> of Bertha Mason, *Jane Eyre*, 1847: 246–247)

Fearful and ghastly to me ... It was a discoloured face – it was a savage face. I wish I could forget the roll of red eyes and the fearful blackened inflation of lineaments.

> (Jane Eyre vocalising her encounter with Bertha Mason,
> Charlotte Bronte, *Jane Eyre*, 1847: 247)

The above event, and the narrative of Charlotte Bronte's *Jane Eyre* more broadly, provides a compelling theorisation of familial domesticity and the regulation of mobility under the British Empire. Bertha Mason, the subject of the above passage, is presented as the first 'creole' wife of Mr Rochester, one of the central protagonists in the novel. Her incarceration in the attic of Rochester's house remains a powerful example of the nature of racialisation and control in Victorian England. This chapter uses the figure of Bertha and her treatment as a way of conceptualising and problematising the relationship between family, borders and empire and its continuity into the present day. Not only is Bertha subject to colonial racism, as we see in the above passage, but her dehumanisation also reveals the complex spatialisation of empire and networking of imperial power through sites of the intimate and the familial. Throughout this chapter, I move to tease out and explore these links.

In Bronte's novel we are told that Bertha was 'brought' to Rochester's English manor house after being wed. Being an heiress of a plantation in Jamaica she is described as a 'creole', or of 'mixed blood'. In Jamaica, Bertha was part of a section of the middle class fostered by the British as a barrier between former black, enslaved and indentured communities and white settler colonialists. Whilst her racialisation in Jamaica was more ambiguous and relatively privileged, on her arrival in England it is revealed that she harbours a madness within her which is presented in terms of the animalism of blackness and oversexuality. We are told by Bronte that such madness is 'inherited' through the mixing of blood, and the degeneracy of the colonial family ('idiots and maniacs over three generations!' declares Rochester). Bertha is subsequently imprisoned in the attic and hidden away from local society, remaining both a living and active danger. We are told, for example, that she has the capacity for extraordinary violence. The novel's ending is conditioned by Bertha's death when she burns down Rochester's manor house, an episode which also leads to the blinding of Rochester. As a parable of intimate social relations, the story ends with the white, empowered protagonist Jane Eyre marrying Rochester as an act of choice and thus 'proper' love. Rochester slowly recovers his sight through Jane's intimate labour, love and care as his 'real' wife.

Through this chapter, I examine, perhaps counterintuitively, what the treatment of Bertha reveals about colonial rule, family and the management of mobility. I explore what Bertha can tell us about the duress of colonial rule, which I consider to relate to the domesticating power of the modern state. I thus set out how family – as the dominant mode of European socio-sexual intimacy – played a role in race-making across European empire. I also examine the role that borders had in taming, domesticating and managing populations deemed familial and non-familial. Just as importantly, I stress how this is reworked into contemporary immigration practices and forms of government in postcolonial states such as Britain.

As many commentators have argued, *Jane Eyre* reveals, quite dramatically, the dual silencing and significance of race to both modern literature and the socio-economic relations of (Victorian) England. It is clear from the above quote that Bertha is represented through multiple accounts of imperial racism – animalism, madness, sensuality – for instance how she is described as grovelling 'on all fours … like some strange wild animal'. She is presented as dangerous, untamed (McKee 2009). Against, this construction, Jane Eyre is presented as the embodiment of the rising bourgeoisie and proto-feminism, shrouded as this is in unmarked whiteness (Gilbert and Gubar 2000). This provides a powerful demonstration of how race underpinned the formation of 'modern' freedoms, individualism and reason through empire. However, whilst the racialisation of Bertha is significant, what is arguably of more significance for this chapter is how she is confined to the attic of Rochester's house. She is kept here under lock and key, as a wild and undomesticated presence within the bourgeois home, until her eventual 'release' when she burns down the house.

Focusing on the spatial/temporal location of Bertha is important. We can firstly consider how Bertha's presence in the attic is symbolic of the authoritarian, paternalistic violence of colonialism and the control of mobility this was often premised on. This tells us important things about the character and place of borders and domesticity. Bertha is *within* the domestic space but presented as a 'wild' element. She is that which must be contained and regulated through carceral practices. She is bound to the attic as the lock, keys, doors, windows 'border' her in. Her movement is violently curbed and regulated as a threat and yet we must remember that she has been able to move across the Empire from

Jamaica to England, enabled as this was through marriage to Rochester and the passage of whiteness this relationship entailed. Mobility – or control of mobility through borders – was of course essential to imperialism, from the flow of capital, trade, administrators, labour to the dispossession of indigenous people from their land.

Whilst we can think of Bertha as 'bordered' in the attic, she is also simultaneously connected to the rest of the house and the British Empire. The novel reveals the many subtle intimacies of empire (Lowe 2015), which collapse down common-sense logics about where colonialism took place. Here we are shown, for instance, how capital circulations and dispossession binds plantation slavery in Jamaica to pastoral England and the 'family home'. Rochester's household is ultimately sustained by Bertha's presence, not merely symbolically but materially. Plantation slavery in Jamaica underpins the wealth of the manor house. We learn from Jean Rhys's retelling of Bertha's story in *Wide Sargasso Sea* ([1966] 2000) that Bertha had 'money'. She is the embodied connection of this structural link to Jamaica and the dispossessive suffering of slavery that continues to finance capital and shape landownership in England to this day (Hall 2013). Here we learn that bodies move or are captured along imperial lines, through the dictates of racialised capitalism (Robinson 1983); just as England (and Britain) itself is constituted as imperial terrain (Burton 1998: 5).

Bertha's eventual death at her own hands is often read by postcolonial feminists as symbolising the violence of white imperial feminism (Spivak 1985; McKee 2009) – that is, how the emancipation of European women (symbolised by Jane) was built on the racialisation of women of colour and white women's complicity with empire (Grewal 1996). To add to this, we should consider how Bertha's death also produces the possibility of heteronormative family. Just as she threatens the possibility of 'proper family' – through her sensuality, darkness and madness – she is also arguably its redemption. It is her death, after all, that allows Jane and Rochester to form a union and have a son. Following Judith Butler (2010), we might consider how Bertha's death is not grievable but instead celebrated. We learn here that not only does the 'wild' element of the household need to be domesticated (through both containment and death) but in doing so this creates the possibility for 'proper' family life and the reproduction of whiteness. Bertha is forced to suffer colonial violence that both imprisons her but equally uses her as a resource to create and sustain European domesticity.

I return to *Jane Eyre* as a site of the material processes of empire and coloniality throughout this chapter. I treat the novel as both an imprint of logics of empire (as a historical text) and a site of theorisation (bringing together abstractions which help us understand complex social phenomena). What is striking for me is how the figuration of Bertha holds together a set of unstable logics which are repeated across metro-imperial space and time – that is, from Jamaica to England, from the past into the present. Borders are shown to concern both the constraint and enabling of mobility (of bodies, relations and commodities); familial domesticity and white European socio-sexual relations are both presented as threatened but also conditioned by racialised 'others' and their move-ment. Colonial violence and dispossession reach across empire from colony to metropole, attached to certain bodies and populations, just as they remain entangled in sites of intimacy such as the 'family home'.

In this chapter I flesh out these tentative connections in more detail. I argue that what draws these processes (mobility, family, racialised violence) together is a compulsion towards domestication that defines the modern colonial and imperial state. To present this approach I build up different readings of Bertha from literatures focused on questions of domestication, colonisation and the family, and borders. The intention of this is to reveal how these literatures can help us build up an intercon-nected analysis and provide a set of tools which I travel with and extend over the next five chapters. To do so I ask three overlapping questions of the figure of Bertha Mason: what does it mean to say that Bertha is subject to 'domestication'? What does it mean to say that Bertha is made 'unfamilial'? And, finally, how is Bertha bordered? The chapter is arranged around answering these three provocations.

Bertha, I argue, is domesticated within the manor house in *Jane Eyre*, but this domestication intimately binds her to the wider (non-fictive) violence of empire and racialised colonial governance, of which bordering is one key tool. To set out a theory of domestication I synthesise work on the domesticating power of liberal states (Owens 2015) with Foucauldian approaches to the family (Foucault 1991; Stoler 1995; Feder 2007). Whilst I show how a Foucauldian analysis helps us understand how family worked as a technique of rule and normalisation central to the management of populations, I argue that such an approach still underdevelops the role that race, colonialism and mobility played in the emergence of modern liberal rule. In drawing upon the work of decolonial and postcolonial and black feminist scholars (Spillers 1987; McClintock 1995; Povinelli 2006; Lugones 2011), this provides a more historically nuanced account of the role of that 'family' has had in creating and sustaining colonial hierarchies of personhood – that is to say the categorisation of people and spaces into the human/not-quite/non-human (Weheliye 2014). I tie this intersectional account of race/humanity to the workings of the modern colonial state, which is constantly attuned to ordering populations around historically produced notions of family.

Whilst in contemporary scholarship the state is understood to sustain the life of the population, I argue that this is anchored to particular heteronormative claims of family (i.e. the domestic in the impulse to domesticate). We know from a long history of feminist scholarship that family worked to serve dominant social relations of capitalist heteropatriarchy and has thus been central to the organisation of violence. But to push this further we need to recognise how family emerged as a means of governing people differently based upon racial geographies of empire (Povinelli 2006; Rifkin 2015). 'Family' in this sense was always a particularistic claim to family as European and predominantly white bourgeois domesticity. We can consider how the figure of Bertha is denied personhood because she can never be part of the European/white family. But she is equally controlled by its parameters, such as being locked in the attic. What drives this chapter is the provocation that 'family' is not merely a site for racist, gendered and sexist ideas to manifest but part of the construction of racial demarcations and central to the operation and drive of colonialism and imperialism.

Once we better understand the role of family in empire-making, we are also better placed to understand the persistence of colonial rule into the present and how it is entangled in policing and creation of borders both within and beyond postcolonial Britain – that is, how the regulation of movement and settlement remain bound to the sensibilities and 'grooves' of imperialism (de Noronha 2018). Borders have been key tools of domesticating states concerned with movement. However, rather than a national history, this is an extensible imperial and globally orientated one (something I evidence in more detail in the next chapter). In thinking of borders/bordering alongside claims to family and domesticity, I want to recognise the role that bordering played and continues to play in hardening categories of race based on distinctions of who can move, who needs to be contained and who needs to be removed. Bordering can be attuned to supporting the movement of people based on claims to family life; or 'making' families such as through citizenship law; or borders can be about restraining movement as a threat to 'proper' family life. Forged through the imperial control of movement, borders continue to work as transit points for colonial ideas about familial intimacy today.

Domestication

It is my contention that we cannot understand the politics of either family or borders without understanding the role of the modern state, as a particular type of domesticating and colonising state. Questions of domesticity have arguably had a renaissance in contemporary scholarship. Whilst there has been a long history of work on the exclusory dynamics of normative domesticity and intimacy from queer theorists and feminist scholars (Barrett and McIntosh 1991; Stevens 1999; Duggan 2003; Oswin and Olund 2010), theorists of government and international order have also begun, tentatively, to bring analysis of the household into their work (Walters 2004; Kaplan 2005; Owens 2015; Weber 2016; also see Hage 1996). In this latter body of work, domesticity is less about cultural norms but about how different scales of government bind the management of the state (the 'public') to domestic spaces (the 'private' and 'familial'). This work has been concerned with understanding domesticity as a particular form of state power, where social relations are crafted out of the use of violence to produce a 'domestic' and thus 'domesticated' social order (Kaplan 2005). In this reading, domesticity is not only a key aspect of liberal political economy (social reproduction, wage labour) but societies are arranged as domesticities, where life processes are administrated based on ideas taken from the governance of patriarchal households (Owens 2015). Drawing on some of these ideas, I firstly want to ask what it means to say that Bertha is subject to domestication.

In *Jane Eyre*, Bertha is subject to bordering practices which keep her contained in the attic – locked away from the rest of the household and wider society. But equally, she is fed, clothed and 'cared for' by her maid, Grace, who is also forced to move with Bertha from Jamaica. Rather than being expelled, Bertha is instead subject to both confinement and care (before her eventual death). Such conditions resemble other nineteenth-century carceral and institutional spaces such as prisons or asylums. Bronte rationalises such containment by pointing to Bertha's unruly and disordered characteristics (her madness, animalism, violent behaviour). Such discipline is far from exceptional but part of a broader logic of modern government (Foucault 1991). To say she is domesticated is to pay attention to how such violence is made to seem necessary to sustain the order of the 'civilised' manor household and, in turn, wider Victorian society.

To consider this a process of domestication is to recognise how the power to domesticate has been central to the operation of modern liberal politics. To Patricia Owens (2015) what defines the liberal state and social relations is the scaling up of household rule to the level of the state, which she argues emerged in the seventeenth century. Noticeably, this occurred as colonial expansion was intensified. The production and sustaining of societal and economic relations rely, Owens argues, on domesticating the life processes of state inhabitants, through despotic means if necessary:

> From this perspective, we might say that 'domestic' government occurs when the inhabitants of household space submit (are forced to submit through violence and other necessities) to the disciplinary authority of a household. After all, 'dominate' is by extension 'one of the derivatives of the Latin word *domus*'. (Owens 2015: 3)

Reflecting Owens's approach to domestication, Bertha's treatment echoes such relations of force: she is forced to submit to coercion, as part of the patriarchal rule of the household administrated by Rochester. What defines modern state rule more broadly is this promise to domesticate those who may potentially resist or disrupt the regulation of life systems and the care of the household (also see Hage 1996). Violence is rationalised here precisely to pacify the internally and externally unruly. But domestication, as a liberal form of power, is premised on a developmental logic. Such violence is justified for the 'progress' and 'development' of the population and its backwards elements. It is not only punishment but also discipline for the reform and sustaining of social order. Bertha takes up the subject position of the undomesticated element within the home which 'threatens' the wider social order. Locking her away in the attic is not just a punishment but an act for sustaining and producing a domestic and 'civilised' order.

In considering modern and liberal rule as domestication, we need to see this as a colonising form of power and one attuned to the claims of Eurocentric civilisation which drove the expansion of empires. Domestication works as a liberal humanist project in which European order is imagined to be universal and universalised through imperialism. Under colonial logics, indigenous lands were viewed as undomesticated but also prime spaces for the bringing and building of social order which could replicate the relations of private ownership, production and labour in the metropole. Domestication is thus attached to ideas of progress; it is the will to produce order in its absence that justifies colonial violence and in doing so links the domestication of societies in the metropole with colonies. Colony and metropole are thus intimately connected but never treated equally (more on which later). The will to domesticate is, therefore, to conquer, dominate, colonise and paternally 'develop' those peoples and spaces who have yet to find their inner domesticity (Kaplan 2005: 26).

When John Locke justified the violent appropriation of native Amerindian land in the seventeenth century it was precisely because of this appeal to domestication – symbolised in pacifying, taming and labouring of a territory that was not so much empty as 'unproductive' and 'wasted' (Gidwani and Reddy 2011). As Anthony Pagden (2003: 183) argues:

> Since the right to unclaimed land was a natural right, any attempt to prevent it from being exercised, by vicious aboriginals, constituted a violation of the natural law. As such they could, in Locke's celebrated denunciation, 'be destroyed as a Lion or a Tiger, one of those wild Savage beasts, with whom Men can have no Society nor Security.' … Furthermore, it could also be argued that even if the aboriginals offered no opposition to the seizure of their lands, by failing to exercise their natural rights to improvement, they have also failed as people.

In considering Locke's justification of the destruction of 'wild savage beasts' we find here a key element of the genocidal logic of domestication – the destruction of those deemed unsuitable for domestic and civilised order (Blaney and Inayatullah 2010). To return to *Jane Eyre*, it is Bertha's savagery and untamed nature which is deemed as ultimately threatening the household. Her death is normalised and merely treated as part of the march of progress and the reclaiming of the household by its more worthy (modern and white) inhabitants – Rochester and, eventually, Jane.

Here domesticity relates to particular forms of developmental violence (Neocleous 2008). Under European empire, domesticity formed part of the conditioning of lands and people for the spread of racialised capitalism through primitive accumulation (Robinson 1983; Marx 2008:

363; Neocleous 2011). This was arranged through forms of dispossessive violence, through territory acquisition, dispersal and land enclosures and the development of 'colonial sciences'. What many of these processes focused upon was the management of movement. James Scott (2017) has highlighted the extensive role that coercion played in the move towards sedentary social organisation and its often contingent and fractured history. The control of movement through emergent bordering was increasingly a facet of European colonial expansion and consolidation from the seventeenth century. This was not merely orientated towards the restraint of mobility (sedentarism or containment) but also the compulsion to move in practices of urbanisation, labour migration, resettlement, plantation and reserve management, and forced migration.

Whilst the gendered household was viewed as essential for the reproduction of social relations in the metropole (at least from the mid-eighteenth century; see McKeon 2005), this was often the opposite in colonies, where domestication sometimes worked to pacify populations into village or household structures (Owens 2015: 173–208). However, it also often worked to create land for settlement and pools of mobile labour, leading to the destruction of kinship patterns. What early nineteenth-century colonial administrators in India obsessed over, was not movement as such but unregulated and 'unrestrained' movement (see Sleeman 1839). Just as with vagrancy in the metropole, it was pilgrimages, roaming banditry, nomads who unnerved the expanding colonial state (Singha 2000). Control over movement functioned within the evolving dictates of imperial capitalism as the opening up of new markets demanded labour to move, often across or within specific European empires. This demanded sites of capture to filter the flow of people through practices such as indentured labourer contracts, medical inspections, work camps, detention and expulsion. As Hagar Kotef (2015) argues, this form of rule necessitated categorising certain types of movement as with value or without value.

Here I have begun to outline how domestication emerged as a colonising mode of power from the seventeenth century. This was organised around the administration of 'developmental' claims to violence, order

and the management of movement (in which we see the emergence
of bordering/borders, which I expand on below). To this end, we can
consider how Bertha is domesticated as an unruly and uncivilised presence (linked to how violent 'civilisation' occurred in colonies) through
the control of movement and the administration of her life systems.
She is provided for in terms of food and shelter but always through the
possibility of normalised violence and coercion. Bertha's treatment in
England shows that domesticating violence is not necessarily attuned to
the geography of imperial expansion but race. Bertha is presented as of
the backwards colonised world and thus in need of further domestication
within English society. This reminds us that whilst domestication took
place in metropoles and colonies, who was subject to different forms of
violence and oppression was rationalised by demarcations of personhood
and humanity (more on this below).

Family and domestication

Whilst some scholars treat domestication as primarily household rule
(Walters 2004; Kaplan 2005; Owens 2015), that is to say in the case of
Jane Eyre Bertha is controlled and managed as part of the household,
I argue that we need to consider how domestication and with it claims
to civilisation and superiority always rely on normative claims to family.
It is my argument that domestication works by privileging and fostering
particular types of domesticity that are deemed familial. To Anne
McClintock (1995), the promise of domesticity that energised Victorian
imperialism was intimately bound to the social and economic relations
of the white bourgeois family. To consider domestication as not just
ordering but also as an appeal to a certain imaginary and practice of
order is to recognise its relationship to unfolding normative and naturalised appeals to family. It also recognises how family in this moment
is specifically related to other intimacies – home, household, marriage,
heterosexual reproductivity and so on. Domestication is bound to the
rise of the heteropatriarchal family that was increasingly viewed as the

model of social relations and civility from the middle of the eighteenth century. To speak of domesticity and domestication is already to invoke the role of family in the historical constitution of the properly domestic/ undomesticated.

What I am interested in is how domesticity emerged as a form of power which institutionalised the family as a key part of social order. I then want to ask what political work the family does in regards to colonialism. This matters because once we are able to appreciate the relationship between family, the colonial state and power, we can better understand the role family played in racial demarcations of civilised/ uncivilised, modernity/backwardness that were so central to empire and the management of movement. So, this leads me to ask: how is Bertha made (un)familial?

We might consider that the treatment of Bertha, her domestication within the home, is far from merely about maintaining order. It is instead concerned with need to discipline her body because of her proximity to family. This relates to the heteronormative impulse to protect and produce the sanctified space of the Victorian bourgeois family home. Bertha is presented as bereft of the appropriate sensibilities that would make her familial – she fails, for example, the normative gendered subjectivity of at first 'wife' and then 'motherhood'. Just as many other subjects and populations are made 'deviant', 'dangerous', 'threatening' because they fail to live up to or threaten the normative arrangement of family, Bertha is made unfamilial. To consider this, is to pay attention to the way that 'family' emerged as a normative set of social and affective relations and the role it plays in colonial/imperial government.

As we know from a long history of feminist and queer scholarship, the family is far from a natural entity, although it has been naturalised (Barrett and McIntosh 1991; Federici 2004). Instead, a dominant understanding of family – universalised around the world through imperialism and apparently neutral claims to the humanness of love – is a historically contingent, particularist set of social relations. To speak of family is not free of power; it is bound to particular European ideas about familial, heterosexual, Christian marriage, intimacy and liberal claims to romantic love and empowerment. To refer to family as I do, is to speak to this history. The provenance and dominance of this notion of 'family' and its relationship to government and the state is worth lingering upon.

Whilst I refer to the dominant idea of family and domesticity as 'European', the emergence of the nuclear family as the dominant mode of intimate and affective relations is historically tied to both the expansion of the modern capitalist state and imperial encounters. Against more diffuse domestic and kinship practices, the family was heterosexualised and increasingly promoted by state and church authorities across much of Northern Europe (Stevens 1999: 218–227; McKeon 2005). Foucault (1991) views this as a central aspect of the shift towards biopolitical governance and liberal capitalist social relations, intensified from the mid-eighteenth century. In his words, at this moment 'biopower bestowed a regulatory function on the one type of sexuality that was capable of reproducing labour power and the form of family' (Foucault 1991: 47). What this means is that the family emerged and was fostered as the 'natural' unit of human intimacy because it was networked into social reproduction and could form an important role in governing. Governing, that is, both desires and sensibilities but also the wider life of populations.

One reason that authorities invested in 'family', through legal regimes of marriage for instance, was because this allowed the organisation of national and imperial inheritance (Neti 2014). The heterosexual family was viewed as the properly domestic and morally superior form of intimate relations – including procreative sex, child care, socialisation – because it was networked into the broader management of the health, vitality and wealth of the population (Berlant 1997). The family could reproduce labour, maintain capital relations and (elite) citizenship through private property, legal inheritance and birth rights (Federici 2004). But natal reproduction (and the gendered labour this entailed) was also concerned with more ambiguous biological inheritance. Older notions of kinship 'bloodlines' were racialised through eugenic science in the nineteenth century (Davin 1978). Reproductive sex, and with it family, was treated as a site for the maintenance of pure racial heritage against threats of 'impurity' such as through miscegenation. To recall how Bertha Mason is racialised in *Jane Eyre* reflects this eugenic logic – her madness is not only inherited but also a product of the dangers of racial 'mixing' (see Stoler 2002).

Within this history, the family emerged as a transit point for concerns about racial health, control and national/imperial inheritance (Cott 2000). Here we can consider how not fitting into the normative intimacies of familial domesticity was enough to be cast as deviant or threatening (Alexander 2006). To be familial, that is to say following the path of heteronormative life and progress, was to be maintained as a moral and social good; against this, to be unfamilial was to be deemed abnormal, threatening and a risk (see Feder 2007; Taylor 2012). This played out differently within metropoles and across European colonies (as I will discuss in more detail below), where people could be deemed 'sexualised threats' (homosexuals, deviants, the diseased) or 'racialised threats' (colonised peoples, slaves, aliens) to family.

Race, family and empire

Working with a Foucauldian inspired account of the family can help us connect its historical emergence to questions of power, the expansion of the liberal domesticating state and demarcations of familial/ unfamilial. This is important because we need to recognise how the institutionalisation of the family has been central to the management of populations, and with this life and death (also see Repo 2013). We should appreciate here how the will to domesticate, and the organised violence this often entails, is bound up with both the normative appeal of 'family' as the dominant unit of not only social reproduction but also intimacy (i.e. wider proximate and socio-sexual relations of 'being together'). However, we cannot stop here. Not only is the conception and history of family that I have begun to tease out here largely Eurocentric but it also relies on an underdeveloped formulation of race.

Stoler's work, particularly *The Education of Desire* (1995), resituates Foucault's account of the sexualisation and racialisation of the family within a more accurate imperial and colonial history. Against Foucault she shows how ideas around the bourgeois family crystallised and were intensified in colonial settings and how this circulated back into European metropoles (also see Stoler 2002, 2016). Intimacy was networked into colonial power and the management of intimacy, and with it the codifica-tion of familial/unfamilial subjects, was played out in colonies as much as within Europe. Stoler (2002) shows how the management of the 'innermost' was exemplified in colonies, for example in formal and informal rules over sexual partners, cohabitation and marriage laws, institutional practices which delineated the coloniser and colonised. Rather than viewing family as primarily linked to national concerns about population, the role of family is better understood in the context of imperial ideas about the future of white colonisers and the future of maintaining, settling and controlling empire.

Stoler's work is wonderfully illustrative of elements of the imperial/colonial coordinates of 'family'. However, her work is primarily focused on expanding and nuancing Foucault's account of sexuality and race, and with this she replicates some of the omissions found in his account of family. Whilst questions of intimacy are transferred to a colonial setting in Stoler's account, race is still often reduced to sexuality. By this I mean that race is often about the threat to heterosexual reproduction and is framed in terms of racial (im)purity. For Foucault, race was about the distinction or 'break' between who could live and who could die within a population. And many scholars influenced by Foucault remain wedded to this rather narrow theorisation (including, I might also add, my own previous work). For example, in Foucault's genealogies of race, 'internal' racial threats (madness, the insane, diseased, deviants) often flatten out what he calls 'external' racial threats – those of foreigners and the colonised (McWhorter 2009; Venn 2009). In Foucault's slightly reductive analysis of race as the 'death function', any form of abandonment or reduction in the sustenance of life can be equated with racism (see Reid and Dillon 2009; Turner 2017; for a critique see Howell and Richter-Montpetit 2019). So, whilst acknowledging that phenomena such as the anxiety caused by eugenics around vitality and racial health was formative of colonial rule, I want to go further and argue that this does not fully get at the longer historical pattern of racial hierarchies, cultural imaginaries and embodied histories of violence that colonialism enacted and that 'family' is equally wrapped up in.

To put it more simply, we need to recognise the role that family played in empire as *European* and *white*. In order to get at this, I turn to other postcolonial, decolonial and black studies accounts of race and family to tease out how appeals to family, as a European construct, continue to form part of the processes of race-making, and with this tease out what is at stake in my assertion that Bertha Mason is made unfamilial.

The human and the familial

We are better able to grasp the power relations of modernity and domesticating power once we examine the manner through which racialisation as dehumanisation was made possible. Decolonial and black studies scholars have argued that we should examine who has historically been brought into the social calculus of 'human life' (Quijano 2007; Wilderson 2010; Weheliye 2014) – that is, the socio-political relations that have disciplined humanity into 'full humans', 'not-quite-humans' and 'non-humans' (Weheliye 2014: 5). To understand how dehumanisation is constitutive of modernity, is to recognise that modernity – and with it, liberal state power, capital accumulation and humanism – rests on the active denial and dispossession of personhood for colonised peoples. Here colonised peoples' ways of being in the world, systems of knowledge, spiritualism, bodies, cultures were rendered incomplete, worthless and absent by European colonial practice and ideology. Decolonial scholars such as Walter Mignolo (2011) point to the legacy of violent acquisition of territory and resources by Iberian states from the fifteenth century to elaborate on this – five hundred years of violence leaves its mark. European colonial science discovered 'Man' in the Enlightenment at the same time it discovered its partial and non-human others (Wynter 2003). These processes relied upon and set in place racial distinctions that did not just view non-European peoples as subservient or as potential resources but also as eradicable and unworthy of subjectivity and personhood. They were denied a place in the family of 'Man' that grew out of humanist and enlightenment ideas of society and politics (Wynter 2003; Lorde 2007).

Ramon Grosfoguel *et al.* (2015), drawing upon Boaventura de Sousa Santos's (2007) notion of the 'abyssal line', argue that race must be understood as the fundamental demarcation between human/not-quite/non-human (although they leave out the middle category). Race was productive of particular spatial and temporal logics maintained by colonialism and its afterlife in coloniality and neo-imperialism. Not only were non-humans 'discovered' through European colonisation but they were presented (and remain presented) as lost and stuck in time – as backwards and undeveloped peoples and geographic zones (Fanon 1961). This is exemplified in the treatment of colonies, which are spaces of endless arrested development and zones of the 'non-human'.

Importantly for us, this spatial distinction between human/non-human worlds is complicated by mobility and bordering. When non-modern and once-colonised people move to the Global North, they remain treated as not-quite/non-humans as we see today. Borders (more of which below) continue to delineate and reproduce these distinctions within metropolitan spaces such as in policing tactics, housing policy and the creation of ghettos, camps and detention centres. Just as in formal colonies, the not-quite/non-human continues to be treated as undeveloped; once in the Global North non-humans are cast as those who 'refuse' to modernise because their culture and kinship practices 'hold them back'. The divide between human/not-quite/non-human is not about citizenship but about who has access to colonially conditioned forms of modernity and humanity. As Grosfoguel *et al.* (2015: 647) argue:

> The zones of being and non-being are not specific geographical places, but rather positions within racial power relations that operate at a global scale between centres and peripheries, but that are also manifested at a national and local scale against diverse racially 'inferior' groups. Zones of being and non-being exist at a global scale between Westernised centres and non-Western peripheries.

What then defines the racial demarcation between human/not-quite/non-human is not geography to Fanon and to Grosfoguel and his colleagues, but instead a relationship to violence. Inferiorised populations, demarcated as non-human, can be subject to structural and arbitrary forms of violence as the norm. Think again of how this is justified in the case of Bertha: violence sticks to her body as it moves across the British Empire rather than being bound within the space of the colony.

Those people defined as human can be subject to violence, but this is rare and exceptional. This structure of violence is so normalised and pervasive that it is barely noticeable to those who occupy the position of the human. Whilst oppression does take place within zones of the human, this often takes the form of struggles over rights (e.g. the labour movement, gender equality, LGBTQ rights). In contrast, within spaces of the non-human (such as the colony, ghetto, plantation, detention centre, refugee camp) oppression more often than not is conducted through systematic and unaccountable violence (also see Mbembe 2003). We might consider here the experience of slavery or the genocide of indigenous peoples structured empire. For contemporary examples, we might instead ruminate on how colonial warfare conducted in the Middle East occurs without accounting for civilian deaths (Gregory 2004), or how refugees, rather than being 'saved', are left to flounder and drown in the Mediterranean on a daily basis as rich European countries and governments watch on (Saucier and Woods 2014).

To Frank Wilderson (2010) what underpins this violence and the hierarchies of the human is the defining experience of 'anti-blackness'.

Chattel slavery, Wilderson argues, was the ultimate form of 'social death' (Patterson 1982), which denied Africans any access to humanity. Importantly, this continues to structure the experience and dispossession of people and communities racialised as black today. We should remember how 'Africans went onto the ships and came out black', argues Wilderson (2010: 38). What defines anti-black racism is the propensity for gratuitous violence and suffering, which structures the zone of the not-quite/ non-human. To Weheliye (2014), an analysis of anti-blackness tells us about the bodied character of colonial racism and who succumbs to normalised and unexceptional violence. This is because anti-blackness also structures all aspects of dispossession – it shapes who has access to humanity (those who are not-quite and non-humans).

Whilst Wilderson (2010: 38) is hesitant to show the contingency of this racialised violence, Grosfoguel *et al.* (2015) suggest that demarcations between human/not-quite/non-human are relatively flexible and rely upon prior histories of racialisation and shifting relations of force. For instance, we could point to the flexibility of anti-Muslim racism that has intensified and expanded after 9/11. Or look at the treatment of Roma citizens throughout the EU who were never 'colonised' formally but are frequently subject to racialised (and with this often gratuitous) violence. If whiteness is bound to the position of the human, blackness remains bound to the position of the non-human; people are racialised between these structural positions (see Mbembe 2017: 4).

So, in examining the rise of domestication we need to stay attuned to how slavery and colonial dispossession continues to shape who has access to humanity and thus what drives distinctions between life and death, rights and violence. Equally, we need to historically situate where practices of government emerged from in the global-colonial order, in experiments of colonial rule, in the management of mobility, in appeals to intimacy that worked across metroimperial space and organised around the movement of inferiorised people. Domestication must be understood to work differently based upon historical and shifting racial markers of the human. This has implications for how we should approach questions of the role of family and the production of 'unfamilial' subjects and populations.

Being attuned to the historical experiences of colonialism, imperialism and their contemporary manifestations helps us better understand the role of family in these ongoing processes. Arguably, the family plays a powerful and constitutive role in the racial markers and delineation around who is human/not-quite/non-human. Rather than a site where preconceived ideas about race are played out (i.e. as contagion through reproduction), ideas about family were hardened in colonial encounters. In turn, the family held together an unstable set of claims about who was civilised/uncivilised, modern/backwards, which rationalised and sometimes constituted the treatment of colonised people as not-quite/non-human. To put this more simply, the emergent model of the European family, and with it, what McClintock (1995) calls the 'cult of domesticity', worked as a means of denying humanity to colonised populations. It was constitutive of racial power as much as it is a container of racist ideas.

In this next section I want to elaborate more on this point and bring us back to the question of Bertha as unfamilial. Below I sketch out how I see the relationship between family, race and colonialism, which is typified with three overlapping but distinct processes: 1) *development*: the equation of family with progress or development; 2) *dispossession*: the dispossession of colonised populations from structures of family/inheritance/social and economic capital; and 3) *control*: the destruction of pre-colonial kinship structures and the imposition of European models of family as a mechanism of pacification and control.

Family as development

As I have previously set out, 'family' is bound not only to bourgeois heterosexuality, but European and white heteronormativity. The presence and conduct of socio-sexual, affective and kinship relations that appeared 'outside' of this mode of domesticity have consistently been cast as incomplete, deviant or absent. Populations were judged on whether

Europeans considered them (in)capable of demonstrating or practising elements of this model of domesticity. This placed people and cultures within a hierarchy of developmentalism based on the codification of family/domesticity (Hoad 2000). Whilst deviant others were constantly discovered within Europe (i.e. the failure of working-class mothers or homosexuals), what structured this hierarchy was discovering whole populations that appeared bereft of 'family life' in non-European and colonised lands. This structured claims around who was to be domesticated and how.

Goody (1990) shows how colonised peoples were categorised as more or less human through what she calls 'marriage taxonomies' (similar to Ferguson's taxonomies of perversion), which compared 'races' by how they related to a template of Christian marriage. African tribal structures, for instance, were long considered incompatible with European marriage (thus colonial administrators developed the legal category of 'tribal' or 'custom' marriage in much of West Africa); Indian castes were often differentiated through an apparent propensity for nuclear family relations (with Brahmins at the top). Alongside this, Eastern Islamic cultures were viewed as particularly deviant, with polygamy and incest thought to be rife.

Such categories were not merely abstract anthropological distinctions or examinations of 'cultural difference'. Discovery of the apparent absence of 'proper family life' often propelled and justified colonial expansion and, with it, violence. In *Sex and Conquest*, Trexler (1995) shows how heteronormativity was at the heart of Spanish and Portuguese material conquest in the Americas. He argues that the apparent 'sodomy of male homosexuality' witnessed by colonialists 'bestowed a right to conquer' on the Iberians. Here, 'Missionaries proclaimed to the Aztecs, Maya and the Incas that sodomy was their downfall and the myth of Christian God had decided to send the Iberians to conquer the Americas because they engaged in homosexual behaviour' (Trexler 1995: 89). Such appeals to deviancy and perversity were performances around which appropriation and violence became legitimated in colonial encounters. Equally, as Rifkin (2015) has illustrated, indigenous American kinship practices were cast as proof of their existence in a 'state of nature' – polygamy, matrilineal, matrilocal residence and pre-marital sex were taken as signs of 'absolute foreignness' to European modernity (Cott 2000: 25). Greg Thomas (2007) makes a similar case for what he calls the sexual conquest of Africa.

Signs of family were equally taken as notes of progress and the possibility of redemption. James Mill (1817: 135) would justify the paternal British colonial project by alluding to the immorality of both Chinese and Indian peoples through the racial marker of dirt and their incapacity for domestic care and labour: they were, he argued, 'both in the physical sense, disgustingly unclean in their persons and houses'. But in the building of the colonial state in India, signs of habitation, of domestic dwellings or 'retarded' family structures shaped how British colonialism was arranged around paternal logics of domestication and the spreading of capitalist social relations (Semple 2013) – that is, compared to the genocidal violence targeted at indigenous populations, or African slavery. Who was considered more or less familial marked out developmental distinctions between not-quite/non-humans, as well as with humans – such as the promotion of white European settlers across empire.

Family as dispossession

Family did not merely create hierarchies of development but also worked as a central aspect of the dispossession of colonised peoples. Perhaps the most notable example of how family emerged as an organising principle of dispossession is how the enslaved and slavery were rendered in relation to ideals of family life. In the constitution and legitimation of slavery, normative claims to family played a vital part of both the conversion of African bodies to chattel and the contestation of freedoms under settler colonialism (Burnham 1987). Not only did the violence of the Middle Passage and the orchestration of the slave trade in the West Indies, America and the ports of England destroy forms of kinship and intimacy but slaves were understood as being incapable of 'family' and through such claims of immorality were subsequently written out of family law and its claims to 'humanity' (Dayan 2011).

Under settler colonialism in America, Burnham (1987) argues that courts declared slaves:

> To be a different kind of human being – innately and immutably immoral (therefore not legally 'marriageable'), too dumb and childish to themselves parent (therefore incapable of childrearing), and sexually licentious (therefore unsuited to 'marriage' and family bonds).

The day-to-day violence of the plantation was often structured around the mutual denial and management of intimacies – between slaves, freed slaves, white workers and plantation masters (Sharpe 2010). Whilst slave women were deemed sexual property and often suffered agonising forms of sexual violence, slave masters sought to promote restricted forms of 'slave family' but often only to complement the extractive system of labour, production and chattel (and satisfying Christian claims to the 'proper treatment' of slaves) (Hartman 1997). Ritualised slave 'marriage' was viewed as having a 'quieting effect on restive slaves' (Burnham 1987) and could be economically profitable through the potential for reproduction. As slaves were written out of family law, they could never legally be parents or hold rights of family unity and so children were the property of the master. This system was shored up by settler colonial law, which identified slave ownership through the very organisation of patriarchal family. As Thomas Cobb argued in 1858:

> Southern slavery is a patriarchal, social system. The master is the head of his family. Next to wife and children, he cares for his slaves. He avenges their injuries, protects their persons, provides for their wants, and guides their labors. In return, he is revered and held as protector and master. (Quoted in Burnham 1987: 194)

'Family life' was legally and normatively coded through white bourgeois domesticity – as a 'moral good' only achievable to some. 'Family' was denied in the precise moment of black dehumanisation because it was already etched around claims to whiteness and European superiority. To Hortense Spillers (1987), this means that 'black family' is not even thinkable within the dominant social calculus; it was rendered an *impossibility*. This has lasting consequences for how we theorise anti-black and colonial racism (with it gender and sexuality), because the historical formation of the family, which emerges as a naturalised social unit, is made possible through the dispossession and denial of affective relations and kinship to specific populations.

Family as control

Spillers's point about the unthinkability of the 'black family' rests on the evisceration of markers of identity that Europeans used to organise social relations, such as gender and sexuality. Such markers of European personhood (being a 'man', 'woman', 'mother' or 'father', etc.) were actively denied through colonial violence and slavery, which again is replicated and legitimated through colonial science and enlightenment thought (Shilliam 2014). To Maria Lugones (2011), colonialism (or what she calls coloniality) is both an evisceration of pre-colonial social and cultural structures and the hegemonic dominance of European forms of intimacy. By this we should consider how European ideas of personhood were used to describe colonised populations as both deviant and/or 'incomplete'. For example, to Lugones, gender and sexuality were imposed on colonised people as forms of European ideology and social relations. To consider how family worked as a form of control, we should recognise that colonised people began to learn of, and perform, themselves as gendered and sexualised. But equally, because of race, this process of subjectification was always viewed as 'incomplete'. It was cast as a deviant version of the European ideal type.

This reveals a double violence: pre-colonial socio-relations were and continue to be constituted as backwards and often violently destroyed or intervened in, just as European modes of social relations were/are imposed through legal codes, colonial administration and inclusion within imperial capitalist markets, production and labour relations.

Here a model of family could be used as a means to reveal the backwards nature and underdevelopment of societies but also as a means to force change on colonised populations imagined to be in need of emulating codes of domesticity.

Debates over how to domesticate colonial populations through forms of developmental violence thus faltered around this vision of heterosexual/ human progress. In parallel to this, colonial rule was often performed through acts of social engineering, such as we see with experiments in social work in colonies (working with some parallels to such interventions in metropoles). Marriage and domesticity schools provided one particular site in the 'civilisation' of underdeveloped societies (see, for example, Mair 1944). Here we can think of the family as relating to particular forms and practices of control.

These different aspects of the role that family played in the construction of colonial rule (development/dispossession/control) are significant because they reveal how the family is both a tool of government and a means of disciplining and delimiting access to humanity. Far from being an internal European process, dominant ideas of who was (un)familial emerged through and out of colonial encounters. In this way, family became a key aspect of racial thought.

Here we consider how the contemporary politics of the family, and with it, heteronormative codes of the 'good life' and 'love', remain bound to this history. The family is tied up with distributions of the human which are constantly recast in modern liberal government. The family is not only bound to modern rule through reproduction but as a cultural configuration which sustains and fosters claims of the human, and with it the centrality of whiteness. Just as decolonial and black studies scholarship demonstrates the continuity of anti-black and colonial racism into the current moment, we need to stay attuned to how this functions through appeals to the family. Family can work as an energising force of colonial rule into the present, precisely because it appears to work freely of its racialised and colonial past. In postcolonial societies that appear to disavow 'racism' as prejudice, such as Britain, family plays a significant role in the reinvention and persistence of modes of colonial dispossession. Family is naturalised as love, care, comfort and thus hides its relationship to past or present violence.

We might turn back to the figure of Bertha Mason, confined to Rochester's attic, to think through how family works here. Rather than as untamed or mad, it is how Bertha is translated in terms of colonial blackness that define her condition and legitimise the suffering she is subject to. This reveals how anti-black racism was anchored across metroimperial space, tied as this was to depictions of evil, corruption and otherworldly deviancy. Bertha, like the swathes of darker-skinned people she is connected to in the colonies and plantations of Jamaica, is precisely without God, beyond the terms of the human. Even if she is 'privileged' in Jamaica (as not-quite-human), she is transformed into non-human on her arrival in the metropole, where she is darkened and presented as a danger. This dehumanisation is organised around biological depictions of darkness which constantly focus on her body and sensuality, against that of the reasoned and objective characters of her white 'superiors'.

However, the racialisation of Bertha is bound to the family home. She is corrupting the white domestic space that Victorian England fetishised. She is already viewed as bereft of family because of her kinship connections to Jamaica, which are cast as not properly domestic but merely a bloodline of toxicity and degeneracy. We might remember, for instance, Rochester's declaration that Bertha's family was 'three genera-tions of idiots and maniacs'. Her mother is presented as a 'drunkard'. Rochester eventually declares to his peers that he should be allowed to 'seek sympathy with something at least human' (Bronte [1846] 1992: 246). As with Burnham's and Spillers's examples of black slaves above, Bertha is depicted as incapable of proper familial intimacy. To this end, Foucauldian accounts of family can only give us part of Bertha's story. They can only help us explain her death as surplus to the reproduction of English society – that is, as a figure of 'abnormality' or 'contagion'. This fails to explain how her body and subjectivity is already rendered impossible and killable through her connection to colonial racism, the suffering of slavery and her incapability of European patriarchal

intimacy and family life. Instead, it is important to understand how
she has already been racialised through these prior attachments as
not-quite-human.

Borders and bordering

In considering how domestication functions, it is also important to
explore the role that borders and bordering played in this form of
government and in colonial expansion. One of the key provocations I
began with is that Bertha is 'bordered'; she is subject to bordering such
as being locked in the attic and contained by the patriarchal and racialised
governance of the household. In this last section I want to linger on
the relationship to borders/bordering and the part that they have played
in colonial rule, family and race-making. This helps us tease out a
particular way of approaching borders/bordering in the book, but it
also helps us situate both the changing nature of colonial rule in our
current moment and the spatial complexity of colonialism – that is,
the intimate connections of colony and metropole, which are central
to the analysis of contemporary postcolonial Britain. I thus ask, what
does it mean to say that Bertha is subject to borders/bordering?

Bronte illustrates how Bertha is confined to the attic through physical
barriers. And yet her enclosure works in parallel with other forms of
bordering that target her body, that tie her to the domestic space of
Rochester's household and that also facilitate particular forms of movement which are paralleled across metroimperial space. We are introduced
to a catalogue of techniques and practices of bordering. Bertha cannot
move as a free subject; she is bound to the rule of her husband, who
is her warden. Here, symbolically, but as I have argued above also
materially, Bertha is bound (unevenly) to the plantation slavery of
Jamaica, a mode of dispossession and accumulation which was structured
around enclosure, confinement but also the facilitation of movement
(the Middle Passage, chain gangs, the enclosure of the plantation) (Browne

2015). Mobility and violence are intimately entangled here. Whilst Bertha could only move to England from Jamaica as the wife of Rochester, equally her only way to escape the confines of the household, her marriage, England, is through her self-immolation.

This helps us think about what borders are and where they go. Borders work as physical barriers and enclosures. Borders work through and on the body, capturing, producing, differentiating people as 'out of place', 'strange', 'uncanny'. Borders work as the dispossession of rights, subjectivity and personhood. Borders work through the socio-sexual relations of the intimate 'couple', where (im)mobility is made possible and restrained though the family. Borders work in multiple scales that rely upon and foster different sites of social authority – the settler state, colonial law, immigration practice, citizenship, the household. Borders do not only work to capture but also to facilitate moving bodies.

Reading Bertha in this way contributes to disrupting the idea of borders as fixed territorial entities, tied to the policing of immigration and sovereign national territory. Here we can consider how borders follow and surveil bodies as part of the domesticating state. However, despite a complex and highly developed conception of the border, studies of borders, both from within migration studies and even from critical border studies, still broadly remain fixated on the evolving and contemporary nature of borders – and in doing so deny their colonial histories and orientations.

Whilst the 'line-in-the-sand' definition of borders has long been disputed and transformed, borders are still largely equated with state sovereignty, the nation state and practices of immigration (Parker and Vaughan-Williams 2009). This work is often necessary because of the dramatic shift in the reach and complexity of sovereign borders in northern states, for instance the extra-territorial character of EU borders (Tazzioli 2014; Vaughan-Williams 2015; Burridge *et al.* 2017); or the outsourcing of border control to private companies (Walters 2016); or the means through which immigration practice has proliferated within and across social government agencies in states such as the UK under polices such as the hostile environment (Yuval-Davis *et al.* 2018; also see Bigo 2006). These all deserve analytical and theoretical attention. Whilst I want to pay attention to contemporary shifts in immigration policy, I also want to treat borders/bordering as part of a longer and evolving process of imperial governance and domestication.

Imperial rule – that is to say the management of empire – and individual colonial administrations were both fixated on mobility long before the invention of immigration law (which we can date to the late nineteenth century in white settler states, and the early twentieth century in Britain; see Ballantyne 2005). Mobility, we should remember, was an important component of domestication. Bordering shaped primitive accumulation and was central to acquisition of territory (Gidwani and Reddy 2011). Following Simone Browne (2015), we need to recognise how the structure of slavery produced lasting experiments in racial surveillance, containment and expulsion, for example in detailed identity documentation, insurance policies and incarceration. Lest we forget that the mass movement of African people to the Americas through slavery represents the greatest forced migration in human history.

These practices to regulate movement under empire not only predate but condition the regulation of movement today. This means recognising two overlapping points:

1) The management of movement evolved out of the concerns of hierarchising and mapping people based on racial categories (whether 'useful', 'valued' or 'dangerous' movement). So, there has been an imperial and colonial logic and orientation which has underpinned bordering/borders – that is to say who can or cannot move. We might call this the ideological dimension of bordering.

2) As well as a historic and ideological orientation towards managing what Lake and Reynolds (2008, referencing W. E. B. Du Bois) call the 'global colour line', bordering practices themselves were honed under colonialism – that is, the techniques and strategies of managing, categorising and regulating who could move and

who could not – and were often born out of the direct control of colonised people (i.e. indentured labourers, slaves, colonial criminals). Even when practices such as vagrancy laws were used in the metropole, they were often experimented with and refined in colonies. We might call this the practical dimension of bordering. In the context of the British Empire, many of the strategies and practices that would become UK immigration policy and the role of border agents/agencies were already honed in (settler) colonies before being transferred back into the metropole (more of this in the next chapter).

Here I want to further elaborate on the conceptual distinction I introduced earlier between borders and bordering, which I use in tension throughout the book. This is to both recognise the *longue durée* of colonial history of the management of movement and also the contemporary power of immigration practices and law. When I speak of borders, I refer to practices which have a specific connection to immigration policy – that is to say the sovereign law of a particular state with regard to migration, settlement and citizenship. When I speak of bordering, I refer to the broader process through which people are made 'out of place'. This is attuned to how bordering was and is constitutive of the broader push to domesticate through colonisation and draw distinctions around people who are familial/unfamilial. Bordering is concerned with the broader means through which movement has been managed and hierarchised through racial categories – human/not-quite/non-human. Borders, to my mind, are a specific subset of bordering which rework, integrate and re-energise bordering strategies.

This distinction is of course contingent, and bordering practices can often become border practices, and vice versa. For example, we might consider how housing policy in the UK has long been an area for the governance of racialised populations. Not only are black, Asian and migrant communities often denied social housing, they are also confined, through intersecting inequalities, to certain parts of urban spaces (such as the top floors of high-rise apartment buildings; see Danewid 2019).

In the Immigration Act 2014, housing law was joined more forcefully to immigration law as it obliged all housing providers and landlords to check the immigration status of their tenants. Here bordering (the spatial governance of racialised populations) becomes institutionalised in the border – that is to say immigration control. Bordering begets borders.

By linking borders/bordering to the duress of colonial rule, it is important to recognise that borders and bordering do not affect all people equally. Borders emerged around the management of racialised mobility, not mobility of people per se. Here categories of citizenship and the division between migrant and citizen are not particularly helpful (although I use these distinctions empirically). Whilst many migrants (i.e. non-citizens) are regarded as unproblematic and 'valued', many subjects with citizenship remain a continual problem – they remain 'unfamilial' and not of 'value' (more of this in chapters 3 and 5). In Britain, long-standing black and Asian communities and postcolonial diaspora remain viewed (and often treated by the state) as migrants, even though they have formal citizenship and have been settled for generations (more of this in chapter 4). Their relationship to the state refracts many of the violent tactics of bordering that we see experimented with on migrant groups such as asylum seekers or irregularised migrants.

What is important here is how bordering is attuned towards making people 'out of place' in ways that reassert colonial categories of the not-quite/non-human, including distinctions about how they do family or how much they have progressed towards familial domesticity. This racialisation can target those who move as subjects of empire – from former British colonies such as Jamaica, Nigeria, Pakistan – but also people who move from peripheral spaces (not only former British colonies) and who are treated akin to subjects of empire (e.g. those from Turkey, Algeria or Central Asian republics) (see Grosfoguel *et al.* 2015). Whilst borders/bordering may affect other populations (i.e. predominantly white migrants or citizens), those populations are rarely the initial target of these practices even if they are pulled into the dragnet of domestication.

Bordering the family

So, finally, what of the relationship between bordering and family? I have teased out some subtle connections above but there are some concrete ties that are worth demonstrating briefly. Put simply, bordering and borders work to both discover and regulate those who become deemed unfamilial. But they also work towards promoting and fostering family. I noted before how the bordering of Bertha Mason tells us of both the embodied dimension of bordering – how it is felt, experienced and targeted on bodies – and also how this is energised by claims to protect or foster family where it is absent. Equally, the claim to hetero-sexual intimacy and marriage that initially binds Bertha to Rochester allows a certain limited form of movement from Jamaica to England. This is important.

As I explore throughout the rest of this book, bordering can work to protect and foster but also delimit affective relations and family. Bertha, we should remember, is bordered into the attic as a threat to the family (the wild, untamed element within). Bordering regulates population health, filtering and managing those who may be threatening. This could be through anxiety over what particular bodies are understood to carry and bring with them when they enter or move across a territory – disease, criminality, immorality or, equally, labour power, resources and skills. Bordering can be targeted to manage who can be intimate with whom in a particular (imperial, colonial and then national) space. We can find this, for example, in rules on 'family migration', which dictate which forms of intimacy, kinships or dependencies can move for family life (see chapter 3).

So, bordering can be initiated in the name of family – for its production or protection – but family can be promoted both to make possible and

to curb movement. Borders/bordering can emerge as a way of capturing
and containing the perils of other modes of sexuality and intimacy, for
example in promoting certain family dependencies to domesticate and
contain the sexual threat of groups. In the context of the movement of
people after formal decolonisation, who was counted as family often
dictated and continues to shape inheritance of rights and who can
move, who can settle and who can claim rights in Britain. As citizenship
is often inherited (such a model has dominated in the UK since 1981),
who is considered a family, through appropriate relations of intimacy,
is guided by histories of racialised sexuality. But this is not only symbolic.
It also works to structure people's material life chances – their access
to resources, capital and labour power – by organising who can inherit
what, who can gain rights of settlement. Who can be a family is one
key site through which inequality is reproduced.

Conclusion

In this chapter I have set out a particular approach to family and borders
through an exploration of domestication. By drawing on theories of
domesticity I have demonstrated how the modern state is a domesticating
state and that domesticity played a central role in empire-making. Using
different readings of the treatment of Bertha Mason in *Jane Eyre* I
sketched out how domestication is constantly energised by a historical
appeal to family. 'Family' was not only gendered and sexualised, I argue,
but was a central force in patterns of racialisation across European
empires. This means understanding how family played into the constitution of some people as modern and civilised (human) and others as
uncivilised and backwards (thus not-quite/non-human). It is my
provocation that such appeals to family remain central to racialised
governance today, often expressed in forms of bordering within postcolonial societies such as Britain. Appeals to family recode and remake
racialised distinctions born out of colonial rule, and in doing so energise
often-violent practices of authoritarian and disciplinary borders and

bordering. I offer that 'family', as a site of racial and heteronormative power, continues to work as a means of development, dispossession and control into our contemporary moment.

Departing from the example of Bertha Mason that I drew upon throughout this chapter, I now look to evidence the role of family in colonial rule and bordering across the British Empire. In the next chapter, I examine a more detailed history of these relationships across metro-imperial space. I look to evidence and nuance my claims about the historical role of family and race-making, and how this was central to the governance of mobility across the Empire and was then brought into immigration practice and policy in the British metropole.

Making love, making empire

On 19 April 1899 a troupe of South African 'tribal' groups landed at Southampton docks on the South Coast of England. Later that month they were due to perform a central role in the Earl's Court exhibition *Savage South Africa*. Local reports claimed that 'among the effects were over 200 natives of South African tribes, a number of Boer families, representatives of the mounted police, and a number of animals' (Shephard 1986: 97). Early film footage, archived by the Colonial Film Project, shows the apparent moment when the groups disembarked. One reel shows a group of 'Zulu' men, clad in 'tribal dress' and clutching spears, performing a choreographed dance for the camera and bystanders (Colonial Film Project 2018). The film shows the group striking an imposing presence, with the merchant docks foggy in the background. Thirty seconds into the reel, a white man in a top hat and dark overcoat stumbles into the frame, stares at the troupe and then leads some of the men further forward towards the camera.

This moment captures a significant imperial encounter. It represents the overlapping of colonial technologies – the camera lens, the white man's instruction, the coherence of the performance – all situated within the wider context of the imperial exhibition (see chapter 7 for more on this, and also Mitchell 2000: 7–13). The arrival of *Savage South Africa* in London tells us how empire was constantly remade not only in 'overseas' colonies but also in encounters within the urban metropole. London is constituted here as part of 'imperial terrain' (Burton 1998: 5) – the site of rebounding and contingent colonising processes (Lowe 2015). The event also stands as a particular encounter in the racialised and sexualised logics of colonialism. It stands, I argue, as an example of the way that mobility, intimacy and claims to family played a central role in both energising and organising colonial rule.

After the opening of the exhibit, newspaper stories circulated regarding the effect of the presence of the 'savages' in London. Exoticised and eroticised accounts of 'savage' behaviour spread as far as the Los Angeles-based *Pall Mall* paper. White women, it was said, were seen disappearing into the tribal tents which constituted the 'Kaffir kraal' section of the exhibition to partake in the 'vilest orgies'. The *Daily Mail* described how 'women of gentle birth, crowd round the near-naked blacks, give them money, shake hands with them, and even go down on their hands and knees in order that they may further investigate the interior of the overcrowded huts' (quoted in Shephard 1986: 101).

Alongside familiar representations of hypersexualised black masculinity (or the 'black peril'), complaints were raised in South Africa on 'racial grounds' (Colonial Film Project 2018) that these 'well-policed natives' posed a significant threat. This was framed as a threat not only to British society but also imperial rule more broadly. The South African press feared that 'nothing but vice in a white skin would satisfy [the 'savages'] thereafter' (Shephard 1986: 97). The exhibition threatened to trouble the sexual demarcations of the 'colour line'. By August 1899 the 'Kaffir kraal' was officially closed to women.

Whilst the press initially raised concerns over interracial sex and the spectre of the 'black peril' (which I return to below), focus began to fall on the coupling and engagement of 'Prince' Lobengula of Matabeleland, with a local white woman, Miss Florence 'Kitty' Jewel. The couple had met in 1898 in Bloemfontein, South Africa, and continued their romance on Lobengula's arrival in London with the exhibition. The *Galveston Daily News* concluded the grave news that 'this little band of savages has brought home to the English people for the first time the seriousness of mixed marriages' (Colonial Film Project 2018). The prospected marriage revealed broader concerns about 'miscegenation', which the *Spectator* argued 'has long been regarded by the Anglo-Saxon race as a curse against civilisation' (quoted in Shepard 1986: 101).

Stoler (2002) reminds us how managing intimacy was central to the power relations of empire. Appropriate behaviours, sexual conduct, proximity and touching all worked as sites of struggle over race, gender, class. As developed in the case of the 'savages' of South Africa, orientalist imaginaries of feverish sexuality, immorality and virility conditioned both the racialisation of colonised men but also the parameters over the acceptable conduct of white women. We can read the crisis surrounding the exhibition as a constellation of fears over miscegenation and racialised 'others' penetrating the white (national) body (Yuval-Davis 1997). But this misses out on the complex ways that claims to family were already bound to the architecture of imperialism and with it the regulation of movement.

It is important to recognise how the fear of interracial intimacy described here was specifically translated into familial and imperial terms. What worried commentators more than interracial sex per se was the promise of interracial marriage proposed by 'Prince' Lobengula and Miss Jewell. Such a union was viewed as 'degrading' the moral and racial claim to white superiority, as well as practices of inheritance and patriarchal rule that structured empire. It equally focused on the impossibility of non-European family and the deviancy of uncivilised kinship practices. The press worried what would happen to Miss Jewell if she wed with this 'dusky savage' (Shepard 1986: 99). Lobengula and Jewell's marriage was not so much presented here as a threat to national integrity as to white colonial power – a power that was 'dissipated by daily familiar intercourses at Earl's Court' (Shepard 1986: 101). The fear was that if such unions were given the blessing of the church and state in the metropole, this promised to weaken the racialised-sexualised power of colonial administration, and weaken violent practices that apparently held native passions at bay all over the British Empire.

In this context, we need to consider how the arrival of 'savages' in London was constituted as a problem of movement across empire – how the movement of certain racialised bodies to the metropole challenged apparently stabilised hierarchies arranged around the (white) family. The closing of the exhibition to women thus became a key governmental move to stabilise fluid boundaries and reimpose a dominant set of ideas around racial intimacy, as did attempts by the management of the exhibition, the local vicar and the Chancellor of the Diocese of London to stop Lobengula and Jewell's wedding. These strategies acted to contain threatening mobility, bodies and intimacy. They were thus acts of bordering. To recognise this is to begin to flesh out how 'family' energised forms of imperial rule, including the regulation of movement.

Making empire

This brief detour through the *Savage South Africa* affair introduces several themes explored in this chapter, which examines how 'family' and 'borders' were entangled and made across the British Empire. Whilst intersecting analyses of race, sexuality and gender which focus on 'perversity' or 'feminisation' are useful tools for critiquing how colonialism was arranged through intimacy, I want to stress how heteronormative family was central to empire-making across metroimperial space (Mendoza 2016). As I outline above, it is the family that energises the spectacle of *Savage South Africa* – the fear of coupledom, reproduction and domesticity. Bearing in mind the relationship between family, domestication and borders I sketched out in the last chapter, I turn in this chapter in more detail to the political work family performed in British imperial and colonial projects (and then into the present). I examine how family worked and still works to energise colonial domesticating power, in terms of making decisions over what bodies and populations are protected, fostered and sustained, and who is abandoned, who is deemed dangerous and who can be stamped out.

Central to questions of life and death under colonial rule were questions of mobility. Sustaining and expanding the British Empire relied on the emergence of borders as a way of managing racialised populations, extracting profit and labour, and with this, forms of socio-sexual relations, intimacy and kinship. This was not only about controlling movement but at some moments enforcing movement, at other times facilitating sedentarism and the active promotion of heterosexual, single-household bourgeois domesticity as the template of 'civilisation' (Rifkin 2015). I extend the argument in this chapter, that 'family' was not only useful as an ideological tool of moral and civilisational judgement (which it was) but also a technology which shaped who could move where, with who and under what conditions.

Drawing on the position I briefly introduced with the example of *Savage South Africa*, I make a further contribution to debates on borders. I propose, against so much of the common sense in migration studies, that bordering practices are imperial in orientation, not national (also see Lake and Reynolds 2008; Bhambra 2017b). Bordering, I argue, emerged not to manage national populations but to manage imperial movement (see El-Enany 2020). Or, to be more specific, it was racialised mobility that was of concern to modern states (Mongia 2018). Disparate bordering practices increased in scale from the eighteenth century to regulate colonised populations who needed to be moved, resettled and enclosed in line with the evolving logic and needs of imperial racialised capitalism, and a dominant liberal heteropatriarchal order which fetishised the European nuclear family. What I propose in this chapter is that the birth of what we come to call immigration law in Britain was already conceived through both an imperial vision of the world and by drawing upon key practices of colonial rule – that is, the practical tools, strategies and knowledge of racialised governance. Immigration law is the institutionalisation of older forms of bordering and the innovation and expansion of borders by postcolonial states. It has thus become a key site through which colonial mandated ideas of family are resuscitated and reimagined. This chapter thus sets the scene for the more contemporary analysis that follows it.[1]

The chapter is split into three parts. Off the back of the *Savage South Africa* case, the first section traces the way that 'family' functioned across different sites of the British Empire: from a means of distributing racial bloodline and inheritance, to the organisation of violent suppression, to the management of movement. This explores how slavery was organised around the absence of family and how black communities were equally seen as a threat to the white imperial order in the mid-nineteenth century, particularly with the Morant Bay revolution in Jamaica. I take up the emergence of bordering practices here and suggest that regulating the movement of indentured labourers after the abolition of slavery became a prime concern of British authorities and settler states alike. This ultimately led to the innovation of bordering and nascent forms of immigration control in the late 1900s.

The second section of the chapter focuses on the developmental promise of 'marriage' and 'family'. Anthropology was central in drawing up global 'family taxonomies' which hierarchised colonised populations based on kinship structures and ideas of perversions. As well as showing how colonial states 'developed' populations through the family, I reveal how ideas around what or who could be family became increasingly important in emergent immigration regimes in white settler states.

The final section brings the discussion full circle by showing how imperial bordering circulated through the metropole. This explores the emergence of British immigration law, which I demonstrate was born out of the push to manage racialised mobility, orientated as this was around the colour line of empire. Whilst bordering practices were developed to protect and sustain the white (or in British imperial language, 'Anglo-Saxon') family, they were also experimented with to surveil the intimate relations of citizens of colour. I end by considering the significance of the British Nationality Act 1981, which ended the imperial definition of British citizenship and bound it to bloodline and kinship.

Blood, inheritance and the family

If the incident of imperial intimacies I began this chapter with raises the question of inheritance and bloodline in relation to British imperial rule, then this is only because this was key to how racial order was constituted across the Empire (Neti 2014). As Robbie Shilliam (2018) has demonstrated, British common law (from the sixteenth century) was organised around patriarchal descent. However, commercial law dominated in colonies. Whilst colonised people were seen as anthropologically bereft of proper family relations, they were equally denied methods of inheritance that were key to legal authority in Britain and the reproduction of social relations. Slaves were denied the right to family law across the British Empire – throughout American colonies, the West Indies and then under American settler colonialism after independence (Patterson 1982: 56–57). As Burnham (1987) argues, under the extensive plantation system that emerged in the eighteenth century, slaves could reproduce but could never be parents in the legally recognised sense. Instead, slaves were rendered commercial property and inherited slave status through their mother (i.e. the mother's master owned her children). Here slavery functioned as an inherited commercial bloodline rather than as a unit of kinship.

Tellingly, from the late eighteenth century, abolitionist critiques of slavery focused on how commercial law and slavery denied patriarchy lineage and posed an 'internal' danger to British moral authority and the 'family of man' that liberal empire was supposed to cultivate (Shilliam 2018: 35). To abolitionists such as William Burke, slavery was not necessarily dehumanising or racist. It instead threatened the proper gendered and sexualised relations of Christian marriage, family and patrilineal inheritance that were so central to British order (Shilliam 2018: 17). The promise of abolition in 1834 rested on the idea that newly freed slaves could be contained and governed by European codes of domesticity and labour in order to rid themselves of the essence of slavery (a point I return to below).

If bloodline organised the structure of chattel slavery and the dehumanisation of enslaved Africans (cutting them out of family law and the possibility of kinship), filial blood also arranged ideas of 'racial types' under British law. Satnam Virdee (2019: 12) describes this legal evacuation of black subjects from family as central to the early foundations of racial categorisation in American colonies from 1607. Not only were slaves and black subjects defined by descent but colonial law punished 'fornications' between slaves, black labourers and white colonialists, with the heaviest measures targeted at relations between white women and men of African descent (Virdee 2019: 12). As Colin Dayan (2011) demonstrates, being categorised closer to 'white' or 'black' was done on parental genealogy (a template that would be copied and refined in white supremacist regimes from the American South to South Africa). The transmission of 'black blood' was viewed as a 'stain' (Dayan 2011: 49). In turn, this decided whether a subject could be born into slavery or could inherit 'freedom'. Under West Indian law, for example, being classed as only having one-eighth 'black blood' made someone legally white and thus 'free' (Dayan 2011: 52). Just as subjects were born into slavery, the children of mixed unions (often free or white men and slave women) could inherit freedom from their father. In fact, the transmission of freedom grew so worrying that in the late eighteenth century in Jamaica, laws were brought in restricting 'mixed' or 'coloured' children from inheriting wealth (Patterson 1982: 146). Under imperial hierarchies of 'humanity', personhood was thus gained or eviscerated through a patriarchal connection to whiteness.

If imperial law shaped both who could be a family and in turn who could be fully human, this worked in relation to how imperial subjects were recognised as familial. Whilst populations within all British territories were conceived of as 'subjects of the Crown' this obscured how personhood was stratified in relation to whiteness, with black slaves at the bottom of this hierarchy. After the Indian War of Independence in 1857, colonial projects were increasingly conceived in terms of the protection and sustenance of an 'Anglo-Saxon family' (Metcalfe 1998; Shilliam 2018: 35–36). The task of colonial power in this period was directed at fostering this family through often-violent forms of capital accumulation and authoritarian government. This intensified already violent racial demarcations around a more explicit protection and fostering of capital interests in colonies and in further linking the metropole with white settler interests.

'Family' here functioned as more than a metaphor; it was an integral aspect of empire-making. Threats to family order could shape and justify how populations were governed. In 1865, black communities in Morant Bay, Jamaica, began an anti-colonial insurrection against the colonial

settler authorities and local elites. The violent suppression of the revolution was later used to debate both liberal and conservative ideologies of
empire in Britain (Hall 2002), but it equally revealed the stark realities
of colonial-racial hierarchies and violence. In a letter to Edward Eyre
(the governor of the colony), Major General Jackson (1865) outlined
the visceral disgust he felt when witnessing 'black labourers' harassing a
'White Lady' during the uprising. Such a moral outcry, which replicated
ideas of the sexualised 'black peril', was central to Jackson's justification
for the extension of martial law and bloody repression over parts of the
colony. It was 'extremely regrettable that the opportunity was not seized
to set an example … with a severe flogging', he argued (Jackson 1865).

The suppression of the Morant Bay insurrection by Eyre and his
generals would become synonymous with the most violent excesses of
colonial violence. Eyre attempted to justify the suspension of the law,
the deployment of troops and the systematic murder of hundreds of
black men and women and the burning of their homes as being necessary
to save 'decency' and 'Anglo-Saxon' 'democratic rule' (also see Hall
2002). Eyre (1865) argued to the House of Assembly a week after Jackson's
letter that the 'peasantry of Jamaica have nothing to complain of';
'rebellion, arson, murder' were merely the products of an 'ignorant,
uncivilised, excitable population' easily persuaded by 'anti-English
rhetoric'. As demonstrated by these connections, intimate domestic order
and the white woman's body were used to configure the dangers of
black rebellion and 'mob rule' (Head 2017). Whilst 'family' provided
an organising principle for categories of humanity and personhood,
colonial power was also orientated towards acts of violent domestication
and dehumanisation in order to protect the 'Anglo-Saxon' family (in
Jackson's case embodied by the lone white woman).

Borders and mobility

One of the key features of Eyre's violent domestication of revolutionaries
in Jamaica was the curbing of mobility of black communities who were

rendered a permanent risk to white settlers under martial law (Hussain 1999; Head 2017). However, such 'emergency' tactics were hardly exceptional and instead indicative of a more long-standing push to regulate movement by colonial states, plantation owners and private companies alike. As I began describing in the last chapter, managing settler and colonial projects across the British Empire was constantly bound to the need to manage movement. The increasing capitalisation and centralisation of the English state in the seventeenth century was built on practices of enclosure and the promotion and restriction of (im)proper movement (Federici 2004; Papadopoulos *et al.* 2008). Equally, experiments to domesticate colonised populations relied heavily on experiments in bordering. Key to strategies of accumulation and the reproduction of labour across the British Empire was the push to discover and categorise disorderly movement – those 'out of place' and 'worthless'. As colonies were more tightly networked into the imperial economy, this bordering worked to the particular demands of racialised capitalism, which demanded often contradictory processes of settlement, containment and identification. As we shall see, this provided a continued site for ideas of inheritance and family to be sustained and reimagined.

Radhika Singha (2000) argues that the East India Company consolidated control over India in the eighteenth century primarily through the regulation of movement. This process necessitated experimentation in colonial government and the birth of many modern policing and border methods. The emergent colonial state began to intensify forms of sedentarism with the hope of controlling forms of 'risky' movement across the Indian subcontinent (see Sleeman 1839 as a key architect of this). Here pilgrim throngs, hunting bands, *daciots* and 'bandits', itinerant communities who travelled without sufficient scrutiny such as religious mendicants, prostitutes and slave traders, increasingly became subject to experiments in enclosure, containment and monitoring (also see Legg 2007). As Singha (2000: 152) highlights, administrators were particularly anxious about the apparent absence of visible social hierarchies and 'verified social antecedents' which allowed colonial subjects to 'conceal or misrepresent their true identity' whilst they moved.

Authorities went to great lengths to capture moving bodies through innovations in policing tactics and the formation of modes of identity capture, categorisation and visual techniques. Browne (2015) argues that the formative modes of identity capture which were initially experimented with in plantation economies – slave ledgers and 'wanted' posters for escaped slaves – provided powerful forms of racial control and forms of proto-visual surveillance (see chapter 6 for more on this). We can see how emergent bordering practices such as these relied on producing stabilised identities that could be categorised, inscribed and made seemingly 'permanent', for example by physically marking risky bodies with tattoos, branding or finding 'unique' markers such as fingerprints, signatures and eventually DNA testing. This push to inscribe identity both on bodies and through the categorisation of mobility underpinned the development of passport technology (see Mongia 1999, or for a different account Torpey 2009).

Managing indentured labour

Bordering worked at key nodal points across both colonies and the metropole to allow some people to move freely and to restrain others (Mongia 2018: 56–85). The control of mobility was networked through the trade and movement of first slaves, then after abolition, indentured labour and convicts.[2] Bordering practices emerged in the context of a variety of spaces, from cotton production in the West Indies and the spice plantations of South India, to English industrial cities and Australian penal colonies. Port inspections, medical examinations, censuses and enclosures during pilgrimages all sought to regulate movement around the dictates of the evolving forms of imperial capitalism and the promotion of the 'Anglo-Saxon' family. Whilst all subjects of the Crown were technically entitled to move across the British Empire, these flows were managed in line with anxiety around the permanent settlement of black and Asian labourers, and hierarchised principles of citizenship (see Harrington 2012; Nahaboo 2018). This was crystallised in the context of white settler immigration policy developed in the latter part of the nineteenth century.

Mobility was equally facilitated and restricted *within* colonial states with the opening up of new markets such as the tea plantation system in North India, facilitated through the Assam Labour and Registration Act 1901, or in the plantation system in Guyana. Indentured labourers, as with slaves before them, could never move freely into or out of the plantation (or the state) (Mohapatra 2004). Without a pass and the relevant identity documents they could be arrested, beaten and even deported. Whilst the management of mobility was organised through the use of vagrancy laws that emerged in England from the seventeenth century, these laws were invariably applied to colonies but with a renewed racialised function.

Regulating movement across the British Empire also necessitated experimenting with more systematic control than vagrancy laws provided. In 1875, for example, the Indian Ports Act was introduced to regulate the flow of indentured labourers out of ports such as Mumbai and Chennai. Further acts were brought in to manage the use of cheap labour in the plantations of the West Indies, on the South African railways and the expanding agricultural sector along the West Coast of America (Shah 2012; Madhwi 2015). Indentured labourers were used by colonial authorities to shore up the cheap supply of labour across the Empire (often as a replacement for slave labour after abolition). Indian subjects were often coerced into signing indentured contracts which meant being shipped to the far reaches of the British Empire in almost slave-like conditions (see Dei 2017: 26; for Chinese indentured labour see Lowe 2015). The management of these subjects created networks of borders from the state of origin through ports and transit points to the receiving territory. It is here, Radhika Mongia (2018) argues, that we need to view the move towards the state's monopolisation and centralisation of bordering and the creation of state-delimited borders.

State bordering took the form of different practices working across dispersed sites, from the administration of labour camps, the legal texts of indentured labour contracts and private shipping company manifests, to the regulation of tropical and venereal diseases, the criminalisation and expulsion of labourers after contracts expired and naturalisation practices (Gutiérrez Rodríguez 2018). Whilst this bordering went against the promise of imperial citizenship and the right to mobility, British authorities often worked in collusion with white settler states to curb and manage 'Asiatic' or 'coloured' mobility – such as the introduction of 'continuous journey' legislation, which restricted entry to Canada for passengers who did not travel on a direct route from their country of birth (for more on how this shaped migration from India see Shah 2012: 198, and Gutiérrez Rodríguez 2018: 22). This reveals how citizenship itself was structured around the ideal of white subjects belonging to Britain and European states (Nahaboo 2018). Bordering might have been increasingly monopolised by states but this was orientated around imperial concerns and the hierarchies of racialised mobility, which were still global rather than national.

Whilst the movement of 'productive' groups such as indentured labourers was viewed as necessary for the extraction of profit, borders worked to maintain the temporality of labourers and to manage socio-sexual relations. In colonies from South Africa and Australia to the Caribbean and Pacific Island states such as Fiji, missionaries and colonial administrators alike continuously raised concerns about the immorality, promiscuity and litigious behaviour of indentured labourers. Reports increasingly circulated in the 1870s and again in the 1900s regarding the behaviour and moral conduct of Indian labourers in labour camps and on plantations (Emmer 1986). This led to the 1875 Indian Ports Act, and later the 1883 Indian Emigration Act and the monitoring of Indian ports of exit, as well as more localised forms of containment (i.e. the pass system, strict laws on movement, punishments for contravening contracts) that were intensified in colonies receiving indentured labour. As Mongia (2018) argues, whilst indentured labourers were viewed as more disciplined, it was those whose contracts had ended or who had escaped, or labourers who were non-indentured that authorities became concerned with. Labourers were presented as a particular type of masculinised-sexualised threat. The focus often fell on the imbalance of male over female indentured and non-indentured labourers on plantations and in camps. This was said to lead to an absence of 'stable' heterosexual unions and was explicitly linked with prostitution, promiscuity and homosexuality.

Here we find an early construction of the single male migrant who would later haunt the racialised imaginaries of nationalist discourse in white metropoles and settler societies throughout the twentieth and early twenty-first century. In a letter to Austin Chamberlain, the Secretary of State for India, Commander-in-Chief Beauchamp Duff (1915: 4) wrote that the 'moral conditions of the India Coolie lines in Fiji are indescribable', and that 'women emigrants are all too often living a life of immorality at the free disposition of their fellow recruits and even the subordinate managing staff'. In response, colonial administrators toyed with promoting the increased influx of Indian women to certain parts of the British Empire to actively promote forms of heterosexual family (Duff 1915: 5). Further laws stressed the need to forcibly repatriate and expel labourers on mass, following the Chinese exclusion laws in America (Tichenor 2002: 87–114). In South Africa suggestions were made for the drawing in of 'local' labour to protect the degrees of racial-sexual segregation that the colonial state was anxious to maintain. In Australia after 1905 any 'Asiatic' (even if a subject of the British Crown) found without the correct identity papers and proof of a contract could be subject to first imprisonment and then deportation. Such bordering was concerned with sustaining the global colour line arranged by the 'Anglo-Saxon' family by making mobile racialised-sexualised labour 'temporary', surveilled and disciplined, and ultimately expendable.

It is important to stress here how bordering was networked across metroimperial space and how claims to family energised bordering. Whilst 'family' was central to the organisation of racial order, bordering equally functioned to quell bodies deemed 'out of place' and disorderly, and to facilitate the mobility of those who possessed 'value' or who needed to be expelled (such as convicts, escaped slaves and non-indentured labourers). This worked across dispersed nodal points all over the

British Empire and was managed by a host of authorities – medics, police, plantation owners, labour camp managers, shipping companies, port authorities. It involved the collusion of imperial as well as local authorities to manage and expand these sets of practices. Bordering practices attempted to regulate movement but this was networked not only through the extraction of profit but through appeals to forms of racialised-sexualised order and the challenge posed in the intimate and affective proximity of certain bodies. Whilst family and kinship could be violently denied in the terms of contracts of indenture, in the foundations of slavery or in the lives of 'black rebels', 'family' could emerge as a technique for taming 'strange intimacies' through moral correction, or in the planned and regulated promotion of Indian women to serve as potential wives for labourers. The sustaining and fostering of imperial inheritance relied on governmental and symbolic power of 'family' (Neti 2014). Not only does this reflect increasingly hardening views about the appropriate limits of interracial intimacy throughout the nineteenth century, but also the way that worthy/unworthy life was encoded around appeals to heteronormative domesticity.

This reflects an emergent and multivariate role for practices which regulated movement: borders could maintain European socio-sexual order (in this case the 'Anglo-Saxon' family). Borders could sustain production, the opening of markets and the extraction of profit. Borders could suppress, capture or expel the disorderly, the dangerous or deviant (such as black rebels or the non-indentured or escaped labourer). Borders could also work to promote the heterosexual family as a means of developing or controlling colonised populations. It is this last point that I return to in the next section.

Family taxonomies, marriage and immigration control

For the features of primitive life, we must look, not to tribes of kirghiz type, but to those of Central Africa, the wilds of America, the hills of India, and the islands of the Pacific; with some of whom we find marriage laws unknown, the family system undeveloped, and even the only acknowledged blood-relationship through the mother.

McLennan (1865: 8)

In a series of letters and reports sent to the Colonial Office in 1872, the Bishop of the African Mission in the colony of Mauritius pleaded with church authorities and British officials to intervene in the problems posed by freed and 'landed' slaves. In Mauritius the black community had steadily grown since abolition, and with the criminalisation of the slave trade, boats and their human cargo were often intercepted and landed on the islands of the Seychelles (Allen 2008).[3] Equally, black indentured labourers were brought to the islands and used to force down wages. Significantly, Bishop William George Tozer (1872) described the population on the islands as being only 'freed in law' but not in essence or spirit: they were 'Heathen Negros' in a state of 'moral, physical and spiritual' arrested development, he argued. Despite the clear historical context of slavery and its abolition, which left these communities first reduced to chattel and then abandoned, the Civil Commissioner's inspection and report that accompanied his outcry focused on the domestic arrangements of the community (McGregor 1873). It placed attention on idleness, consumption of alcohol, and the half-naked and half-feral children running malnourished through encampments. It focused on the non-normative intimacies practised within the community and the condition of their huts that were 'dark with no ventilation' (McGregor 1873). 'Whilst mild and easily manageable', missionaries and civil authorities alike complained of the lack of spiritual uplift needed to 'elevate Africans into humanity' (Tozer 1872). Tellingly, one of the proposed practices of this 'uplift' was visualised in the absence of 'legitimate' (i.e. Christian) marriage.

Tellingly, domesticity and with it, 'marriage' were used as central tools in the management of black communities in Mauritius, as was true of large swathes of the British Empire. This provided several functions. The apparent absence of normative kinship (in this case Christian marriage and single-household monogamy) performed a racialising function to reveal the 'absences' of black and African people. The absence of proper domesticity was seen as reflective of their inability to throw off the 'essence of slavery' (Shilliam 2018: 55). Furthermore, the uptake of Christian marriage worked as a domesticating tool. Firstly, it was used to explain the precise spiritual and moral failure of their condition (such as idleness and the malnourishment of their children); secondly, Christian marriage was proposed as a solution to their predicament and a means of 'humanisation'. Domesticity here was viewed as a way of finally throwing off backwards kinship structures and 'developing' towards European modernity.

This reveals the varied role that marriage (and with it, normative claims to family) had in shaping and maintaining colonial order and with this imperial movement. Marriage categorised state-sanctioned forms of kinship, inheritance and access to citizenship. But in doing so it produced claims to civilisation and social development (Peterson 2014b). State investment in marriage was often carved out in a European setting alongside Christian authorities who committed to monogamous legal and spiritual forms of partnership and heterosexual family life (Cott 2000). In overseas colonies, Christian marriage served as a normative template against which other intimacies were judged (Neti 2014). Whilst liberals claimed that marriage was universal, this always worked to frame Christian marriage as an ideal against which other intimacies were viewed invariably as partial, deviant or threatening (Attorney General Dar Es Salaam 1951).

In this setting, anthropologists attempted to 'discover' whether local cultures practised 'marriage-like' rituals (Goody 1990) which could be sanctioned by the colonial state, thus conferring varying degrees of legitimacy and, with it, personhood. In this sense, they provided a taxonomy of family forms and perversions. Debates over the status of marriage became increasingly important in the early twentieth century as the scripting of who was or could be married was central to decisions over what constituted 'family' and with this an array of potential rights to British imperial citizenship and movement across the Empire.

Family as dehumanisation

It is important to recognise the afterlife of slavery that drives the encounter in Mauritius and in the role of marriage and family more broadly. As noted earlier, claims to family worked to organise, rationalise and challenge slavery. As I noted in the last chapter, this means recognising, as Spillers (1987) argues, that dominant claims to family were central to the dispossession of Africans in reducing them to chattel. Here the organisation of gender relations and domesticity was not so much imposed upon African people through colonisation and enslavement but worked to eviscerate their personhood and claims to humanity (see Thomas 2007: 31). Spillers (1987) famously argues that, black (women) slaves were not so much gendered as *ungendered*. The categories of heteronormative family used to explain non-European people and their status as (in)human merely produced black women as a series of absences – (failed) women, (failed) mother, (failed) body.

It is important to see the (un)gendering that Spillers talks of as working alongside the creation of taxonomies of family and marriage across European empires. In many respects, the (un)gendering of black slaves is bound to and structures the hierarchy of who could be familial and thus properly human. It was this unfamilial 'essence of slavery' that black communities in Mauritius were unable to shake off. This anti-blackness connects to the way that nineteenth-century anthropologists sought to investigate and categorise non-European peoples. Colonial anthropologists such as John McLennan (1865) and Lewis H. Morgan (1877: 186–275) mapped and taxonomised marriage and family forms, which served to instruct colonial authorities on the legitimacy and desirability of non-European kinship structures. The categorisation of marriage and kinship forms was nearly always linked to temporalities of bourgeois European modernity. Eastern marriage forms could be windows into Europe's past (see Goody 1990) or, as with the native population of America, reveal the perverse and deviant social practices which could threaten to degenerate human 'progress' and 'development' (Rifkin 2015). Here the (un)gendered black slave represented a key series of absences that other peoples were categorised in relation to.

This was increasingly viewed in stark evolutionary terms. From the mid-nineteenth century, racial science and particularly colonial anthropology argued that marriage forms were suggestive of the evolutionary development of a society and its relative progress from 'simple' to 'complex' patterns (Benedict 1935; Mead 1964). It was argued that evolutionary patterns rested on an evolving form of heterosexuality:

> From an initial state of 'promiscuous intercourse', there had arisen, in sequence, the 'Communal Family' (founded on the intermarriage of brothers and sisters); the 'Barbarian family'; … the 'Patriarchal family' (founded on the 'marriage' of one man to several wives); and the 'Civilized Family'. (Hoad 2000: 140)

Deviant, perverse and decadent forms of intimacy – 'traditional' kinship, polygamy, promiscuity, same-sex intimacy – became aligned with pre-modern savagery. This was depicted as threatening the linear development of humanity towards its blossoming under the civilised family of European modernity (also see Benedict 1935: 189–191). To McLennan (1865: 8), particular bonds of legal intimacy could only be a product of a modernised society as 'marriage laws, agnatic relationship, and kingly government, belong, in the order of development, to recent times'. The most primitive of societies, argued McLennan (1865: 9), were those that could only recognise blood relationship through the mother – challenging or ignoring the template of European (and particularly British) patriarchal lineage. This temporalisation and spatialisation of family forms, from 'savage' to 'civilised', did not just replicate pre-existing racial categorisations but was also part of the ongoing process of colonial race-making. Here the 'discovery' of kinship forms that replicated European Christian marriage could be used as a sign of the potential for development of a society or its retardation (again see Amadiume 1987; Thomas 2007).

Family as development

Hierarchical family taxonomies were central to the geopolitics of empire. In the same way that the absence of family in the enslaved was used to organise their dehumanisation, anthropologists focused on matrilineal, polygamous and tribal structures to reveal how African society remained 'undomesticated' and primitive (McLennan 1865: 10; Amadiume 1987). Goody (1990) demonstrates how 'Near Eastern marriage' was placed in this hierarchy, defined as it was by strong and often violently imposed communal ties. As with African 'bride pricing', Near Eastern marriage was viewed as a means of financial exchange and formative of an overzealous and 'cruel' patriarchal culture. Orientalist interpretations of Islamic law also pointed to the apparent feature of forced or intra-family marriage where 'universal taboos' such as 'incest marriages' were actively promoted (Goody 1990: 321). The 'Asiatic marriage' form was recognised as a deeply religious and ancient series of rites. Certain religions and castes were labelled as emulating nascent forms of European domesticity such as Sikhs and Brahmins (Goody 1990: 17; on the role of religion and sexuality in colonial India see Nandy 1988 and Chatterjee 2010). Against this, 'traditional' practices such as polygamy, child marriage and purdah were viewed as a sign of backwards and uncivilised tendencies in other lower caste Hindu and Islamic communities (Gowans 2003).

As marriage was increasingly desecularised by liberal authorities throughout the twentieth century, what remained of these hierarchical taxonomies were distinctions between what Povinelli (2006) calls 'genealogical communities', where family forms were bound to tradition and ritual, and those forward-facing 'autonomous subjects' who practised marriage as a symbol of romantic love, choice and contractual exchange. This was used to explain the relative (under)development of societies globally and the resistance to progress that lay hidden in intimate relations (see chapter 3 for more on this).

The alignment of 'family' with a particular evolutionary geography meant that colonial projects either worked to contain deviant familial forms (through their rejection in law) or to promote normative alternatives. This was demonstrated in the promise of abolitionists and missionaries in Mauritius that black populations could alleviate their position or be redeemed through marriage and domesticity. Debates over how to domesticate colonial populations through forms of developmental violence thus faltered around this vision of heteronormative progress. To some administrators such as Henry Maine, progress would occur organically as 'marriages arranged by caste and kinship would give way to marriages based on individual contract' (Mody 2002: 228). However, at the beginning of the twentieth century more interventionist approaches became viewed as necessary. Acts such as the Concubine Act 1911 and the Child Marriage Restraint Act and Age of Marriage Act 1929 were developed to criminalise and punish non-normative intimacies across the British Empire. Other domesticating strategies were crafted in welfare and social work projects of home-making, such as in the construction of 'marriage schools' where Ugandan women were taught how to sustain patriarchal gender relations (see Mair 1944), or in the creation of model villages in India that were designed to teach 'backwards' populations proper forms of domestic governance and rituals of hygiene.

The shift towards the active promotion of marriage and family forms in the early twentieth century reflects broader imperial strategies of domestication and a push by British authorities to develop colonies as decolonial movements agitated for independence and were violently pacified. As with welfare programmes in Britain, the production of domesticated households, patriarchal monogamy and childrearing were viewed as central to economic development and producing desirable workers, as well as quelling revolutionary fervour (Owens 2015). Heterosexual, monogamous sex within marriage and the rearing of children were viewed as vital aspects of moral uplift and taking up wage labour.

In the Colonial Office's 1959 report on the future of Commonwealth development, H. L. Elvin was resolute that economic prosperity was tied to developing civilised family structures and suppressing 'traditional practices' such as polygamous marriage. 'These things will go', he argued, 'just as certainly as Africa will move forward to participation in full modern life' (Elvin 1959: 12). Such ideas echoed the logic of the 1942 Moye Report on development in the Caribbean. The Colonial Office's welfare strategy proposed the creation of an entrepreneurial agricultural sector which relied on Caribbean women taking up patriarchal domesticity and rejecting the more extended kinship structures that sustained many communities.

In the push to develop and 'modernise' colonies, a key site for the promotion of (as well as hierarchisation of) family forms was also found in increasingly centralised border practices, especially those that pertained to the movement of racialised labour.

Intimate borders

Whilst technically all subjects of the British Crown had the right to travel across the Empire, as I described above this right was increasingly delimited by border practices from the 1870s, often in parallel with rising white nationalism in settler colonies. Immigration law increasingly restricted the movement of Asian labourers to settler colonies, but once contracted and registered, indentured labourers still held the right to travel with their families. This meant that at various points across imperial space border agents, medical inspectors, law makers, ship crews, ticketing agencies and so forth made decisions about whether subjects could move, or settle, based upon the proof of family ties to registered labourers and 'settled persons'. In doing so, this provided colonial states with the opportunity to monitor and shape what cultural forms of kinship and intimacies were legally and culturally recognisable as 'marriage' or 'family'. At the same time this created a site to make certain intimate relationships possible over others.

In South Africa the Immigration Regulation Act 1913 made provision to limit and regulate subjects at entry points such as major ports but also made provisions to detain labourers travelling without an official registration (i.e. a valid labour contract or official papers). Registered labourers and merchants could travel with their families. However, what complicated this right was the struggle over whether polygamous marriage could be included as 'family' (Mongia 2018). The normative idea of 'family' in South Africa was explicitly codified in the Immigration Regulation Act 1913 as Christian, monogamous, heterosexual marriage and included biological parentage of children under 16. And yet, imperial law upheld the right to polygamous marriage. What this produced was a complex network through which border agents in South Africa and other settler states tried to limit and deny the right of passage for Asian labourers and their kin on the basis of the suspicion that they were not 'real families' (see Shah 2012). Following the 1913 Act, officials in the Transvaal were given increased powers to inspect the papers of suspect aliens and take fingerprint and biographical records at transit points such as train stations (see Chamney 1915). Although family members were allowed to travel with registered labourers, colonial administrators were anxious about the true identities of subjects travelling and working under the guise of 'children' or 'spouse' status.

Communiques during the 1910s reveal the extent to which immigration officers, medical inspectors and port authorities were tasked with judging the validity of these embodied family claims (Chamney 1915; Horsfall 1915). Unaccompanied Indian youth were the target of particularly intense scrutiny. M. Chamney, the principal immigration officer in the Transvaal, recollects in a letter to the Colonial Office his experience of interrogating 'hindoo minors' crossing the province. They were, he recounts, well versed in performing the 'lies' needed to escape detention by claiming particular parentage or using communal ties to secure registration and documentation (Chamney 1915; also see MacDonald 2012). In another account, 'children' waiting to be interrogated by port police in Cape Town were deemed 'suspect' because of an inability to speak English and because they provided ambiguous claims about who their fathers were. In such contexts, administrators consistently stressed the logistical nightmare of the 'family' loophole and the problem of disproving parentage of 'Asiatic' children 'who often did not look to be related' (Chamney 1915), particularly where formal records of Indian marriage rites and parentage were not consistently available or documented.

In an early rendition of border inspections and the struggle over family immigration law that would follow, we can consider here how particular cultural imaginaries coalesced in the categorisation of who was a 'genuine' family, and in the bureaucratic process to categorise and authenticate 'suspicious' intimacies. The white colonial gaze was confounded by linguistic differences and apparent physiological characteristics of 'biological family members' (Immigration Regulation Act, SA 1913, Chapter 2, 4.1). It was similarly perplexed when confronted with intimate relationships that were not codified by state registration such as marriage and polygamous marriage rituals. Such doubt over the legitimacy of Hindu and Islamic marriage rites feed into other orientalist imaginaries of Indians as sneaky, disguised and possessing communal ties which confounded the policing of the colonial state (see Sleeman 1839). To officials, the complex kinship structures that they were asked to adjudicate on were indicative of a more general moral and cultural malaise. This reflected how 'the Indian community does not desire finality' - 'finality', that is, in the clear categorisation and appropriate parental and gendered relationship of bourgeois (white) domesticity (Chamney 1915: 12).

Border decisions over who could be family were shaped by what a family was supposed to look like, but they equally conditioned who could move with whom. As we see with the above cases, non-adherence to normative kinship meant exclusion from the rights of imperial citizenship and settlement based on family life. But equally, bordering shaped who could be familial through historical frames of intelligibility - in their affective relations, movement and behaviours, people could be judged to be familial or not.

Such heteronormative ordering was an inherently violent project. Negotiations over what 'family' could be were sites of disciplinary violence (including deportation, imprisonment, abandonment, separation of kinships and family members). This was not merely reflective of the fumbling of administrators and the absence of appropriate means of

paper identity but part of micro, everyday practices through which
questions over personhood were continually arranged by normative
ideas of family. In the end it is only the corporeal intimacies privileged
as white that could be offered sustenance, protection and public legiti-
mately through imperial citizenship. It is significant here to note that
whilst the imperial state temporally and formally granted polygamous
marriages legal status across the Empire, this was short lived and was
radically overturned by the British state in the 1960s with the increase
of Asian subjects moving to the UK.

Whilst family taxonomies provided colonial administrators with
knowledge of population development, this was always arranged, as I
proposed above, around the absences of the figure of the black slave
who was without family. This was always contrasted against the idealised
patriarchal domesticity of white coupledom. Other intimacies were
deemed to be 'imitations' or 'shams' which were stuck in time. Heteronormative family not only configured the colonised as living in a
'European past' but often as inhabiting a separate time from humanity
proper (Agathangelou and Killian 2016: 8). Scrutinising these sham
intimacies and the potential for developmental progress would be a
task for border practices over the course of the twentieth and twenty-first
centuries (see chapter 3). This happened as bordering was intensified
in northern states, which were increasingly focused on the movement
and settlement of people from colonies to the European metropoles.
In the next section I turn to how the different bordering tactics of the
British Empire 'came home' and were domesticated within the metropole
and postcolonial Britain.

Revolt(ing) intimacy and empire 'coming home'

In June 1919 a string of violent mob attacks on black communities
living in Liverpool became termed a 'race riot' (May and Cohen 1974).
Over the course of the month, numerous clashes between white and
black sailors took place across the English city. This unrest further

extended into August when the police themselves went on strike and set forth a series of violent protests which were eventually quashed by the deployment of three army battalions, several naval destroyers and a battleship on the River Mersey. In the aftermath of the so-called race riot, commentators sought to place the event in the spiralling unrest that was growing across the British Empire, with the rise of pan-African consciousness, decolonial social movements and the Bolshevik revolution (May and Cohen 1974). The causes of this unrest were also put into a now common logic of colonial racism: the 'black peril' – the apparent threat that black men posed to white women in the port city. White men (both local and alien) were seen as defending, in the words of *The Times* newspaper, their race and the 'instinctive certainly that sexual relations between white women and coloured men revolts our very nature' (quoted in May and Cohen 1974: 114).

In a bid to suppress further violence and regain order, the police instituted a series of mass arrests and the detention of seven hundred black subjects 'for their own safety' (May and Cohen 1974: 114). The Superintending Officer of Liverpool's port then introduced special registration cards and fingerprinting of 'alien' seamen. In doing so, authorities appropriated technologies of criminalisation and identity capture that had been experimented with in colonial India and across settler plantain economies. As with previous restrictions on 'aliens' this did not *legally* affect British subjects. However, black sailors were frequently defined as 'alien seamen' by the local authorities until they could prove otherwise (a task that was nearly impossible, as carrying a passport was not a requirement of travel from colonies to Britain). Despite outcry against this policy by black community leaders, immigration orders increasingly became viewed as a useful device for suppressing racial disorder in the UK's port cities, and in turn disciplining black bodies. In the Aliens Order 1920, deportation of 'aliens' was formalised and streamlined, and then in the Special Restriction (Coloured Alien Seamen) Order 1925 specifically targeted people of colour for expulsion. Deportation of black British subjects again worked by proxy, as anyone *suspected* of being a 'coloured alien seaman' could be deported.

Given the arbitrary nature of these powers, they were frequently used to police, harass and punish black communities living in port cities across Britain.

Colonial domestication was again at the heart of this encounter, as the bordering practices that had been honed across the British Empire found new uses in the metropole. Here the racialised distinctions that made up imperial citizenship were reformed as black and Asian subjects were deemed 'unworthy' of the right to settlement and movement. Internment, detention and deportation, tools that were experimented with across the Empire, were reasserted to both police and expel racialised communities within Britain in the name of white supremacy. In the face of decolonising movements and the unravelling of order in certain parts of the Empire, emergent immigration laws (alongside older modes of policing and social government) were increasingly viewed as vital to reassert the appropriate sentiments of white intimacy and racial segregation 'at home'. Whilst this was not the first time that bordering practices had targeted black and other racialised communities in the metropole (see Wemyss 2009), the Special Restriction Order set a precedent for immigration law that would intensify across the twentieth century and through formal decolonisation.

Immigration and the colour line

From 1905, centralised British immigration law drew upon border tactics and logics that had been experimented with across imperial space, in the formation of a 'national' border regime. Imperial in history and in orientation, immigration law began to focus on the cultivation of white Britishness – whilst remaining tied to wider claims of the imperial 'Anglo-Saxon' family. Whilst initially orientated towards the policing of 'aliens', particularly Jewish refugees arriving from Russia and Eastern Europe after the succession of pogroms in the 1890s, the state border regime began increasingly to focus on British subjects of colour.

As colonial practices were turned further 'inwards' to refocus on Britain and racialised communities within the metropole, claims to family played a powerful role in this re-alignment. Debates over the limits of race relations, national identity, social and economic order, welfare and policing were played out in debates over appropriate forms of intimacy, sexuality and domesticity of people of colour. For instance, in the eugenics-inspired 'Report on an investigation into the colour problem in Liverpool and other ports' in 1930 the authors argued that 'black seamen were twice as likely to carry venereal diseases, and that mixed race or "half caste" children were more likely to be sickly' (Eddo-Lodge 2017: 20). In the categorisation of 'English' or 'Negroid' children, the report drew on colonial ideas surrounding bloodline and inheritance as well as facial measurements from eugenics to warn against both the risk of 'colour' and 'racial mixing'.

Anxiety about the racial composition of Britain was configured in the scrutiny placed on colonised people arriving in the UK. Immigration management increasingly became a site to play out the protection of white patriarchal domesticity by restricting mobility based on race. This did not begin with the larger scale movements of people from the Caribbean and the Indian subcontinent, and the now famous arrival of HMT *Empire Windrush* to Britain in 1945 (see, for example, Wemyss 2009). However, bordering was certainly scaled up and intensified in post-war Britain. Family immigration law worked with other bordering mechanisms, such as policing, health, education and welfare, to establish a template for the type of intimate relations that could be tolerated within and that could move to Britain (see Jackson 2015: 161). In 1947 the British government, in a bid to consolidate imperial ambitions against decolonising movements, changed citizenship law so that any subject within a British territory was promised the right to move to, work, settle and claim full citizenship rights in the UK.[4] The structure of various immigration laws from the 1960s onwards, and forwarded by all the main political parties, was to dismantle these rights until they were eventually overturned in 1981. Gurminder Bhambra (2017b) argues that this process was one of converting 'citizens' into 'migrants' (also see Karatani 2002).

As with the movement of racialised labour across the British Empire, bordering in the UK worked to support demands for an influx of a cheap and exploitable work force, at the same time as restrictions were increasingly imposed because of the fear of chaotic 'race relations' brought about by 'coloured immigration' (Hansen 2000). It is worth remembering that it was not movement per se in this period that led to the introduction of extensive immigration restrictions. For example, some two hundred thousand people settled in the UK from Southern Europe between 1945 and 1948, and this led to no overhaul of the immigration system (Bhambra 2017b). Such large-scale resettlement is almost entirely forgotten in dominant histories of immigration because it was predominantly white. Instead, it was the movement of those racialised as non-white that needed to be managed (Gilroy 1992).

From the 1960s, bordering practices fluctuated from facilitating the movement of family members of Commonwealth citizens, to delimiting the mobility of family members because of raised anxiety about the 'unfamilial' character of black and Asian communities (Webster 1998). Whilst patriarchal family structure was viewed as producing a compliant, orderly workforce and containing racial disorder (through the 'threat' that black and Asian men posed to white women), alternative kinship structures were viewed as the remnants of underdevelopment, 'primitive' culture and 'savagery' (Turner 2014).

The Immigration Act 1962, for instance, restricted Commonwealth citizens' right to move by making employment a mandatory requirement of entry into the UK. However, 'family members' were guaranteed special status and could reportedly move 'freely' (until this was ended in 1968). As I have already demonstrated above, evidencing who was family to claim the right to settle replayed distinctions over who was properly familial within imperial and evolutionary hierarchies. Debates in Parliament circulated around how Caribbean families could provide evidence of family connections because of the frequent absence of proper marriage or evidence of kinship (Hansard 1961). Fears that polygamous marriages would allow multiple partners and dependents into the country were equally recycled (see also Foreign Office 1933). In the 1962 legislation, 'dependent' family members were overtly classed as married wives and children (Home Office 1962: 7–8) or dependent elderly relatives, making the entry of husbands or male fiancés more difficult (a practice which would later be intensified in the now infamous 'primary purpose rule'; see chapter 3) (Smith and Marmo 2014). This essentially led to the outlawing of non-normative family structures from imperial/British citizenship.

Equally, border agents working at airports and ports were given discretionary powers to decide whether a person had a 'reasonable' family relationship to a settled person (Home Office 1962: 8). Replaying the restrictions placed across the British Empire, such strategies provided new tools for surveillance over the intimate relations of colonised subjects. These border practices also worked to *produce* certain types of family, that is by making heterosexual kinship and marriage a mandate of citizenship and settled rights.

Citizenship, bloodline and inheritance

Whilst family immigration law worked to surveil intimacies (a point I take up in more depth in chapter 3), citizenship was increasingly organised throughout the mid-twentieth century around the defence and promotion of the white 'Anglo-Saxon' family. This family had both a national (i.e. British, or more specifically English) and imperial white constituent (i.e. tied to settler states or 'dominions').

In order to dismantle the rights claims of Commonwealth citizens of colour, successive British governments from 1968 to 1980 pushed to define British citizenship in terms of biological inheritance. Firstly, in the 1968 and 1971 immigration acts, the right to abode was restricted to those who could prove a line of descent to a parent or grandparent born or naturalised in Britain. This was finally consolidated in the British Nationality Act 1981, which ended the (now much reduced)

rights of Commonwealth citizens to residency. After 1981, British citizenship was defined by being born into citizenship through an ancestral
connection to Britain (and not the Empire). Citizenship was thus actively
reimagined as a structure of bloodline and kinship in line with key
imperial claims about race. Whilst formally eviscerating the rights of
millions of Commonwealth citizens, the Act preserved the connection
of white subjects to British citizenship as they were more likely to be
able to evidence an ancestral connection (i.e. to the 'Anglo-Saxon' family).
The privileging of white mobility and the simultaneous containment
of people racialised as non-white was managed through binding heterosexual family further into the codes of citizenship.

It is telling that after the Falklands War, Margaret Thatcher would
in 1983 grant the Falkland Islanders 'special citizenship status'. She did
this whilst recalling that they were of 'British stock' (Thatcher 1982).
It is worth dwelling on the how the inheritance of whiteness or blackness
worked in this setting. Thinking through this racial claim to 'British
stock', we should consider that the British Nationality Act was more
than a reorganisation of citizenship as 'national belonging'; it was the
reimposition of an older patriarchal colour line which had sustained
the British Empire. Just as inheritance worked to 'pass on' slave status,
or encode people as white and 'free', reproduction was institutionalised
as the site for the (non)transference of British citizenship and the
organisation of inherited rights into the polity. Citizenship was legally
bound to both the reproductive white family and the racial scientific
fantasy of bloodline. Just as claims to family dispossessed colonised
people of their personhood across the Empire (as undomesticated and
'deviant'), this worked to dispossess millions of former colonised people
of their right to settlement in Britain.

As the British Nationality Act passed through Parliament in 1981,
black protestors in London were actively railing against both police
violence and the institutional racism of the British state in what became
known as the Brixton Riots. Imogen Tyler (2010) argues that we should
see a direct connection between the passing of the Act, which made
Commonwealth subjects into second-class citizens, and revolts by black

political activists taking place in the London borough (also see Andrews 2018). Just as immigration and citizenship law stripped people of their rights and managed racialised communities as 'internal others', the police functioned as an occupying colonial force to violently contain, suppress and punish resistance (Jackson 2015).

It is significant that in the aftermath of the Brixton Riots, the Scarman Report would eventually admit that the event revealed discriminatory policing tactics against black communities, for example in the use of colonial bordering tactics such as the 'sus' vagrancy laws to crush protests or in the mass incarcerations brought about by the authoritarian practices of Operation Swamp (Jackson 2015). However, Lord Scarman also laid the blame for the violence at the feet of the black community in Brixton. One of the causes of the riot, he argued, was the violent tendencies of black youth who grew up in 'single parent families' (Amos and Parmar 1984). Violence, ultimately, was a product of a lack of domestication – the key to this being (failed) black motherhood. Not only would citizenship now be inherited as a bloodline, but this faltered around the absence of black motherhood, a key factor in the inherited 'essence of slavery'. It is telling that as the British government re-institutionalised the racialised sexuality of the Empire into citizenship law that (failed) black motherhood would be presented as the site for the reproduction of social ills.

The British Nationality Act 1981 was one of many examples of how the logic and orientation of bordering practices of the British Empire became nationalised and brought more closely in line with the British nation state. Whilst still locked to an imperial mapping of the world, bordering practices increasingly focused on both policing communities of colour within Britain and restricting the possibility of movement into the country. We must consider this process as a set of acts of colonial duress – the adaption and intensification of Britain as imperial terrain, and a process of internal colonisation reaffirming the racialised governance that structured colonial administrations globally (also see Turner 2018). Whilst colonial rule was further intensified and bound to the policing of once-colonised or peripherised communities within

Britain, the cultural and social landscape of Britain worked to deny such linkages, either through a disavowal of the Empire (as 'past wrongs'), or a nostalgic harking back to the lost privileges of whiteness found in more explicit appeals to white nationalism. In such a context, as I shall argue over the next few chapters, appeals to family continued to work both to stratify people as modern or backwards, domesticated or undomesticated, and to hide the colonial and racialised coordinates of such work.

Conclusion

This chapter has demonstrated some of the intimate historical connections between family and bordering that circulated from British colonies to the metropole. 'Family' emerged as a key technology in sustaining and fostering colonial projects and in the nineteenth century became increasing bound up with the regulation of movement. Family worked here as a governmental mechanism to shore up whiteness, but equally it was central to the domestication, surveillance and suppression of colonised people and the regulation of their mobility. Claims to family, as I have previously proposed, ultimately structured claims to humanity.

I have argued that bordering, as it expanded the regulation of movement in the nineteenth century, rather than being a nationalistic project was in fact imperial in orientation. Bordering was both an imperial and colonial project. The regulation of movement was central to colonial states' bid for order (as illustrated in India and Jamaica). Bordering functioned to facilitate and control the mobility of slaves, mobile people and indentured labourers through the shifting dictates of imperial capitalism and racialised sexuality. Bordering here must be seen as more disparate than state-sanctioned immigration law or the management of 'migrants' or 'aliens'. It was forged in the management of escaped slaves, rebels, criminals, nomadic communities, prostitutes, indentured labourers – some who had legal status to travel, others who did not. Equally, bordering was practised by multiple social authorities, not only the imperial, settler or colonial state, from shipping companies, medics, labour camp inspectors, to missionaries, police and plantation masters. The regulation of mobility across the British Empire was orientated towards the management of the global colour line by discovering and controlling people 'out of place'. This was institutionalised in the late nineteenth century by settler states in nascent immigration law, but imperial authorities colluded and supported such bordering (such as in the 1875 Indian Ports Act). Whilst concerned with containing, identifying and expelling '(un)productive', 'dangerous' or 'deviant' subjects, bordering practices were frequently energised by appeals to heteronormative family, a key lynchpin of (settler) colonial order.

Fleshing out the approach to family and domestication I began in the last chapter, I have demonstrated that family – or more specifically the claim to a heteronormative, monogamous (white) nuclear family – energised colonial projects and, with this, bordering practices. Family took on multiple roles in empire-making; it functioned to dehumanise and *dispossess*. Personhood was arranged through bloodline, such as in the case of slave law. but people could also be judged as more or less human based on where they fell within family taxonomies. That is, whether they emulated Christian marriage and bourgeois domesticity. Family could also be *developmental*. Populations could be 'brought into' civilisation and be 'developed' by the facilitation of familial and patriarchal domesticity. Family could be *control*. Claims that the 'true family' was European and white led to the management of interracial intimacy, just as suspicious intimacies (such as polygamous marriage and extended kinship structures) were intervened in, suppressed and expelled by colonial states.

Throughout these processes, 'family' became key to how mobility was perceived and regulated. Bordering and then borders (immigration law) worked to protect and defend (white) family life, either to foster or protect it (such as the example of the masculine/sexualised threat of black sailors in Liverpool); borders worked to delimit and intervene in intimacies viewed as unfamilial (polygamous kinship, unmarried or same-sex couples); borders worked to shape and produce familial relationships (such as promoting the movement of the wives of black and Asian Commonwealth citizens). By being attuned to different archives of bordering, I have illustrated how various forms of colonial knowledge and practice informed what we know as 'family' and its absences. Different claims to family were not merely a set of contingent and 'culturally located' ideas about kinship, but instead a site of racialised power where struggles over personhood, life and death, inclusion and abandonment were played out.

By ending with a focus on British immigration law, I have emphasised how colonial rule worked across metroimperial space but was contingent upon local struggles. In examining the codification of citizenship and immigration law in the UK, I have argued that this was a reinscription and adaption of imperial and colonial government to the particular demands of white supremacy and familial order. From the 1920s, centralised immigration became a key site for the ongoing domestication of colonised peoples. Immigration law and the bordering this entailed was orientated towards delimiting the right to settlement of Commonwealth citizens of colour. And equally, facilitating the mobility of white subjects of the 'Anglo-Saxon' family (often from settler states). Furthermore, bordering practices, often bound up with but not exclusively driven by immigration law, were frequently drawn from experiments of colonial rule. Consider, here how practices of detention and deportation were tested and honed across the British Empire, such as in the control of indentured labourers, and then circulated back 'home' to manage growing racialised communities in the mid-twentieth century. Following the role of bordering and family across the Empire, immigration law became a key site for the rehearsal, reimagining and intervention into non-normative intimacies in the UK. In doing so it provided a means of controlling the movement of colonised subjects but also a means of producing and shaping what family could be.

As I will go on to explore in the next three chapters, the ongoing border regime in the UK continues to be forged through, and equally to reinvent, colonial rule as an intimate spectacle. This means recognising that the reasons why people move are intimately bound to empire, in the same way that practices that regulate movement equally work along and resuscitate 'imperial grooves' (de Noronha 2018).

Notes

1 This chapter was based on archival work undertaken from 2016 to 2017 at the National Archives, Kew; the British Library, London; and the Bristol Archives.
2 I talk less about the role of convicts in the regulation of mobility in this chapter. The creation of penal colonies provides another fascinating history of movement, often arranged around ideas of failed whiteness and the regulation of 'internal others' within Britain, orientated as this was towards projects of settler colonialism (such as in Australia). For more on this see Walters (2002), Wolfe (2006) and even Turner (2016).
3 The British Crown Colony of Mauritius included the contemporary territory of the Republic of Mauritius, Rodrigues, the outer islands of Agaléga, St. Brandon, Chagos Archipelago and Seychelles.
4 Devising the newly titled Citizen of the UK and Commonwealth.

3

Shams

Sham marriages have for too long been an easy target for migrants seeking
to circumvent our immigration rules, often assisted by organised criminals.
Registrars are frustrated when they marry couples who are obviously
sham; we need more effective tools to deal with it.

Immigration Minister Mark Harper
(quoted in Home Office 2013a)

In 2014 the Home Affairs Select Committee convened for a special
session on the issue of 'sham marriages'. It aimed to explore those 'in-
genuine' marriages of 'convenience' imagined to be performed for the
'benefit of gaining immigration status/advantages' (Home Office 2013b).
In the Home Affairs session, expert witnesses were called to testify on
the 'threat' that sham marriages posed in modern Britain. Within the
session, Labour MP David Winnick suggested that 'all of us are agreed
upon the dangers of sham marriages and want to see an end to them'
(Home Affairs Select Committee 2014). Following this 'common-sense'
logic, shams were presented as a dangerous practice that not only
undermined the immigration system but created a mockery of marriage
itself and those engaging in it 'truthfully'. Immigration, the story goes,
does not simply threaten British society but it does so by undermining
the normative institutions of marriage and family.

So, what is so dangerous about sham marriage? And in turn, what
is a 'sham'? Who is a 'sham'? And what do 'shams' do? In this chapter
I trace the way that fears about shams have driven a style of government
in contemporary Britain built on demarcations of 'genuine' and 'sham'

intimacies. Starting with immigration rules around family migration, I reveal how this has connected up with broader practices of domestication from social work to counter-terrorism. The sham, I go onto argue, has become a transit point for ongoing modes of colonial rule and the dispersal of what I call 'intimate borders'.[1]

Built on the promise to protect heteronormative life, the right to family is enshrined in international law and historically in states' immigration policy. However, as I proposed in the last chapter, wealthier northern metropoles and settler states have consistently used European ideas of family to regulate the movement of people – especially in the case of movement to Britain from ex-colonies. From the late 1990s family migration (in the main, people moving on the basis of familial dependencies) was increasingly viewed as a problem for European states because it promised a right to permanent settlement and citizenship. Following the practices of monitoring Commonwealth citizens' familial relations that we saw in chapter 2, the emergence of concerns around sham marriage in the UK worked to bolster the state's ability to restrict who counted as 'family' in immigration law. With the rise of the Conservative-led coalition government's policy of the 'hostile environment' from 2011, this route was increasingly viewed as site for 'illegal migration' and 'criminal activity' (Home Office 2013a). It was increasingly presented as being akin to an existential security threat.

Whilst sham marriage has been increasingly criminalised, this equally rehearses concerns about what intimacies can be tolerated by the British postcolonial state. In the latest overhaul of the family migration route in 2011, then Home Secretary Theresa May led the reform of the family migration visa by arguing that the changes to the visa, which involved introducing a minimum income requirement for non-EU spouses/partners, were about making sure couples were 'genuine' (Home Office 2011a: 3). The visa focused on evidencing whether the affective and domestic bonds between a couple were both 'genuine' and 'subsisting'. Being a sham was not only making an intentionally 'fraudulent' claim for the benefit of immigration status but falling short of moral and economic claims to bourgeois domesticity (see Turner 2014; Carver 2016).

It is significant for our discussion that the reforms were preceded by a series of (perhaps now familiar) concerns that Bangladeshi and Pakistani communities were *over-represented* in family migration figures (Home Office 2011b). It was also thought that the practice of 'international marriage' could be used as a route for forced marriage, human trafficking and the reproduction of 'unintegratable' communities (Gill and Mitra-Kahn 2012). In the 2014 Home Affairs Select Committee session that I began with above, it transpired that the *real* danger of sham marriages was non-EU subjects marrying EU citizens for the benefit of residency and settlement. Far from a technical issue about circumventing immigration law, the idea of the sham has been loaded with suspicion regarding the 'backwards' kinship practices of former colonised people and their mobility. This continues to drive bordering practices today.

Policing the sham

In this context, we need to consider the slipperiness of the sham and its appeals to danger; foremost, how it brings together different racialised-sexualised markers concerning suspicious movement, suspicious kinship and suspicious communities. As we see above, the sham is not only sham marriage but also slowly reveals itself to be about 'sham intimacy'. If the migrant is always suspicious – that is, a fraud or sham – intimacy is a particular site of danger (Ahmed 2016). The fraud of the migrant can be easily hidden (it is assumed) within the private confines of coupledom and the family. The job of the state becomes proving this fraud through the monitoring of the intimate relations of those claiming rights to see if they are 'genuine'. But the sham is not only framed by a broad suspicion of the migrant. The sham is highly racialised. It mobilises a historical suspicion about the fraudulent and 'backwards' intimacies of non-European peoples born out of empire – foremost here, the (im)possibility of Asian and black family life. We thus need to be aware of how concerns about sham marriage bleed into sham intimacy, which translates into sham families.

This chapter sets out to explore the different points of contact that the sham brings together. It does so by reading the sham as one site for the reworking and reforming of colonial modes of domestication in contemporary Britain. I argue that a key point for the transference of empire-making within Britain is through 'intimate bordering' – the fostering or abandonment of bodies and subjects made a sham or 'out of place' by their relations to ideals of the modern family. Tracing the work of the sham helps us get at some of this, in particular by revealing how heteronormative claims to family continue to draw lines around who is civilised or backwards; whose intimacies are suspect and subject to intervention, scrutiny and containment. This works to police not only migrant subjects on the move but also racialised communities with settled rights in Britain.

If, as I argued in the last chapter, family taxonomies were central to how colonial projects were justified and directed under formal empire, I argue that a hierarchy of 'family forms' are just as central to the racialised treatment of Asian and black communities today. Whilst heterosexual family units were viewed as necessary for the development of the colonised population and the settlement of Commonwealth citizens in Britain during the mid- twentieth century, migrant families have been increasingly viewed as troubling the national-civilisational order. 'Family' is treated as a site for the reproduction of cultural difference, in which Islam is made highly visible.

From the late 1990s policy makers became increasingly fixated on the 'hyperpatriarchy' of Muslim families – especially with regard to the treatment of women and in debates around forced marriage. Whilst these concerns still drive immigration policy and family visa regimes, as I will show, they have increasingly fed into the question of the 'integration' of settled Muslim communities. After the onset of the Global War on Terror after 2001, the problem of suspicious intimacies has been increasingly bound into counter-terrorism strategy. Reworking the family taxonomies I presented in the last chapter, the markers of the modern or 'genuine' family are now found in appeals to liberal choice, romantic love and domestic governance. It is these seemingly 'deracialised' principles that are increasingly used to govern mobility and rights claims as well as the policing of settled communities within Britain.

In the first part of this chapter I explore the short history of intimate bordering in the UK, connecting this to the regulation of Commonwealth citizens through immigration law that I began in chapter 2. I then go on to demonstrate that what often drives this bordering is a particular gendered configuration of the unintegrated female migrant/citizen. Following Cynthia Weber's (2016) proposal that we should examine the 'worlding' that particular figurations perform, I trace how the figuration of the unintegrated woman dominates debates around the sham and thus immigration and integration more broadly. I show how suspicions about the sham intimacies of Muslim communities have been networked into social work and the UK's counter-terrorism programme Prevent. This provides an emergent site for the reworking of colonial forms of rule which work through different forms of intimate bordering.

The (re)emergence of the 'problem' of family migration

In the UK what reignited the recent anxiety around sham marriages was the lifting in 1997 of the infamous 'primary purpose' rule, which governed the movement of married or unmarried partners into the UK from 1979 (Menski 1999). The primary purpose rule meant that couples had to prove that the move of a partner to the UK would not result in an economic benefit or advantage. This in effect created an explicit colour bar on family migration after 1979. It made it extremely difficult for non-white male partners from ex-colonies to secure settlement as they could nearly always be seen as 'gaining a benefit' (Wray 2015). As with the Immigration Act 1971 and British Nationality Act 1981, primary purpose was set up in a way so that it privileged the movement of white spouses from Anglo settler colonies and those within the European Economic Community.

Whilst primary purpose was configured around the threat of male Commonwealth citizens, intimate scrutiny was still placed on feminised bodies. Smith and Marmo (2014) detail how border agents at Heathrow Airport during the late 1970s used their discretionary powers to inspect the 'suitability' of fiancées arriving from India by carrying out 'virginity tests', which took the form of the physical inspection of these women's hymens. During this period, as we might remember from the last chapter, family dependents and fiancées could travel to live with a Commonwealth citizen settled in Britain. Border officials were tasked with disproving this relationship. The highly invasive inspection of women's genitals reimposed orientalist notions of chaste and passive South Asian women; no Indian bride, the logic went, could marry without being a virgin (Levine 2007). Discovering who was a sham in this setting reduced South Asian women's bodies to objects of flesh to be examined (Spillers 1987). The mediocre attempts by British authorities to either apologise or rectify these wrongs reveal a broader normalised distain for the body of the colonised. It should be noted that in Enoch Powell's now infamous 'Rivers of Blood' speech (in 1968), whilst it was the figure of the sexualised and violent black man that Powell warned was a threat to British society, it was the female 'migrant' who was cast as the reproducer of unBritishness. Just as it did across the Empire, the natal feminised body provided a key site for playing out concerns about 'race relations' and the reproduction of difference in Britain. And this continues today.

When the New Labour government withdrew the primary purpose rule in 1997, this heralded almost immediate calls to re-monitor the movement of migrant partners for settlement. This was in part precipitated by the rise in the number of partner applications from former colonies. For example, applications from Pakistan went from 1,960 in 1996 to 5,080 in 1998 (BBC 1999). What stimulated this anxiety was a series of interconnected fears regarding the social landscape of 'multicultural' Britain. In this setting, sham marriages became fused to the regulation of immigration through issues of 'integration', the 'problem' of settled minorities communities and specifically 'cultural practices' of forced marriage.

We can trace the emergence of the prominence of sham marriage to the Immigration Act 1999, which stressed the urgent need for closer scrutiny of migrants moving for 'family life'. Whilst the New Labour government of this time was rhetorically invested in celebrating 'multicultural Britain' and supporting ethnic minority rights, this Act immediately worked to restrict the movement of subjects from outside of the EU. Border officials were tasked with monitoring whether a relationship was a marriage of 'convenience' by assessing whether a couple had an intention of living together. Civil registrars were also obligated to report 'suspicious' marriages to the Home Office.

These techniques were later supplemented with increasing scrutiny over the 'genuine' and 'subsisting' nature of the relationships of those claiming a right to settlement through the family migration route. After 1999, sham marriages became a normalised concern across governments of all political leanings. To reflect some of these changes it is worth noting that in 1999 partners travelling for family unification (as partners of British citizens or those with leave to remain) had to prove their intention to live together and the nature of their 'continuous' relationship. By 2014, couples had to prove that they were participating in a 'genuine' *and* 'subsisting' relationship according to strictly regulated income, language and cohabitation requirements (Charsley and Benson 2012).

What is a sham?

So, who is caught up in the sham? What cultural figurations energise it; give it 'colour' and fleshiness? How does this work to shape particular border strategies? During the re-emerge of the 'problem' of family migration in 1999, a BBC *Newsnight* report and subsequent article provided details of the emerging crisis around shams (BBC 1999). In doing so it exemplified the connections that were emulated across numerous policy documents, immigration acts and legislation over the next seventeen years. I read this report as a manifestation of the dominant ideas that are attached to shams, which become enshrined by the legal apparatus of the British state during the 2000s.

The BBC report is described as an investigation into 'Fighting arranged marriage abuse'. Its key task was in explaining to the British public how 'cultural practices' of arranged marriages – linked in the report to Pakistan and Asian communities in Britain – were often 'shams' for the benefit of mobility and settlement. Quoting an official in the British High Commission in Islamabad, the report argued that: 'There is no doubt that a lot of the girls are being forced to bring husbands into Britain against their will but we are powerless to do anything about it' (BBC 1999). Marriages, we are told, particularly in Asian and Muslim culture, are forced upon girls through family and community pressure and for the benefit of male patriarchs. It is worth quoting the article at length to reveal the connections it makes visible:

> The 'problem' is that the present Labour government scrapped the hated 'primary purpose' rule in one of its first initiatives after coming to power in 1997. Labour wanted to appease the sensitivities of Britain's ethnic communities. Under the old system, officials at the High Commission could ask couples intimate questions about each other ranging from favourite toothpaste brands to preferred sleeping positions to determine whether the 'primary purpose' of the visa application was a marriage of convenience or based on true love. The change in rules had an immediate effect. In 1996, there were 1,960 applications for entry from Pakistan to Britain from would-be husbands. In 1998, after the law was changed, there were 5,080. (BBC 1999)

Here the rise in applications after the end of primary purpose is presented as evidence of the rise of sham marriages. Suspicion is cast over the family relations of anyone travelling from Pakistan. Colonial ideas of the 'backwards' kinship practices of colonised people are then bound to social problems within the UK, in particular the treatment of women in 'ethnic communities'. We are told that 'forced marriage' (collapsed into 'arranged marriage') is an increasing risk to social order: 'The police in Bradford, where the Asian community add up to 19% of local people, are overwhelmed by appeals from Asian women for help' (BBC 1999). The article voices concern regarding primary purpose; however, the overhaul of the policy is presented as merely an attempt to appease minorities ('appease' being a word that in the British context is frequently linked to the historical appeasement of Nazi Germany in the 1930s). Intimate bordering such as passing judgement on the right to mobility based on knowledge of toothpaste and sleeping positions is suddenly presented as entirely reasonable and necessary.

Importantly in this report, 'marriages of convenience', 'arranged marriage' and 'forced marriage' are frequently slipped together as if they are the same thing. Ann Cryer, MP for the northern English town of Keighley, is quoted in the report as arguing for the state to step in to immediately stop the 'cruel practice of making their girls go back to Pakistan to marry first cousins or those to whom their family owe a favour' (BBC 1999). Her remarks show how the sham was bound to the apparently 'backwards' practices of Asian communities. British Asian patriarchs, she argues, have such little respect for women's rights that 'girls' (always infantilised) are merely traded for 'family favours'. Just as orientalist anthropologists sought to delineate the 'Eastern' marriage form (Goody 1990) – with its propensity for incest, hierarchy, honour and absence of love – Cryer discovers the modern expression of this orientalism. Most shockingly for her, the 'Eastern family form' is found alive and well in her constituency in West Yorkshire.

This report ties together various types of shams. The sham expands to more than the circumventing of immigration controls also to include forced marriage. Because of the cultural location of forced marriage, it became linked to the practice of intercontinental, diasporic and arranged marriage. As forced marriage was transformed into an issue of mobility and women's rights, it shaped the family migration debate and the remit of policy-making. In this period, forced marriage came to exemplify the generalised oppression of women within so-called 'ethnic communities' (Wilson 2007), both within Britain and in 'backwards' colonised spaces such as Pakistan. The sham became enlisted in a set of equivalences, putting the problem of the Asian and then (later) Muslimified body and kinship practices front and centre (Razack 2008). Through the figuration of the deviant forced marriage, all other marriage forms conducted by these communities become shams.

Policing shams

> How can you tell if a marriage is a sham, that is if it isn't beauty and the beast?
>
> Keith Vaz MP, Home Affairs Select Committee Meeting,
> 24 June 2014

Ann Cryer's warning in 1999 that the 'cruel practice' of forced marriage would lead to social and civil unrest foreshadowed future governments' commitments to deal with sham marriage. Here the practice of international relationships and particularly arranged marriages were presented as always 'risky' to women (Gill and Mitra-Kahn 2012). A push to criminalise forced marriage was accompanied by bordering techniques which increasingly focused on scrutinising the intimate relations of those travelling for family unification. In the context of the War on Terror and the hypervisibility of the 'problem' Muslim, the debate around the improper intimacies of minority communities also began to energise wider imperial forms of violence. The reconstruction of anti-Muslim racism after 2001 made deviant intimacies and patriarchal violence a particular problem of Islam (Cowen and Gilbert 2008). The domesticating role of the colonial state was energised to reform and modernise such intimacies through the regulation of mobility, interventions into Muslimi-fied households and, with this, the staging of a war of 'civilisations'. All this coalesced in various ways around the paternalist role of 'protecting women's rights' (Farris 2017).

In 2003 migrant partners were refused access to public funds of the welfare state and had to provide certification that their houses were not 'overcrowded' (Gedalof 2007). English language proficiency became a requirement of partners in family unification cases by 2010. Such policy changes were saturated with racialised logics of control. For instance, whilst justifying the new crackdown on sham marriages in 2002, Home Secretary David Blunkett argued that Asian communities practising arranged marriages should choose potential spouses from within the British Asian community, rather than risk putting their daughters in danger (BBC 2002a). Changing their 'traditional' practices was a fair demand, according to Blunkett, because 'those who come into our home – for that is what it is – should accept those norms' (quoted in Brown 2011). Not only were Asian communities 'guests' – forever unwanted migrants – but they were undermining the 'genuine' family home of white Britons.

Whilst campaigners struggled to criminalise forced marriage in legislation (until 2014) – mainly because of resistance from black feminist groups (see Larasi *et al.* 2014; Wilson 2014) – depictions of forced marriage bolstered further immigration practices focused on shams. In 2008 the age at which someone could sponsor a migrant partner was raised to 21. The proposal was viewed as a way of limiting forced marriage as younger adults were viewed as overly susceptible to the pressure of both their family and community (Home Office 2007). In turn, it reminds us that communities practising intercontinental marriage will always remain *immature*. And furthermore, that forced marriage travels to Britain from former colonies.

The hypervisibility of forced marriage was greeted with thoughtful concern from many black and Asian women's associations, many of whom argued against criminalisation and the conflation of forced marriage and immigration (see Southall Black Sisters 2001; Wilson 2007; Razack 2008; Larasi *et al.* 2014). This was often ignored by law makers. Instead, paternalistic and often overtly colonial logics saturated discussion of shams in this period. For example, during the unveiling of civil legislation against forced marriage in the House of Lords, Lord Lester argued that the amendment was a direct continuity of reforms to eliminate the 'barbaric' practices of sati and child marriage in colonial India (Hansard 2007). Colonial nostalgia here begets contemporary coloniality.

Family visa rule changes

In 2012, in a move that many commentators viewed as the return of primary purpose, the Conservative–Liberal Democrat coalition government introduced a complete overhaul of the family migration route. Here the multiple delineations of the sham coalesced to re-energise further intimate bordering. Whilst Pakistani and Bangladeshi communities were made hypervisible within Home Office reports (see Home Office 2011a; 2011b), the government made it explicitly clear that community practices of arranged marriage would be protected in future changes. Instead, policy makers focused on creating an 'objective' template of what a 'family' *should* and *could* be (Home Office 2011a: 7), so as to regulate marriages of convenience, forced marriage and 'in-genuine' and 'un-subsisting' relationships all at once. However, this 'objective template' of partnerships was informed by a particular white, bourgeois imaginary of liberal romantic love, household governance and equally energised through a fear of suspicious and deviant intimacies.

Changes to the family visa after 2012 meant that in order to live with a partner from outside the European Economic Area (EEA), British citizens and settled persons had to earn at least £18,600 a year, effectively barring 47 per cent of those working in Britain from applying. The non-EEA partner also had to prove a higher standard level of English than previously accepted, and the couple was forced to evidence cohabitation (or proof of intention of cohabitation). Theresa May, then Home Secretary, made it clear that this new visa system was about distinguishing between 'genuine' and 'in-genuine' relationships, and about providing a material and objective test that these relationships were 'subsisting' (Home Office 2011a). The changes to the visa were equally accompanied with more stringent reporting duties tasked to registrars administrating marriage; they were given a checklist to investigate whether the marriage they were due to perform was one of 'convenience' or 'forced' (Carver 2016: 273).

The 2012 regime effectively works to regulate the possibility of a whole host of undomesticated intimacies moving for settlement. It does so by testing household income as an ingredient of a 'subsisting relation-ship'. But it equally judges applicants on intimate histories of their lives together in ways that emulate specific norms of heterosexist 'progress', such as through evidencing marriage, sharing private property, cohabita-tion, savings, reproduction, childrearing, shared language (see Turner and Vera Espinoza 2019). In this setting, the sham works to queer certain groups as outside of the 'modern' family and nation. Whilst same-sex couples can increasingly be included in legal rights to family life, if they emulate the domestic arrangements and progressive imprint of liberal consumption, monogamy and choice, this works to exclude a host of other intimacies and practices of kinship which are marked as unfamilial (for parallels see Puar 2008).

Because of the way that forced marriage conditioned the reforms and the apparent 'over-representation' of South Asian communities in histories of family migration (Sirriyeh 2015; also see Home Office 2011a: 43–45), the Home Office's 'objective template' needs to be seen as a site for producing and monitoring racialised-sexualised deviancy. The visa does this by also excluding other non-normative intimacies such as non-married homosexual couples, multiple-partner relationships, non-cohabiting couples, the poor/workless, which are also managed by the distinction of the 'genuine' or 'sham' couple.

It is important to recognise that the push to discover shams through complex categories of domesticity has had a dramatic effect on visa application and refusal rates. Between 2007 and 2015 applications for all forms of migration for family life fell by 52 per cent. Family unification figures (i.e. those moving to be with a British citizen or settled person) also show a dramatic decrease of 41 per cent in the same period, from 53,300 in 2006 to 21,600 in 2015 (Blinder 2017). With the introduction of high-income requirements in 2012, refusal rates for family unification rose from 16 per cent in 2011 to over 40 per cent in the last quarter of 2012 (Blinder 2017). Such rates of refusal are seen as a success by the Home Office in both meeting targets to lower immigration and in the context of the government's hostile environment to weed out scams and sham marriages.

To appreciate the colonial racialised-sexualised logics at work here, it is worth noting how refusal rates for family unification visas differ starkly based on country of origin. For example, the refusal rates in 2016 for family unification of partners from Pakistan was 40.6 per cent, Nigeria 49.1 per cent and India 31.8 per cent; meanwhile, the refusal rate for those from the US, Canada and Australia varied from 10 to 14 per cent (Home Office 2016). If mobility was arranged around an explicit imperial colour line throughout the nineteenth and mid-twentieth centuries, this is reimposed starkly here. The imperial colour line regarding movement and settlement is organised around whether intimate relations are deemed 'genuine' or 'sham'. Whilst appearing to be about economic and technical criteria, the visa is able to function as tool of racial governance, and it does so in classic neoliberal fashion by appearing to be 'without race' (Goldberg 2008). This is not about race, the story goes – merely about 'genuine' and 'subsisting' family forms (for an alternative reading see Kofman 2018).

The body and the border

The manner in which claims to family are increasingly evaluated and evidenced in this regime of intimate bordering is important. Just as previous border regimes focused on the body in order to read and assess shams, so does this one. 'Proving' that someone is not in a 'genuine' relationship involves a commitment to both an ideal of coupledom (culturally located) but also an assessment of the feelings of love which are viewed as innermost – that is, as embodied and affective (D'Aoust 2018). The enhancement of registrars' obligation to report suspected sham marriages and civil partnerships (from 2014) reflects the affective and embodied politics of assessing the 'non-genuineness' of couples. Civil registrars across Britain must now assess *every* couple who want to register a marriage or civil partnership. But of course, given the existing racialised-sexualised coordinates of the sham, this *all* is disingenuous. This assessment can occur during the interview conducted when applying for a ceremony or on the day of a ceremony itself (Home

Office 2014a). If reported to the Home Office, sham couples can have their ceremonies interrupted, their union revoked and face criminal prosecution and deportation. Since 2014, EU nationals involved in sham marriages can also be considered for deportation. This is significant, as prior to this such practices focused on non-EU nationals (Home Office 2015: 14).

The strategy of Home Office officials arriving to break up ceremonies is a reminder of how central the spectacular protection of heteronormative institutions alone is to the politics of shams (D'Aoust 2018; Wemyss *et al.* 2018). Just as border officials judge the embodied intimacy of the couple, eye contact, affection, body language, shared languages, caresses, handholding, kissing all become features of the 'look of love', which registrars now use to assess a couple who may be sitting in a municipal waiting area or embarking on a civil ceremony (Home Affairs Select Committee 2014). Here the 'paper identity' of a visa assessment slips over into judgements made about the deeper 'truth' of the migrant's body and its relation to others (White 2014).

It is worth remembering how imperial regulation of movement often fixated on the racialised body to evidence and reveal inner and intimate 'truths'. Border officials in South Africa policing indentured labourers at the turn of the twentieth century relied upon judgements as to whether a child looked like they were related to an accompanying adult. Such judgements conditioned whether a child or dependent could be allowed to travel with a family member and claim the rights of a British subject. This was coded through skin, eye or hair colour, dress and their mannerisms towards each other. Shah (2012) reminds us of how disease screenings in North American ports from 1870 surveilled the migrants' body for the inner truth of their productivity. Here urine and stool samples provided an 'inherent truth' of whether a migrant would be a burden on the state through disease, immoral practice or 'unsuitability' for labour (Shah 2012: 200). The invasive 'virginity tests' performed on South Asian fiancées at UK airports in the 1970s demonstrated how the colonised and feminised body is expected to reveal intimate truths that 'paper reality' (a passport or visa) obscures. In this context the push to re-centre bodily relations in the assessment and evidencing of shams, in both the spectacle of the wedding ceremony and the registrar interview, follows a history of such bodily scrutiny and, with it, ways of seeing (see chapter 6 for more on this). Such intimate bordering is always about capturing but also permitting the 'inner truth' of the potentially devious body and its affective relations.

The sham in late liberalism

As I have set out above, the sham does a lot of work to energise intimate borders. It intensifies scrutiny over migrants' bodies and the policing of racialised communities, limits the possibility of international intima-cies, and it regulates an evolving colour line around family unification to the UK. It makes judgements on proximities and the potentiality of 'family' within the now national space. This means breaking up, separating and intervening in kinship and intimate relationship that appear unfamilial. In the last chapter I discussed the centrality of taxonomies of marriage and family forms to colonial government, particularly the way that family forms were networked into legal systems of colonial states (private property, inheritance, marriage) and then into the regula-tion of imperial mobility (through ports of exit, entry, labour camps, shipping mandates). The parallels to the function of the sham deserve teasing out, and in doing so they will help us think through a colonial and racial rather than only national orientation of intimate borders and the violence they reproduce.

Whilst the intimate bordering attached to shams is considered to be about fraud and the violence of forced marriage, it is equally energised by developmental logics of 'liberal love' and tenses of modernity and backwardness (Povinelli 2006). As I have previously discussed, nineteenth century family forms were organised around an evolutionary hierarchy of humanity, with the white heterosexual family at the top and black kinship patterns at the bottom (see Hoad 2007: 56; Sharpe 2010). Arguably, this template of heteronormative 'progress' continues under the guise of the 'modern family', defined as it is by liberal notions of choice, consumptive domesticity and love. It is these colonial hierarchies of intimacy/family/humanity that are reasserted through the policing of the sham and UK visa rules.

Berlant (1997) argues that what is central to liberalism is the autonomous, bodied intimacy of the liberal subject, who through mythologies of private/public and inner sanctuary (see McKeon 2005) is presented as having a pre-political/social capacity for love. Romantic love (often heterosexualised) is viewed as the pillar of modern liberal subjectivity because it relies upon the festishising of 'choice' and the passion of 'intimate' emotions (which are internal to the individual subject), as well as coalescing around heteronormative appeals to childrearing and parenthood. Here we should consider how liberal love becomes a particularly powerful way of reasserting secularised forms of Christian marriage as the template of domestic modernity and progress. Whilst these claims to liberal love are 'universal' (i.e. everyone has a capacity to love in the same way), this is built on distinctions between liberal/ progressive and backwards/illiberal intimacies, which equally replicate the distinctions between the white and black family (Collins 1998). To Povinelli (2006), 'progressive', forward-looking (autonomous) subjects choose their intimate relations and reproduce out of love. Against this, 'backwards' cultures – what Povinelli calls 'genealogical communities' – are instead bound by tradition, obligation and duty. They are rendered underdeveloped, stuck in a distant past without 'value'. Here who is backwards- or forwards-facing, who has value, is arranged around supposedly universal claims to intimacy (such as the claim that the UK visa is about 'genuine couples').

As we can witness with the above examples of the role the sham performs in UK immigration practices, who can access rights is organised around how they match up to the (white) 'modern family' – that is, how they emulate notions of genuine intimacy and domesticity. This is detailed in visa regimes where applicants must prove they are 'genuinely' intimate by evidencing that they are a 'romantic couple', with the particular affective and behavioural bonds this assumes, such as communicating and feeling towards each other in ways that are intelligible to the state (D'Aoust 2018). Evidence of appropriate domesticity is then judged on evidencing cohabitation, consumption, private property, economic productivity, wage labour. This became enshrined in legal and bureaucratic practice with the 2012 family unification visa changes with the new income requirement and tests of 'genuineness'.

This system arguably provides a new taxonomy of family forms where people are placed in a hierarchy of worthy/suspect/unworthy intimacies. Here bodies and communities (such as South Asian and Muslim communities) can be demarcated as 'backwards' because of an adherence to 'tradition' and 'cultural practices' which are viewed as working against the evolutionary empowerment of women, minority sexualities and apparently universal race-blind values of romantic 'autonomy' or 'choice'. They are cast as always/already imminently suspect. These notions of the 'modern family' thus produce racialised effects without appealing to race. Because the modern family is naturalised as universal, against which everything else is a sham, people are racialised by their relationship to 'backwards' kinship practices. They are judged as to whether they have 'developed' towards the template of the modern family. Far from being objective, the current template of family within the UK visa system directly polices people moving from ex-colonies such as Nigeria, Bangladesh and Pakistan. This is the ongoing coordination of 'family' as racial governance.

In order to assess where people fit within this reworked taxonomy, authorities rely on further colonial practices of intimate bordering. Judgements are made concerning the 'look of love' by border agents, registrars, lawyers. Such judgements are networked through cultural notions of what is properly familial and appropriately intimate. This is *colonial* not only because of the continuity of orientalist representation. This form of liberal government shares a series of logics, knowledge and practices which are recalibrated and adapted across imperial time and space, and continues to shape who has access to modes of reproduction – that is, who is sustained and fostered and who is excluded or abandoned.

Once we take the dynamics of where the majority of applications for family unification originate from into account, we need to see this within a history of imperial citizenship. We should remember here that the revoking of imperial citizenship in 1981 turned Commonwealth citizens into migrants without rights to settlement in the UK, which they had held, up until this point, through historical birth right. The movement of people for family life is in part driven by the necessity of diasporas (created by empire) to sustain themselves. What the discourse of the sham does is obscure the fact that until 1981 and prior immigration acts, these communities had a right to move and settle in the UK. And that bonds of kinship, histories of mobility, the material grooves of dependencies across the structurally unequal 'commonwealth' continue to shape who moves where.

The emergence of the discourse of shams energises the racial-sexualised hierarchies of empire (by deciding who is genuine/sham). It equally hides the way that colonised peoples have been dispossessed of legal heritage and rights, and the unequal structure of racialised/imperial capitalism which enriched the metropole at the expense and dispossession of colonies, which remain impoverished (for a parallel argument see Andrews 2018: 28–33). Think for a moment why many of the poorest former colonies, such as Bangladesh, remain such large contributors to family unification. This is no accident.

The imperilled and unintegrated woman

'Liberal love' plays a significant role in how hierarchies of civilisation are readdressed in contemporary government. But what equally drives the bordering process around shams is a particular racialised-gendered figuration of feminised victimhood. This is the figure of the unintegrated female migrant. This figuration does a huge amount of political and cultural work to sustain the domesticating force of colonial government – it gives bordering *life* and *flesh*.

To Weber (2016: 28), 'figurations' are repeated tropes, images and imaginaries that come to dominate social meaning and produce common-sense understandings about political phenomena. As Razack (2008) has argued, it is the 'imperilled Muslim woman' who propels so much of the debate surrounding forced marriage across Europe. In this section, I want to sketch out how variations of this figuration are located within the bordering moves attached to the sham, but also in the wider cultural and political landscape of late liberal Britain. I show how the unintegrated woman was increasingly Muslimified post-2001, and became known as a victim of traditional patriarchal culture. After the 7/7 bombings in London and the growth of 'homegrown' radicalisation, this passivity has been translated into complicity and active engagement with the reproduction of terrorism. This shows the extent to which intimate borders not only shape immigration policy around shams but also wider forms of rule such as integration and security strategies.

The imperilled brown woman holds a significant place in the annals of colonial government, often rehearsed in the axiom of 'white men (and women) saving brown women from brown men' (Spivak 1988). If the figuration of black womanhood was haunted by the afterlife of slavery, oversexualised and unchangeable, the 'brown woman' was known as underdeveloped but often 'saveable' – invariably *not-quite* rather than *non-human*. The reformist agenda of imperial feminism focused on the particular predicament of colonised women who were viewed as an un-emancipated and underdeveloped form of femininity in places such as India (Mohanty 1984; Grewal 1996). As Mohanty (1984) argues, the figure of the colonised and underdeveloped woman has historically worked to shore up white, feminine subjecthood as 'progressive' (also see Lorde 2007). In this context, white femininity is viewed as supported and sustained by the 'modern family' (as a less patriarchal and emancipated sexual arrangement); against this, underdeveloped femininity is presented as trapped within the structures of backwards kinship, patriarchal violence and the third-world home.

Sham marriage is depicted as working at the expense of women. Women can be at risk of importing patriarchal husbands from abroad. However, the more dominant figuration of the 'at-risk' woman is as the newly arrived migrant-housewife. To MP Ann Cryer, defending the push to criminalise forced marriage, the problem is that 'Asian girls who are *brought in* as wives are frequently abandoned by their husbands and their in-laws' (BBC 2002b, my emphasis). Here the feminised subject is coerced and passive to demands of patriarchal culture. She is only ever a *wife* and only ever 'brought in'. But she is also risky because she is assumed to be *unintegratable*.

From 1999 this at-risk femininity shaped bordering strategies which were intensified after the onset of the War on Terror. Reflecting the higher percentage of women who apply through the family migration route (Blinder 2017), borders increasingly focused on the need for female migrants to 'integrate' and 'partake' in British society. It was assumed that as male migrants were expected to work, they would learn English. Against this, the female migrant was assumed to be housebound – removed from the labour market, unable to speak English or learn 'British values'. The removal of welfare benefits in 2002 for non-EEA partners focused on this 'problem', as did the requirement to speak English and take the British citizenship test prior to naturalisation (see Turner 2014). Such strategies were viewed as 'supporting' the figure of the non-English-speaking housewife into the labour market and out of the ghettoisation of minority communities (Home Office 2011a). Deploying ideas of 'undeserving' welfare scroungers, the female migrant was viewed as needing coercive support to reach her 'potential' and 'contribute to British society'. To Theresa May, this was why an objective test of intimacy was needed for family migrants (Home Office 2011a). Just as testing migrants' knowledge of British society became a requirement of citizenship, emulating practices of intimacy and cohabitation became a requirement for settlement and proof of a potentiality for harbouring '(un)British values'.

The gendered character of these bordering practices has been shared in other areas of social government, particularly with regard to integration.

In 2016 the 'Integration Tsar' Louise Casey authored a government report which mirrored the concerns of previous immigration policies but focused on settled communities of racialised citizens. In the report the 'dangers' of communities living 'separate' or 'ghettoised' lives was viewed as a failed strategy of a too-generous family migration regime (Casey 2016). What made this problem worse was that 'minority' women, it was supposed, were failing to integrate into British society (also see Cantle 2002). Muslim women, the report argued, exemplified this trend. They were presented as lacking opportunities in the job market, bound to domestic duties, rarely speaking adequate English and tied to the demands of reproductive labour.

We can thus place Casey's report in a tradition of both imperial feminism but also an example of what Farris calls 'femonationalism', where the discourse of feminist works to energise white nationalist stigmatisation of 'unprogressive' and 'anti-women' cultures (Farris 2017). To Casey, the oppression of women is structured by the Muslim community and household where 'women are treated as second-class citizens' (Casey 2016: 120). Whilst women themselves were to blame for this social breakdown and tasked with their own emancipation, the ultimate responsibility for this lagging behind was the patriarchy, misogyny and homophobia of Islam.[2]

What is significant about the Casey report is that it works to silence the patriarchal structures of contemporary liberal capitalism, forces which often push women into precarious and reproductive labour and the way that immigration practices enhance this gendered and raced precarity and vulnerability (Anderson 2013; Tepe-Belfrage and Montgomerie 2016). Instead, oppression is deemed cultural (Razack 2008). To Casey, this is about 'cultural values' and behaviour: 'The harms and inequalities [of non-integration] are often a result of practices and behaviours that are out of step with modern British values and in many cases the law' (Casey 2016: 120). What Casey views as the fault of patriarchal Islam in creating 'unintegrated' and 'unlawful' bodies and spaces (the urban ghetto and the immigrant household) also became tied to the risk of terrorism, as 'unintegrated' communities and failed households create a further risk of 'radicalisation' (Casey 2016: 46). The unintegrated (Muslim) woman is described here, as she is more widely, as both 'at risk' and 'risky'.

Haunting these depictions of the unintegrated (Muslim) woman are past colonial figurations which join up and reveal her predicament. The unintegrated (Muslim) woman is spatialised within the confines of the household – that is, hidden away from the proper public space of the labour market, civil value and emancipated (white) femininity. Shades of light and dark become important metaphors of civility here, just as they did with debates concerning purdah, the harem and sati in British India (Grewal 1996). The murky space of the unintegrated household is a site of cultural dangers – where English is not spoken, where 'tradition' rules, where claustrophobic patriarchy oppresses expression, individuality and eventually love. The path to modernity is throwing open the shutters and letting the light in.

Just as failed black motherhood was defined by an absence of patriarchy, the suspicious intimacy of the Muslim family is too much patriarchy. As her relations are only ever a sham, the Muslim woman is unable to experience (or is held back from) progressive intimacy and the choice of liberal romantic love – linked to both the financial autonomy of work and 'breaking free' of her community bonds. She is unable to contribute to the value of the nation and liberal progress. The task of authorities is rationalised by intervening in these intimate relations and modernising them.

As Razack (2008) argues, the unintegrated (Muslim) woman can be 'saved' and offered shelter in the national 'home' but only if she renounces her community and reforms. This paternalistic dynamic dominated during the early 2000s, promising 'inclusion' and support to modernise (Wilson 2007). However, with the extension and expansion of counter-terrorism logics across numerous areas of social government, the Muslim woman is increasingly cast as dangerous and in need of more disciplinary domestication. Tactics of 'integration' found in the Casey report increasingly mirror the concerns of the security services and the production of the British Muslim community into a 'suspicious community' after 9/11 and the London bombings of 2007. The notions of women not speaking English or no English being spoken in the home fixate on fears about the socialisation of children as future citizens (Casey 2016: 55, 58, 117); getting women into the labour market is a battle of values to get minorities to 'contribute' to the nation; learning British values is viewed as essential for containing and battling 'radicalisation' within the home.

This heterosexual futurism increasingly locates (Muslim) motherhood as a socio-biological threat to the civilised nation. With the 'rise of Islam' figured as an existential threat to white European and British order, this has connected to an increased interest in Malthusian demographic science where European Muslims are presented as 'taking over' other settled communities (see Sherwood 2017).

Casey (2016: 9) poses this threat in terms of how 'international marriage' brings in new and 'unintegrated' migrant bodies who fail to adapt to British ways of life (bound as they are to backwards spaces):

> Rates of integration in some communities may have been undermined by high levels of transnational marriage – with subsequent generations being joined by a foreign-born partner, creating a 'first generation in every generation' phenomenon in which each new generation grows up with a foreign-born parent. This seems particularly prevalent in South Asian communities. We were told on one visit to a northern town that all except one of the Asian councillors had married a wife from Pakistan. And in a cohort study at the Bradford Royal Infirmary, 80% of babies of Pakistani ethnicity in the area had at least one parent born outside the UK.

The social problem here is directly presented as a cycle of reproductive takeover. Geographies of race (those 'strangers' coming from elsewhere) meet the push to whiten and civilise ('integrate') existing minority communities. The resistance of citizens of colour to integration into the nation is revealed in the *will* to sustain their strangeness through intercontinental marriage and reproduction – symbolised in the 'wife from Pakistan'. The sham is less about these marriages being 'of convenience' or even 'in-genuine' or 'forced'. The sham here is the reproduction of racialised bodies birthed by the 'unintegrated' (Muslim) woman.

Here what underpins questions of shams in immigration policy are not only concerns about marriages of convenience but also about the maintenance of a broader domestic order. The undomesticated/ unintegrated Muslim woman is central to the restrictive immigration policies and changes to family migration visas. But this equally energises and drives broader racialised concerns about the demography of contemporary Britain, and the reproduction of settled citizens with questions of security. From being 'at risk', and a subject of interventionist tactics to 'save' her, the unintegrated woman is increasingly viewed as 'risky', a threat to be managed. This reveals how intimate bordering joins up across different areas of government, affecting migrants and racialised, settled communities in connected ways.

Counter-terrorism and intimate borders

Logics of reproduction, natalism and heteronormative intimacy that I began to uncover above have played an increasingly vocal role in the contemporary deployment of counter-terrorism in Britain. This connects up with the way that the War on Terror has been fought through the enforcement of heteronormativity (and homonormativity) globally (Puar 2008). For instance, it has long been suggested by security services and the judiciary that incidents of forced marriage could provide information on the whereabouts of Islamic extremism and terrorist activity (Wilson 2014). Crown Prosecutor Nazir Afzal argued in 2014 that there was a distinct correlation between 'hotspots of radicalism and hotspots of honour-based violence':

> If you went in the Special Branch of the Terrorist Unit and looked at their map, you would see significant links, significant correlation [to incidents of forced marriage]. So, maybe there is something about ... extremism, the way people think around those issues, that links in with what happens with women in their families too. (Quoted in Wilson 2014)

Through this logic, 'extreme' beliefs which lead to terrorism are born out of what happens in families. If you follow the treatment and body of the unintegrated woman – at risk of forced marriage – you will eventually find extremists/terrorists, so the narrative goes. Of course, such a bonding together of concerns about the treatment of women to questions of terrorism is hardly novel. Feminist and postcolonial scholars have shown how the feminisation and sexualisation of 'others' has structured the Global War on Terror, driving imperialist 'saviour complexes' and the wider grammar of suffering/violence (Rao 2014; Richter-Montpetit 2014; Welland 2015; Weber 2016). UK counter-terrorism has reproduced these global dynamics. However, since 2010 and the extension of the Prevent strategy, 'family values' have been increasingly weaponised as a means of finding and combating terrorists (Puar and Rai 2002; Cowen and Gilbert 2008). Here the figure of the unintegrated (Muslim) woman is not only constituted through victimhood but also as an alive and present danger.

Prevent and sham families

Over the course of the late 2000s the development of UK counter-terrorism, working in tandem with the deployment of counter-insurgency practice in the colonial wars of Iraq and Afghanistan, would begin to focus on preventing threats of 'extremism'. In various evolutions of the project, this has meant focusing attention on Muslimified households and the intimacies within them for signs of 'radicalisation'. After the 7/7 attacks in London, counter-terrorism authorities stepped up their implementation of the anti-radicalisation programme known as the Prevent strategy. Originally conceived to promote a form of self-governance over Muslim communities and organisations in the UK, after 2010 Prevent increasingly drew upon the recent experiences of counter-insurgency in Afghanistan and Iraq (and Northern Ireland, Kenya and Malaysia) (Sabir 2017). Prevent focused on extending responsibilities for reporting extremism and radicalisation, seen as the underlying cause of violence, onto a host of social government bodies.

From 2015 any public-facing organisation in the UK has had a legal duty to report possible incidences of radicalisation, defined as espousing or being socialised into 'extreme views'. As I have argued elsewhere, if counter-insurgency is known as 'armed social work', then in the UK social work has become a natural ally of counter-terrorism (Turner 2018; also see Owens 2015). With new reporting obligations, social work (alongside health, educational, welfare service) became a key tool in monitoring radicalisation born out of suspicious intimacies.

In 2015 Birmingham City Council became the first authority in Britain to add the risk of radicalisation to their categorisation for assessing 'troubled families'. Troubled families are families that can be subject to disciplinary interventions by the state based on a number of socio-economic and behavioural factors, from intergenerational worklessness to child truancy (see Casey 2012; Crossley 2016; Turner 2018). This inclusion, it should be noted, came in the wake of the 'Trojan Horse' scandal, in which reports claimed that certain schools in the city were teaching and practising 'radical' forms of Islam (even if the reports were later discredited). The inclusion of radicalisation into the definition of troubled families reflects how social workers nationally are now expected to monitor the familial relations of households for signs of radicalisation. Issues of child protection and safeguarding vulnerable individuals are now built into the official guidance on how to spot 'those being drawn into terrorism'. As Prevent duty guidance reveals:

> The Counter Terrorism and Security Act 2015 places a duty on local authorities to give due regard to support people from being drawn into terrorism. This includes identifying individuals at risk of being drawn into terrorism, assessing risk and developing appropriate support to address that risk. The government states that this needs to be incorporated into existing policies and procedures; in particular the need to do this within local authority safeguarding is highlighted. (HM Government 2015)

The 'assessment of risk' as to whether someone is being radicalised is thus networked into the existing logics and practices of social work.

Social workers are seen as a key resource here because of the way that they can access the 'private' interior of households and observe the function of the family. Child safeguarding is a particular focus in counter-terrorism practice because young children are viewed as distinctly *at risk* of being radicalised and taking up 'unBritish values'. This has been intensified through elite claims linking terrorism with child abuse, as demonstrated in an article in the *Telegraph* in 2014 where Boris Johnson, then Mayor of London, argued that the radicalisation of children urgently needed to be treated as a form of such. Following this, in 2015 a UK court ruled that that the parents of a 16-year-old girl were emotionally abusing her through exposure to 'ISIS propaganda' (McKendrick and Finch 2015).

As with the risk of forced marriage, terrorism is continually presented as a cultural problem in which Muslim parents teach their children the dangerous practices of Islam and intimately socialise them into deviant/ terroristic activities. Here the take-up of terrorism is not cast solely in terms of dangerous masculinity (see chapter 4) but as a feminised process of socialisation within the family, in which motherhood is made highly visible. Practitioners' training guides for Prevent make this fear of proximity and reproduction explicit (see Smitherson and White 2017). It is suggested that 'high-risk indicators of radicalisation' are not necessarily holding or expressing 'extreme views' but living in proximity to someone expressing extreme views (Smitherson and White 2017: 10).[3] Further emphasising the socio-sexual and affective dimension of child radicalisation, it is often viewed as a form of 'grooming' (for more on this see London Safeguarding Children Board 2018 and the next chapter).

Social workers are supposed to jointly assess 'risk of extremism' as they identify other risks such as child abuse, absence of care, domestic violence. Here factors which may be used to assess radicalisation or the *potential* for radicalisation in the bodies of children are often linked to existing imaginaries of the intolerable (familial) practices of Muslim communities. For example, 'medium risk indicators' of radicalisation are whether a child is 'at risk from harmful cultural practices ... e.g. FGM [female genital mutilation], Forced Marriage, removal from education, honour based violence, abuse linked to faith or belief, etc.' (Smitherson and White 2017: 11).

Radicalisation is constituted here as a 'cultural process' attached to Islam. Radicalisation emerges from other intolerable 'cultural practices' again symbolically attached to the 'sham families' of Muslim communities. Radicalisation is child abuse; radicalisation is born out of the milieu of the Muslim family; existing familial problems (family breakdown, alienation, generation conflict) become in this way translated into terrorism. This mirrors claims that littered the Casey report, in which the figure of the unintegrated (Muslim) woman provided a breeding ground for radicalisation. If the unintegrated woman migrant risked reproducing unBritish values in her home and through the body of her children, here the intimate space of the Muslimified home is a radicalising space. Just as sham marriage is presented as a danger of immigration that threatens 'real' marriage and family, the War on Terror becomes fought within the home of the sham family.

Unsurprisingly, whilst social work guidance notes stress that 'extremism' should be interpreted broadly as including far-right or even environmental extremism, 90 per cent of all referrals to Channel (the 'community' arm of Prevent) in 2015 were of Muslims. The intimate bordering that social work now performs can be orientated towards intelligence gathering; it can lead to the targeting of subjects for anti-radicalisation programmes, just as it can be about taking children into care. As radicalisation is treated as an issue of national security, the intimate surveillance of social work is bound to mundane and exceptional forms of security – arresting, imprisoning and even deporting subjects thought to be a threat (Kapoor 2018). Precisely because of the way that terrorism is viewed as secretly 'bred' within spaces of failed domesticity – such as the proximity of children to 'extreme' views – the Muslimified household becomes reconfigured as a space of (un)known dangers, but also as a site of preventative management and control.

As I have demonstrated over the course of the last section, the figure of the unintegrated (Muslim) woman is able to capture a host of related anxieties about the intimate family 'problem' of racialised communities, of postcolonial British society, mobility and insecurity. As with the threat of sham marriage, the sham family and sham mother present multiple dangers which demand intervention by the state in ways that mirror past forms of control. The unintegrated woman is at risk and always risky. She must be 'helped' and protected but also protected against. Tied as she is the failure of the Muslim family, she (and her household) becomes a site to struggle over, domesticate and reform for the future of heteronormative order and the preservation of Britishness. In keeping with the global/imperial logics of the War on Terror, she is cast as a failure by not being part of the modern family and yet she is viewed as threatening it through her 'backwardness'. In doing so she risks threatening not only British society but the order of (white) Western civilisation.

Conclusions

Discussions of sham marriages have had an increasing amount of attention in academic scholarship and within the media (for example see Wray *et al.* 2015; Kofman 2018; Wemyss *et al.* 2018). Much of this work and media attention has focused on how family migration policy has taken an evermore restrictive direction, leading to the break-up, detention, separation of international and migrant families. The detention of families in centres such as Yarl's Wood and the separation of children and parents seeking asylum on entry to the United States under the Trump administration has brought such policies into starker focus. Liberal, pro-migrant rights activists and media campaigns have tended to focus their attention on repealing these laws and practices by highlighting how immigration rules break up and destroy 'real' families. Campaigns such as the 'Divided Family Campaign', 'Bring them Home' or 'Love Letters to the Home Office' constantly invoke heteronormative images of family life to demonstrate what is threatened by these intimate borders.[4] I approach this work with some caution.

In this chapter I have instead shown how the sham has poured scrutiny on the intimate relations of migrant subjects and settled communities alike. In viewing 'family' as central to empire-making, both historically and within contemporary Britain, I have explored the political work that appeals to family (and in this case the modern family) make possible. For example, it is a claim to 'genuine' family life that continues to drive intimate bordering practices such as scrutiny of migrant families, or social work interventions regarding radicalisation. In light of this, it is of course important to recognise who is allowed access to family life and to map out where family rights are eviscerated (as many pro-migrant campaigns do). However, calling for a defence of family rights without scrutiny of the history of the Empire, fails to get at the heart of the problem we are dealing with in Britain and other northern states. By appealing to save 'real' families, this fails to appreciate the multiple subjects who are queered and racialised through an appeal to 'real' families. Instead, this chapter has explored how an appeal to protect 'real' families and cast others as shams already drives colonial power.

In tracing the multiple reincarnations of the sham – sham marriage, sham intimacy, sham family, sham motherhood – I have shown how demarcations around the 'genuine' or 'sham' family energise different intimate borders, from immigration and integration strategy, to social work and counter-terrorism. I have shown how the sham is concerned with delineations between 'genuine' families and suspicious intimacies. Whilst the idea of the sham emerged in relation to immigration practice and the mobility of people for family life, the idea that people can be distinguished into those who are properly familial and those who are shams has many manifestations. It is not only migrants that are policed here through scrutiny of sham intimacy. As I showed with the discussion of forced marriage, reforms surrounding the discovering and capturing of sham marriages not only concerned mobility but the domestication of settled racialised communities within the UK. Whilst immigration policies have produced evolving forms of intimate borders to regulate international marriage and partnerships, integration strategies, policing, social work and counter-terrorism operations have coalesced to discover and monitor 'sham' families.

Whilst focused on protecting the nation from intolerable and unBritish intimacies, this domestication remains colonial in orientation. Orientalist representations of backward, savage and under/oversexualised peoples still drive the treatment of those moving to and living within Britain. Here 'family' remains a significant transit point for colonial power because of the way it disguises racialisation. Who is a sham is organised around a liberal and progressive notion of the 'modern family'; defined as this is by autonomy, romantic love and consumptive domesticity, and 'contribution'. It is this liberal and outwardly deracialised account of family that arguably organises who is properly 'familial' or 'unfamilial' – that is, who is sustained and fostered and who is dangerous and subject to exclusion and abandonment. For example, it is the treatment of women that distinguishes Muslim communities as 'backwards', and their inability to 'evolve' their kinship practices that marks these communities as suspect. As with family taxonomies under the British Empire, this reworks a civilisational tense, where people are racialised as being 'underdeveloped' based on supposedly universal claims to intimacy, romantic love and liberal values. This is then used to organise access to rights and citizenship of both migrants and settled communities alike.

The figure of the unintegrated (Muslim) woman continues to marshal the contemporary domesticating state, both in its push to police the movement of people and equally to integrate minorities. The constitution of feminised victimhood of course has a longer paternalist imperial history. However, what marks out the figuration of the unintegrated (Muslim) woman is how she is treated as both at risk and risky. If the passive Muslim housewife was once viewed as a victim, in need of saving, she has increasingly been constituted as a threat – that is, as a natal reproducer of terrorism within the sham family. Just as failed black motherhood occupied a site for the reproduction of social disorder throughout the twentieth and early twenty-first centuries, the Muslim woman is increasingly viewed as someone to be contained. The Muslim woman can reproduce but increasingly cannot be a genuine mother.

Thus, whilst we need to be attuned to questions of how families are separated, we must also be aware of how intervention, separation and violence is done in the name of family. If family was offered a means of *developing* the unintegrated woman, under counter-terrorism and renewed visa policies it is increasing used as a form of *control.*

We can consider here how claims to protect against shams continue to organise varying degrees of violence – the separation of international kinship structures, the deportation of those who fail to gain the correct visa or fail the application, the criminalisation of those who are deemed a sham. Alongside this we can place wider practices of the hostile environment, the joining up of immigration rules with housing policy and healthcare, for example, or the increased use of immigration raids on places of work and within homes to criminalise and push people into detention (Corporate Watch 2018: 65). Such hostility joins up with the increasingly intense policing and surveillance of Muslim communities and households through both the work of security officials and social workers. Not only does the surveillance of sham families lead to intervention by social workers in cases of child protection (which can mean the removal of children from a home) but intelligence gathering and reporting by social workers can lead to criminal prosecution, counter-terrorism raids, detention without trial, passport removal, the possibility of more state violence and even extradition (see Kapoor 2018). Here sham marriages are not only a danger but the sham family becomes extraordinarily dangerous.

Whilst intimate bordering attached to the sham concerned discovering and regulating suspicious intimacies, what I turn to in the next chapter is how the family is also tied to 'monstrous intimacies'. Here I take up in more detail what is done in the name of protecting the 'proper' family. I do so by examining how the liberal and progressive appeals to the modern family are always/already bound to whiteness. I explore what is done in the name of protecting the white family, which is viewed as 'under attack' from racialised others. To do this I examine the increasing trend of citizenship deprivation in Britain, a practice which I argue tells us much about the 'sticky' nature of contemporary borders.

Notes

1 This chapter is based on archival research undertaken by the author at the National Archives in 2016 and 2017, as well as a discourse analysis of immigration policy documents, integration strategy documents and social work guidance between 1999 and 2018. In order to examine the material, I draw upon Weber's (2016) work on 'figuration' to study how the sham is imagined and brought to life, attached as this is to a particular embodied gendered figuration of threat and 'victimhood'. This pays attention to the performative and 'worlding' role that powerful imaginaries have in shaping state practice – such as immigration law. As Weber (2016: 28) argues, 'figurations emerge out of discursive and material semiotic assemblages that condense diffuse imaginaries about the world into specific forms or images that bring specific worlds into being'. For further discussion of this methodological approach see Weber (2016: 28–29).

2 The hypervisibility of Islam in Casey's report is striking. For example, in a four-page section on religious 'regressive attitudes', only two lines at the end of the text are devoted to the Jewish and Christian faiths – and even then, mostly in parentheses as an afterthought. Meanwhile, four pages of extensive detail outline the 'regressive attitudes' held by Islamic communities in the UK.

3 Revealing the flimsiness of the definition of 'extreme', an 'extreme view' is defined as even '[refusing] to acknowledge other viewpoints' (Smitherson and White 2017: 10).

4 Joint Council for the Welfare of Immigrants campaign 'Bring Them Home': www.bringthemhome.org.uk/; Love Letters to the Home Office: http://lovelettershome.org/. Also see BBC (2018b) for another example.

4

Monsters

In February 2016 the British news media doggedly reported on the conviction of five suspects charged with the sexual abuse of minors in the northern English town of Rotherham. Since revelations of child sexual exploitation (CSE) emerged in the press in 2012, the very word 'Rotherham' (and to a similar extent the name of another northern town, Rochdale) had steadily become synonymous in the public imagination with CSE or 'grooming' scandals. The scale of the abuse transformed these convictions into a site of moral panic, with authorities suggesting that approximately 1,400 children in Rotherham alone could have been targets of exploitation over a fifteen-year period (Jay 2014). However, what framed this scandal and energised the parameters of the moral panic was a competing set of racialised and sexualised imaginaries and logics. This worked to make the scandal one that concerned multiculturalism, citizenship and 'integration'.

Despite the fact that two of those convicted in Rotherham were white women, the news coverage focused almost exclusively on the background of the male perpetrators who, whilst all holding British citizenship, were described as 'Asian', 'Muslim', 'British Pakistani'. The victims of such abuse were almost uniformly presented as 'white girls'. As with previous cases of 'street grooming' this led to mass outpourings of anger, disgust, hate and revilement. Such emotional circulations coalesced around easily available tropes which relied upon codes of orientalist deviancy and the symbolic power of interracial rape: the 'monstrous' and 'evil' paedophile, the 'Asian grooming gang', the patriarchal, women-hating Muslim man. This took place alongside the steady whitening of the female victims, who were transformed from marginalised and dismissed 'child prostitutes' (a common category used by police and local authorities) into 'daughters of the nation'.

Speaking after the trial in Rotherham, the victims' solicitor David Greenwood made it clear that what happened in the town was not a unique case but one that was endlessly repeated throughout the whole of modern Britain:

> This trial is just the first of many and is the tip of a very big iceberg. From the work I have done, it appears that gangs of Asian men have been operating to sexually abuse young white girls in Rotherham, Oxford, Keighley, Bradford and Rochdale. (Quoted in Cusick 2016)

This abuse was termed endemic and systematic. Unlike other examples of child abuse and paedophilia, which tend to be presented in terms of unique contexts and circumstances (Wilson 2018), what happened in Rotherham could act as stand in for Bradford or Oxford. Why? Because this involved 'Asian', 'Muslim', 'British Pakistani' men and the very presence of these racialised signifiers meant that we are already supposed to know why these tragic events happened. As former cabinet minister Jack Straw would argue, to many Pakistani men these white girls are merely 'easy meat' (BBC 2011).

Seizing the opportunity to capitalise on the public mood of outrage surrounding these convictions, then Home Secretary Theresa May immediately pledged that those convicted of CSE, but more specifically 'street grooming', could and *would* be deprived of British citizenship and then deported. Through applying long-standing powers to deprive naturalised citizens of citizenship, renovated under successive counter-terrorism and immigration acts (see Home Office 2002, 2014b; HM Government 2006), the Home Office (quoted in Chambre 2016) reminded the press that 'citizenship is a privilege not a right. The Home Secretary can deprive an individual of their citizenship where it is believed it is conducive to the public good to do so.'

From 2002 to 2016, eighty-one subjects were deprived of their citizenship. In 2017 it was reported that in that year alone a further 104 were stripped of their rights. These figures also reflect the expanding number of people who have their passports removed by the state, and there are countless more who have had naturalisation and indefinite leave to remain applications refused, nearly all for issues relating (however loosely) to 'terrorism' (see Kapoor and Narkowicz 2019). The technical reasons for deprivation of citizenship are often linked to a clause regarding the 'public good' and/or charges of fraudulent claims (McGuiness and Gower 2017: 3). In 2018 the government continued to push for legislation which made it possible to strip *anyone* of citizenship, whether a naturalised citizen or born into citizenship, disregarding the international legal precedent over statelessness (Ross and Galey 2014; Anderson 2016; Javid 2019). In the context of this short history, the apparently exceptional acts of criminality relating to grooming became rendered as another form of terror. This justified the exceptional act of removing a subject's citizenship and threatening to send the perpetrators, in the celebratory tone of one newspaper, 'back to Pakistan' (Scheerhout 2017).

In the fall out from the convictions, we can begin to see how events in Rotherham (and other cases of grooming nationally) shaped and energised numerous bordering practices – imprisonment, deprivation of citizenship, potential deportation. What was significant about this event is how 'exceptional' powers of deprivation of citizenship were targeted at these criminal citizens. The expansion and intensification of deprivation of citizenship raises the question of the (im)possibility of British citizenship after empire.

Following the way that I discussed the practice of intimate bordering in the last chapter, here the border not only targets those with precarious migrant status but also those with settled rights and citizenship. Here we can see how borders transform the right of citizenship from a status of relative permanence into a different kind of temporal and bodied relationship to the state. From having settled rights, a citizen can become subject to immigration law as a migrant. They can suddenly become akin to an 'illegal' migrant who can be subject to deportation. Through the threat of deprivation, the border can permeate and transform supposedly settled rights and make certain populations *deportable* within modern Britain (De Genova 2002). Significantly, this practice does not affect everyone (it is not every criminal that is subject to deprivation). Deprivation 'sticks' (Ahmed 2004) to certain bodies and slides off others.

In this chapter I want to examine how the case of Rotherham (and the scandal of 'grooming gangs' more widely) reveals how borders stretch, follow and 'stick' to certain bodies and populations. In doing so, this tells us about the limits of citizenship and how the British state continues to administrate through colonial and authoritarian techniques when it comes to certain populations. It also tells us how such practices are equally rationalised and justified based on colonial claims to who is or is not properly familial. If intimate bordering was central to the management of 'suspicious intimacies' that I examined in the last chapter, the 'sticky borders' I explore here are bound to 'monstrous intimacy' – that is, intimacies that are energised by disgust, revilement and hate. As with the case of the grooming scandals in Rotherham, monstrous intimacies are cast as intolerable and used to justify the use of exceptional authoritarian measures, such as deprivation of citizenship, used primarily against Muslimified populations and racialised citizens deemed to be without 'value'. As I go on to claim, monstrous intimacies are bound up with the endangering of the (white) family, which must be protected at all costs and through whatever means necessary.

In focusing on what the case of Rotherham tells us about contemporary citizenship, I ask what conditioned the promise to deprive CSE offenders of their citizenship, and in turn what allowed this to be celebrated with such glee. This follows into the next chapter where I examine where the power of deprivation came from and consider how this particular bordering 'sticks' through the shifting parameters of colonial notions of the (non)human.

The case I chose to explore here is a difficult one because of the violent nature of the crimes committed. However, the scandal of grooming has been made to *feel* exceptional in ways that are not comparable with other cases of CSE and this deserves careful attention. The presentation of the exceptional nature of these crimes tells us important things about the character of race in contemporary Britain. Equally, it tells us about how both race and racial violence enacted by the state and white nationalist organisations is hidden as the logical consequence of 'defending' the (white) family.[1]

In the first section of the chapter, I examine how racialised masculinity plays a wider role in the contemporary political landscape in Britain and Europe, from the 'refugee crisis' to the war in Syria, to grooming gangs. I use these as examples to illustrate the relationship between monstrousness, violence and sticky borders. In the second part, I focus in more detail on the grooming scandal in Rotherham. Whilst detailing how the scandal was constructed and responded to, I consider emotional attachments around grooming to be important, primarily because grooming was made to seem so scandalous and exceptional as an event of incomparable violence. In using Sara Ahmed's (2004) work on affect I explore how the act of grooming was rendered so monstrous, and how the thinkability and feelability of this violence conditioned how bordering practices stuck to those who were convicted of grooming. In order to evidence this, I look at both the wider media and state treatment of 'grooming gangs' and the body of 'confessional' (non-)fiction literature and novels published in the immediate aftermath of the grooming scandals. I suggest that we can only understand why the deprivation of citizenship becomes an option in such cases once we understand how grooming is presented as a site for the sovereign and emotional protection of the white (national) family against perverse others. This is shaped by the place of the family at the heart of white nationalism and colonial racism. If heteronormative ideas of family organise who is 'unfamilial' and suspicious in modern Britain (as I argued in the last chapter), this equally organises who endangers the 'real' family and how these dangers should be eradicated. Relating to the

historical use of 'family' under the British Empire, I demonstrate here
how family is still wrapped up with *dispossession* (of rights and life).

Of violence and monsters

Before going into the specifics of the events in Rotherham, they deserve
to be situated in the wider context of racialised masculinity and the
part it plays in the social landscape of twenty-first-century liberal states.
Asylum seekers crossing the Mediterranean, gang violence, knife crime,
child refugee resettlement schemes continue to be framed through a
narrative of dangerous black and brown men (across Europe, Australia
and North America in particular). Just as with the examples of the
'black peril' I explored in chapter 2, this relies on claims to sexual
deviancy and the risk this poses to family life.

In 2016 the rise in the number of male asylum seekers in Cologne,
Germany, was blamed for a spate of 'sexually predatory' attacks on
women during New Year's Eve celebrations (Smale 2016). Child refugees
arriving in the UK as part of resettlement schemes have been consistently
hounded by the British press who presented them as 'burly lads' rather
than 'real' children (see chapter 6 for more on this). These reports went
on to suggest that (child) refugees posed a sexual risk to 'school girls'
and painted visions of such figures hanging around outside school gates
(Greenhill 2016).

Equally, 'gang culture' has been blamed by London's Metropolitan
Police for a rise in knife crime in the city and for the civil unrest which
broke out in 2011. Here black teenagers are rendered a particular type
of masculinised danger. 'Black culture' as well as the reported absence
of father figures and single-mother households are commonly cast as
causal factors of this violence (see Starkey 2011).[2] Powerful circulations
of deviant sexuality and race are materialised through these examples:
the lusty, over/under-sexed colonised subject of orientalist obsession,
the impossibility of 'childhood' for brown and black subjects, the failure
of the black household and family. Following my previous discussion

of figurations, it is worth thinking here of how the figure of the dangerous brown and black man does important political work in driving colonial domestication.

Such figurations of dangerous masculinity persist as easily available means of explaining complex societal relations. They are able to sustain racial hierarchies and work on fears of proximity. They also work in the context of the evolving dictates of racialised capitalism where once useful populations of cheap and expendable labour have been made redundant and causally viewed as replaceable, surplus and 'undeserving' (Shilliam 2018). Here figurations of dangerous masculinity work to make populations even more precarious and subject to coercion from the state. This enhances existing inequalities and maximises profitability through the dual function of precarity and control (Lewis *et al.* 2014).

This is continuously animated by how whiteness is bound to *threatened innocence* and blackness to *sexual danger*. Such attachments work to fuel disciplinary practices of incarceration, stop and search, and restrictive immigration policies based on delimiting the movement and freedom of black and Asian men (see Elliott-Cooper 2016). We might consider here how immigration detention rates reflect wider patterns of imprisonment in the UK, where black and Asian men are disproportionately represented by almost exactly double.[3] Sexuality and renderings of deviancy play an important role here. It is worth remembering that the hardening of modern racial categorisation and its governance has nearly always taken place around fears of intimacy and proximity (Stoler 1995). It is in the possibility of affective relations and sexual conduct that racism finds life.

This appeal to dangerous deviancy does important work in organising scales of the human. The 'bogus asylum seeker', 'black youth', 'Asian grooming gang' and equally the 'jihadi terrorist' are figurations that can arguably transform subjects into 'monsters'. The monster is a complex figure of modernity. Richard Kearney (2003) views the rise of the culture and aesthetic of monstrousness as a product of tensions and boundary-forming in the Renaissance, which produced the monster as a thing which was neither human nor non-human. However, monsters play a particular role in colonial governance. Monsters propel fear; they mark the difference between the human/not-quite/non-human and work to both demand but also silence exceptional violence against them. To Foucault:

> The monster's field of appearance is a juridico-biological domain. The figures of the half-human, half-animal being …, of double individualities …, of hermaphrodites … in turn represented that double violation; what makes a human monster a monster is not just its exceptionality relative to the species form; it is the disturbance it brings to juridical regularities (whether it is a question of marriage laws, canons of baptism, or rules of inheritance). The human monster combines the impossible and the forbidden. (Quoted in Puar and Rai 2002: 118)

Monsters are coded through particular sensibilities and emotional circulations – fear, intrigue and repulsed fascination being key psychological phenomena (see Halberstam 1995: 8–10). The 'double violation' that Foucault speaks of is helpful for thinking through the contemporary colonial power of the monster. Monsters both disturb and sustain social order and necessitate the policing of boundaries. They threaten order but their eradication services its renewal. This codes violence into monstrous violence and then legitimate violence, which is called upon to protect against and destroy the monsters in the name of 'normality'.

Missing from Foucault's account is the explicit attachment of monstrousness to race and the ease through which racialised bodies can be transformed into monstrous bodies. To Puar and Rai (2002) the monster is always a sexualised monster. This is because they actively threaten the hetero-domestic order of nation, family, household, thus their sexuality is always known through violence. It is a violent and uncivilised sexuality. Halberstam (1995: 3) views the monster as 'embodied violence': 'The monster itself is an economic form in that it condenses various racial sexual threats to nation, capitalism and the bourgeoisie in one body.' Tracing the contemporary racial codes of the monstrous, Christina Sharpe (2016) reminds us of how anti-black racism was constantly energised under slavery (and under Jim Crow and beyond) by depictions of the unstoppable strength of the male slave, as an inherently violent and physical beast. The 'lust' of the black slave towards white women propelled both the eugenics obsession with miscegenation, and the depiction of *all* interracial intimacy as symbolic and physical rape. To invoke Fanon (1961: 32) here, we should remember that 'the colonist turns the colonised into the quintessence of evil'. Monstrousness thus sticks to certain bodies over others and demands exceptional violence to contain and eradicate it. The monster can work to demarcate between the human, not-quite-human and non-human.

The monster and the drone

Monsters play a particular role in the machinery of contemporary war and the geographies of heteronormativity and racism that accompany this. Tracing some of the contours of these dynamics shows how grooming is always/already networked into broader regimes of coloniality and violence. Just as the War on Terror has relied on policing of and intervention in 'suspicious intimacies', as I explored in the last chapter, the logic of this global 'war' has frequently relied upon invocations of the monster: from Al Qaeda and the Taliban through to the Islamic State in Iraq and Syria (ISIS) as new and evolving visions of evil (Puar and Rai 2002; Friis 2017). Significantly, the movement of European citizens to fight in the war in Syria and to join ISIS has expedited much of the public discussion about citizenship deprivation in Britain from 2010 onwards (BBC 2017; *Guardian* 2017; Hansard 2018). Fears that 'ISIS recruits' with British citizenship would return to cause destruction in the UK (and in other EU states) led to high-profile calls to deprive those travelling to Syria of their passports and stop them returning. In 2019, as the last strongholds of ISIS fell in Syria, the British government intensified the use of deprivation (for example, the case of Shamima Begum; see Javid 2019). Here affiliation with ISIS was to be rendered 'pathologically evil', as within the popular imagination ISIS represents the return of medievalism, known through markers of extreme orientalist savagery and illegitimate violence (such as decapitations and crucifixion; see Friis 2017).

In 2015 Reyaad Khan and Ruhul Amin were reported as the first British citizens to be assassinated by RAF drone strike whilst fighting for ISIS in Syria. After the attack it was revealed that in 2012 the British state had also killed Bilal al-Berjawi and Mohamed Sakr whilst they were in Somalia. Prior to the attack they both had their citizenship removed (Woods and Ross 2013). After Khan and Amin's deaths, the *Sun* newspaper ran with the headline 'Wham! Bam! Thank you Cam', in response to Prime Minster David Cameron's ordering of the strike. Against the monstrous violence of 'jihadi terrorism', this violence was *felt* to be not only appropriate but in fact worthy of being celebrated. The government (and their lawyers) argued that these subjects became enemy combatants, situated as they were within 'war zones' (see Webb 2017). We learn here that the exceptional act of joining ISIS begets the exceptional act of removing citizenship, which is then accompanied by a spectacular yet normalised act of violence and death.

In 2017 Gavin Williamson, the secretary of state for defence, intensified the logic of this violence by arguing that all British citizens in Syria fighting for ISIS should be hunted down and killed: 'I do not believe that any terrorist, whether they come from this country or any other, should ever be allowed back into this country,' he said. 'We should do everything we can do to destroy and eliminate that threat ... A dead terrorist can't cause any harm to Britain' (quoted in Elgot 2017a). In this account of colonial war, the only good terrorist is a dead terrorist. The complexities of the Syrian civil war and the myriad of people involved in the conflict – humanitarian workers, theological converts, travellers – all become rendered 'terrorists'. We might consider here how monstrousness 'sticks' and transforms one-time British citizens into drone targets and bodies that need to be eliminated.

Monstrous violence is accompanied (and makes possible) 'legitimate' state violence. This has particular gendered and racialised-sexualised codes. Staying with the subject of the war in Syria, it is telling that questions of citizenship deprivation, extreme violence and the monstrous have been almost entirely absent from the discussion of white British citizens who have joined Kurdish or other non-ISIS militia in Syria. White 'fighters' or 'amateur soldiers' returning to the UK have faced prosecution in court (rather than deprivation of citizenship or state-sanctioned death) and those who have died have been repatriated in ways that mimic that of the 'fallen soldier' (Murphy-Bates 2018). The parallel is significant: whilst for some subjects the rights of citizenship are eternal – not even deprivable in death – the removal of citizenship is a precursor to abandonment and then death for racialised others. How is it that some can experience social death in life whilst others do not experience social death in death?

War, the monster and grooming

Following these circulations of legitimate versus monstrous violence leads us eventually back to grooming scandals. In his preface to the book *Easy Meat* (McLoughlin 2016), self-confessed libertarian and far-right campaigner Gavin Boby offers a vignette which asks what a group of trained soldiers might do if they discovered the 'truth' about Asian grooming gangs in Britain.[4] In answering, the vignette offers up connections between citizenship, violence and war in the UK, which plays to a particular constituency of white nationalism. Boby goes on to describe how disgruntled soldiers could begin to explore vigilante justice by violently murdering the 'bearded thugs' and 'Asian perpetrators' of crimes against white women (McLoughlin 2016). The book asks readers to consider the normality of this violence and its immanence. Boby's account asks the reader to consider this martial violence as a necessary outcome of grooming. The argument presented is that this is only a natural reaction to state inaction and the real threat posed to white women (who are, of course, portrayed in patriarchy familial terms as 'wives', 'mothers', 'sisters') by 'Asian men'. Violence is merely the protection of the white nation by its warrior sons. Boby's martial fantasy of white supremacy ends with the breakdown of law and order and the start of a 'race war' on Britain's streets. War comes 'home' through the sexualised terror of the brown man and the just violence of the unmarked yet white 'soldier'.

What is concerning is how Boby's fantasy is actually far from extreme. In fact, it plays to a significant set of circulations that have become central to bordering practices in the UK and also connects up with many accepted narratives which have underpinned state policy towards grooming. Here the monstrousness of ISIS slides into the case of grooming in Rotherham through a continuum of racialised sexuality and violence. As a practice, the deprivation of citizenship binds together different monstrous bodies which blur the boundaries of colonial war from Syria and Somalia to Rotherham. They become linked together because of what is done to citizenship through bordering: deprivation is used to stop subjects returning to the UK, so they can be expelled and deported, so they can be killed with impunity. These sites are also joined together because of the way that they are rendered places of the monstrous. The 'Asian grooming gang' and the 'ISIS recruit' are made knowable as cultural problems of Islam – rendered a monstrous threat to the West. These events elide and collide as they work to animate further racialised violence which is either condoned or enacted by the state. Here the figure of the monster walks the border between citizen/non-citizen, human/non-human, and life/death.

Grooming, affect and the white (national) body

If monstrousness makes particular circulations of colonial violence possible, I want to probe in this section what underpins particular figurations of the monster. I do this by turning in more detail towards the way that grooming in Rotherham and beyond have been made sense of. By 'made sense of', I am interested in how these events are made socially meaningful but also, working off the *affective* dimension of sense, how these events are made 'feelable' through particular atmospheres and emotional circulations. This traces the affective politics of grooming by bearing in mind how the connection between events and their thinkability and feelability are historically produced. In following Ahmed, we should consider how emotions circulate to materialise particular political forces (Ahmed 2004: 11). I find this a productive way of exploring how the call to deprive convicted sex offenders of their citizenship was first made possible, and then welcomed with such glee. It helps us understand why, alongside monstrousness, borders follow and stick to certain bodies and not others.

From 2010, widespread media, public and policy debate in the UK began to focus on grooming as a new criminal act. As Cockbain (2013: 23) argues, this was presented as a new form of 'racial crime threat', with what became known as 'street grooming' inextricably associated with 'Asian sex gangs' who were imagined to be deliberately seeking out white girls for repeated and horrific sexual abuse. In January 2011 *The Times* carried a story titled 'Revealed: conspiracy of silence on UK sex gangs'. The article claimed to have discovered the emerging crime of street grooming, a particular form of CSE where vulnerable girls (and to a lesser extent boys) were targeted by groups of people (*The Times* 2011). These 'Asian gangs' falsely befriended children and young women through the promise of access to alcohol and recreational drugs before raping and abusing them, often for a number of years.

Rotherham was presented as the centre of this new crime wave, which was described as a 'plague on northern English towns' (Cockbain 2013). Part of the coding of the scandal was a focus on the lack of response by the authorities who, it was claimed, were failing to tackle widespread cases involving Asian male offenders sexually abusing white British girls for 'fear of being branded racist' (Cockbain 2013; Jay 2014; Casey 2015). The charge was made that 'multiculturalism' in Britain had caused this. Not only was this blamed on the perverse actions of ethnic minority men but it was 'political correctness' and 'respect for community difference' that allowed such crimes to go unchallenged. Whilst evidence emerged describing the heterogeneous character of victims, who were from variety of backgrounds (Peach *et al.* 2015), the dominant framing of the victims of grooming was as 'white girls'.

Whilst previous stories of sexual abuse and rape garnered much less public attention (Wilson 2018), this developed into a 'scandal' with the government launching several independent investigations into the abuse (Jay 2014) and the running of local government services in Rotherham (Casey 2015). Indeed, the push to deprive of citizenship those convicted of grooming is directly animated by how this was deemed so scandalous. Scandals here can be thought as a 'moral panic' or a crisis in a particular moral order – that is, the exceptional moment that breaks apparently settled norms (Johnson 2017: 705–706). This scandal had particular racial and gendered codes, into which ideas of monstrousness were animated – firstly, through the presentation of CSE and grooming as a crime against whiteness; secondly, as a crime which emerged out of an inferior and deviant culture and underdeveloped sexuality. This relied on the resuscitation of colonial imaginaries of the dangerous brown man lusting after white women, but also the 'backwards' nature of Asian and particular Muslim family and communal structure, which was viewed as a causal factor underpinning sexual exploitation.

To appreciate the precise nature of how grooming became a monstrous crime is to understand the role that outrage and disgust play here. Outrage and disgust are particularly vital emotional states to study because of how they circulate and drive certain attachments of violence to particular bodies (how they make things 'stick'). To Ahmed (2004: 11) it is vital that we appreciate how emotions stick and create attachments, and in doing so 'create the very effect of the surfaces or boundaries of bodies and worlds'. Outrage and disgust at what happened in Rotherham can be seen to be mobilised by particular attachments to the 'surfaces and boundaries' of whiteness and white nationalism. Such attachments are only made possible through the way that perversity and deviancy are bound onto the body of racialised men and wider racialised communities. Here the whitening and feminisation of the victims, the focus on childhood innocence, the darkening and pathologising of the perpetrators, the claims to white family, all become features which animated the particular bordering practice of deprivation.

The cultural politics of the white family

The far right in Britain has been particularly adept at seizing upon and mobilising the emotions of outrage and disgust around grooming. For instance, the white nationalist organisation the English Defence League (EDL) campaigned in many northern towns after 2011 under the mantra that authorities had failed to protect white girls from 'Islam' and 'Muslim men'. Here 'white girls' were presented as forever under attack by 'rapist foreigners' whose attacks on white female bodies were viewed as part of an attack on 'British' and 'European' culture. This was often presented as a 'rape jihad' (EDL 2019).

Whilst the EDL may be an extreme and relatively small organisation, their position is significant because of how it makes explicit the attachment between whiteness and abuse, which is repeated more broadly. Despite the liberal authorities' condemnation of the actions of the EDL and their position, more mainstream media outlets and state authorities have in many ways shared with the EDL a familiar analysis of grooming. The mobilisation of the far right in Rotherham has been linked to numerous attacks on the local Muslim population. This has led to at least one reported death, that of 81-year-old Mushin Ahmed (Mitchinson 2015). South Yorkshire Police have often been complicit in failing to protect the local Muslim population, not only by allowing far-right marches by organisations like the EDL to go ahead but also by arresting anti-racist protestors defending their local community (Wilson 2018).

Such racialised violence has been justified by the EDL as a form of 'protection' against 'grooming gangs' (akin to the 'soldiers' in Boby's account above). Speaking in Newcastle in 2016, one campaigner argued that:

> I've seen the devastation in their eyes. And I look at them – and I try not to show pity. All of these girls who have suffered and are still suffering, they have brothers, they have sisters; they have mums, they have dads, they have aunties and uncles, grandparents; and a wider circle of friends who watch *their friends* decay and rot away into oblivion. (EDL 2016)

These sentiments alone appear to be concerned with the plight of vulnerable women and may seem initially unproblematic. However, this suffering, pity and decay are bound to national rot in the EDL's ideology – multiculturalism, political correctness, toleration of 'others' are all central to the emotions of 'decay' and 'suffering' attached to grooming. Rather than being concerned with violence done to women, this suffering is converted into the violence done to *whiteness*.

The emotional circulations around grooming are consistently bound to white nationalism and white femininity. It is significant that in this speech, 'rot' is witnessed and felt by or on the family. What is so central to the scandal of grooming is that these are *white girls* raped by *Asian men*. To Peter McLoughlin (2016), what is significant about 'grooming gangs' is that these perpetrators always come after 'our girls'. As Yuval-Davis (1997) has argued, feminised bodies constitute a symbolic and biological role in the reproduction of race and nationhood, and, as with colonial fears about 'miscegenation', remain pervasive sites of anxiety and control. Disgust over the rape of 'our girls' in such accounts is framed as a rape of white Britishness rather the violation of individual bodies. In this context the sexualised violence of grooming is also tied to anti-Muslim racism (such as in the articulation of 'rape jihad'). White women must be 'protected from Islam' for the continuity of 'us' and sustaining the purity of the white family and national home.

This is significant for how wider nationalistic atmospheres abounded after the events in Rotherham. In this context, violation is made 'feelable' (made disgusting and outrageous) through the signifier of the 'foreigner' and the terroristic penetration of the white (national) body. Violation is translated into the experience of men who must protect the family as the nation. Feeding into the wider logics of colonial warfare in the War on Terror, the response to such threats is martial. The EDL, for instance, are in the habit of calling themselves 'footsoldiers' (EDL 2019).

Writing the (white) family

Feminised whiteness drives these explicit white nationalist projects (such as the EDL) through strategies that connect up with anti-Muslim racism that is central to the contemporary War on Terror. But what is more significant is how feminised whiteness also saturates the affective mood of disgust and outrage surrounding grooming more broadly, and how this happens in sites that are not explicitly linked to projects of white nationalism. Whilst most analysis of grooming has tended to explore dynamics in the mainstream media (Cockbain 2013; Tufail 2015), I now want to examine how (non-)fiction has played a role in building and dismantling emotional attachments around the 'grooming scandal'. One product of the attention on grooming has been the publication of an expanding body of confessional books on the subject. Since 2010 thirteen novels concerning grooming have been published in the UK, as well as the release of one BAFTA award-winning television miniseries, *Three Girls* (Lowthorpe 2017). The rise of the confessional novel has a much older lineage (see Halberstam 1995) but we can view this as part of a cultural trend that emerged in the 1990s when books and television programmes on paedophilia began to dominate bookshelves and occupy schedules in both the UK and US. This reflected broader shifts, particularly in Anglo-American culture, where the 'monstrous paedophile' became a metaphor for the imagined threats to 'family values' posed by globalisation, immigration, demands for LGBT and minority rights and 'excessive' forms of consumer capitalism. The publications on grooming add a particularly racialised dimension to the existing figuration of the paedophile monster in works of (non-)fiction and, with it, shifting threats to the white nuclear family and childhood innocence.

The creation of this body of work is in and of itself a significant cultural development. It begs questions of the role of the confessional novel in neoliberal societies, as well as the political economy of publishing and programme commissioning. What is also significant is how cultural artefacts like this circulate affective moods (Closs Stephens 2016), through images but also through thick, personalised description in autobiographical accounts of rape – including sights, smells and sounds of deeply violent acts.[5] They thus provide a site of 'truth-telling' that is arranged through both the production of an 'authentic' voice but equally an affective relationship between narrative and reader. They thus deserve our attention for what they tell us about the wider scandal of grooming.

What is striking about this body of literature is its close-knit consistency. After reading several of these books, the familiarity of the narrative becomes uncanny. Almost all of them mirror each other in tone, style, content, format and imagery. The majority function as autobiographical accounts (although a large proportion are ghost written), which makes the 'personal' experience of these narratives speak to a 'deeper' truth of the individualised confessional (Mills 1995). Despite how they are marketed as 'autobiographical', it remains important to approach these artefacts as sites of social narratives and as nodes in broader affective regimes. These books are commissioned, edited, made publishable within a particular economic and cultural domain where both sex and violence are commodified, made readable and profitable. To consider how affect functions in relation to these artefacts means exploring how sentiments and emotions circulate through this work to create particular types of attachments, boundaries and 'surfaces' (Ahmed 2004: 23–28). In asking how the violence is made thinkable and feelable, I am interested in how the books are aligned to particular ideological positions and how this produces emotive states and feelings towards 'others'.

Innocence, whiteness and the child

What is, of course, politically significant is who is allowed to speak through these cultural artefacts – who they are speaking *to* and what this *does*. The narrator in the majority of these books is depicted as a survivor of abuse. However, they speak from a position of both white feminised victimhood and also childhood innocence. Nearly every novel on the subject of grooming begins with detailed descriptions of the domesticity of the patriarchal family home. We are then introduced to the maturing of their body and sexual relationships through school, before the eventual encounter with abuse. This is always enabled through the presence or development of a relationship with a boy or man of colour. In most cases the author lingers on the 'Asianess' of this figure, which equally works to embolden the whiteness of the home and domestic space of protection the author emerges from. Significantly, even if this initial relationship is not abusive, it is often narrated as the facilitation of abuse. Thus, as a genre these books relay a particular failed heter-onormative temporality attached to the white family. It is in life beyond the parameters of the paternal home that deviancy begins (whilst in fact most abuse takes place *within* the family home). It is the danger of both emergent female sexuality and interracial intimacy that leads (logically) to abuse.

The enlisting of the voice of the 'child' is a tactic of this genre which produces outrage through the 'loss of innocence'. But it is worth exploring the racialised and gendered codes of both 'childhood' and 'victimhood' because they relate to how grooming is made intelligible. One of the many striking things about this genre are the front covers, which set up and bolster the already assumed positionality and bodied character of the narrator. Of the thirteen UK novels on grooming available through Amazon.co.uk, all are covered with an image of a young white woman or girl. The bodied placement of the cover image is important: some are of very young girls who would be socially known as 'children', others rely on more heavily sexualised images of young women, often with skin exposed, wearing full make up, staring into the camera, often with doe-like blue eyes. Not a single cover references a woman of colour (we should remember that some things are not feelable in the same way; some things do not stick). This vision of white innocence is then immediately juxtaposed with the title of the book, which bolsters the immanence of violence. Such titles include *Violated, Exploited, Broken and Betrayed* and *Girl for Sale*.[6]

The authority of the narrative of abuse is thus made feelable through the affect dynamic of whiteness, which joins together 'white girls', 'innocence' and 'violation'. Abuse here is made recognisable through the fragility of the body of the 'white child' who, as Lee Edelman (2004) argues, is always cast as the defining symbol of 'reproductive futurism' and 'social hope'. But this white childhood also works as a frame for the sexualised male gaze. Take, for example, the autobiographical book by Emma Jackson. In 2010 her account of sexual abuse was published as *The End of My World*. The front cover depicted a young girl of around 10 years of age with her head in her hands. In 2012, as grooming was firmly placed in the public eye, the book was republished as *Exploited*. The new cover featured a soft-focus shot of a (partially) naked blonde adolescent, staring into the camera with dewy blue eyes. The framing of such images plays an important part in the politics of grooming. Not only does the violent sexualisation of the cover relate to the sensationalism of grooming ('exploited'!), but it also works to equate sexual exploitation and rape, firstly with dangerous female sexuality (the more sensuous and nude position of the young women) and then with the penetration of purity, white, blonde femininity, by men of colour. Violence becomes recognisable and feelable as the body of the white girl is again made both risky and threatened.[7]

This construction invites the reader to adopt an emotional attachment to the young, feminised body in a way that relays rage and disgust towards the perverse other. This joins up with the broader logics of grooming scandals propagated by elites. For example, MP Jack Straw argued in 2011 that what drove Asian men to rape white girls was that they were 'fizzing and popping with testosterone' (BBC 2011). Here rape is presented as an *outcome* of Asian communities' underdeveloped sexuality and kinship, where they are held back by arranged marriage and sexual conservatism (and the unavailability of their 'own' women). But it also renders rape and abuse a product of *lust* and unvanquished aberrant desire rather than an act of violence and power.

Through these cultural artefacts, outrage and disgust are bolstered as affective moods which solidify attachments to the white nation and bind violence to other 'perverse' bodies. Readers are addressed to share in the experience of threatened white innocence (embodied in the figure of the 'pure' child and the sexualised adolescent). This becomes clear in the formatted ending of each book where, without fail, the author sets their story in the wider context of grooming and racial politics in the UK. Their experience is then rendered a 'truth' of the dangerous masculinity of brown men.

Whilst every novel pays lip service to an anti-racist stance, this is then logically denied by an assessment of the cultural motivations of the perpetrators. For example, in *Girl for Sale* (2015) the cause of abuse is the misogyny of Asian men who have no respect for women. In *Stolen Girl* (2013) the issue is the availability of white girls for Asian men and the heightened danger is that they can disappear to Pakistan at the drop of a hat. In *Violated* (2015), abuse and eventually murder are rendered products of a culture of honour attached to Islam. The authors approach these explanations as if they are self-evident truths. Here misogyny and hate of white women is located culturally; it is of 'Asian' and 'Muslim' communities, tied to religion, hyperpatriarchy, diasporic practices (just as with forced marriage). The borders of the white nation are brought to life here in an uncanny mirror to the mobilising energies of the far right, which again is conditioned by claims to the white family central to the organisation of the British Empire.

In describing acts of abuse and sexual violence, these narratives are almost always coded through epidemiological senses of race (Fanon 1986). In one passage in *Violated* (Wilson 2015: 266) the victim walks through a 'predominantly Asian area' of a city and is physically sick at the smell of the environment. Another describes the stench of curry on the breath of her attacker and the way that perpetrators would speak in Urdu or Punjabi. It is here that disgust becomes an entangled affect regime. It is impossible to separate the racial demarcations of the perpetrators body and wider cultural environment, and wider Asian and Muslim community, from the act of abuse (on the politics of disgust see Ahmed 2004: 82–100). Throughout these novels, sexual violence is not only rendered otherwise (it is of 'Pakistan', 'West Africa', the 'Wild West') but also specifically inhuman. Perpetrators are frequently 'hunters' or 'lions of the Savannah' who come to stalk their prey (Anonymous (Girl A) 2013: 329). They are beasts who live on white flesh. As with other energising forms of coloniality, animalism is again the crossing of the monstrous into the human world.

'White girls'

What makes whiteness such an accomplice in the translation of criminals into monsters, and such a significant part of the story of grooming more broadly is its flexibility. What we witness in strategies which 'make sense' of grooming and sexual abuse (such as the artefacts above) is the transformation of victims into 'white girls'. This first involves a social and institutional silencing and forgetting of abuse 'within' communities and against women of colour (Thiara *et al.* 2015). Despite convincing evidence to the contrary (Gohir 2013), grooming is only rendered meaningful and feelable as an interracial crime which is done by 'Asian men' on 'white women' or 'girls' (also see Apna Haq 2018; Wilson 2018). Unlike sham or forced marriage, sexual abuse and grooming do not stick to women of colour. Secondly, this process of victimisation involves the whitening of vulnerable children from a multitude of social backgrounds.

Reports have detailed the extent of institutional failures of multiple social agencies in Rotherham and other towns where young girls and boys reported sexual abuse and rape for up to fifteen years, with little or no action from authorities (see, for example, Jay 2014; Casey 2015). Official reports on institutional failures in Rotherham consistently showed that most of the girls who suffered sexual abuse were known to the police and frequently dismissed as petty criminals, 'child prostitutes' or 'little whores' (Jay 2014: 69, 112; Casey 2015: 34–35, 47). It has also been revealed that during those fifteen years, 67.5 per cent of perpetrators of CSE in Yorkshire were white (Drew 2016). Most of the young people who were victims of CSE were already marginalised and vulnerable, in care and predominantly from poor communities. This reminds us that whiteness is flexible. It is bodied. But it must be worked upon and crafted. These young people were not always 'white girls'.

White heteronormative power works by privileging able-bodied, heterosexual, bourgeois white men. For these girls to eventually speak, be heard and have their stories recognised, they had to be discovered to be 'white'. And they could only be discovered to be white through the monstrous racial crime threat of grooming. By this, I mean that they could only be translated as white once they were established within the sexualised and racialised grammar of the protection of the white national family (as daughters, sisters, wives, etc. in need of protection). The 'whitening' of these girls and the frame through which 'their' story is told is saturated in whiteness because that was the only way it could become intelligible and listenable within wider codes of coloniality (i.e. as a wider threat to the white body, white family, white nation, white civilisation). The discovery of monstrousness involved a translation of 'child prostitutes' into daughters of the white familial nation. At the same time, this eviscerated the voices of other women and girls (as well as men and boys) who were subject to abuse but who did not fit within this structuring of monstrous intimacies.

Conclusion

Defending Theresa May's decision to strip naturalised citizens and dual nationals convicted of sexual exploitation or grooming of their citizenship, a Whitehall legal adviser argued: 'There are no limits. It is not just potential terrorists who face losing their UK citizenship. Those involved in serious or organised crime, and who hold dual nationality, can expect similar justice' (quoted in Cusick 2016). In the context of the racialised logic of grooming scandals and the anti-Muslim racism we see in the War on Terror, 'there are no limits' must be read as a specific threat against those who citizenship is already brought into question as 'suspect' populations. As we have seen, even when white British citizens fight for Kurdish 'terrorist' groups in Syria they are shielded from the deprivation of citizenship. The bordering practice of deprivation, which destroys the settled rights of citizenship and can lead to deportation, 'sticks' to certain bodies and slides off others.

The stripping of rights of those convicted of CSE was justified by the exceptional 'monstrousness' of these acts. But what is significant here is how, just as with terrorism or forced marriage, grooming and sexual abuse stick to 'Asian' and 'Muslim' bodies as serious and exceptional crimes. It is not only the crime of CSE that makes deprivation of citizenship necessary and even celebrated (as in some parts of the media) but this relies upon the existing perceived deviancy of racialised populations who are already cast as unfamilial. To add to this, the case of grooming not only relied upon colonial ideas of deviancy (as we saw in the last chapter) but it is made sense of through the threat that racialised populations pose to 'proper', white, British family.

That the deprivation of citizenship is energised by the monstrousness of grooming reminds us of how interracial intimacy has remained a site of both extreme and normalised colonial violence. This violence, energised by racialised sexuality, has taken the form of lynch mobs claiming to defend white women against black rapists, explicit bans on interracial marriage and 'miscegenation' laws across the British Empire, anti-Muslim attacks, beatings and murders in the wake of grooming scandals. Particular imperial codes of the white European family have been used to justify white terror (Razack *et al.* 2010; Richter-Montpetit 2014) – think, for instance, of Eyre's justification for the massacre of black protestors in Morant Bay. Authorities harness and draw upon such racial violence to govern colonised populations. As I have argued, appeals to family continue to animate colonial bordering in Britain today. This means that borders can stick to certain people, even if they have citizenship – to remove their rights, to deport them, to line them up in the sights of an RAF drone. In analysing the role of 'family' in such bordering moves, we can appreciate how 'family' plays an ongoing role in practices of *dispossession*. Defending the white family involves marshalling particular forms of 'legitimate' – that is, state-sanctioned – racial violence.

Grooming, I have illustrated, is made monstrous through the feelability of this violence, which is again made possible through a distribution of 'racist sentiment' (Hook 2005: 74). This violence can only be made sense of as *worse* than other forms of sexual abuse and rape (i.e. those carried out by white criminals) through the exceptionalism of interracial sexual violence as a threat to whiteness. This not only obscures violence and abuse done to women of colour (see Imkaan 2019) but obscures other structural conditions which made grooming possible such as deregulation, night-time economies, wider forms of patriarchy. As with forced marriage, this merely recycles a racist and culturalist analysis. The valorisation of whiteness, in the aid of white nationalism, creates the double bind of forgetting the everyday violence that affects many women of colour (Thiara *et al.* 2015), whilst equally readapting colonial racialised masculinity and claims of the undomesticated family to make new forms of legitimate violence possible.

Set in these terms, deprivation of citizenship works as a particular form of exceptional punishment. It is about securing the white family from the terror of the racialised monster through enacting the violence of deprivation. Here borders mark out and distinguish people as deviant and monstrous. The demarcation of the monster meets up with the sovereign power of the state to deprive a subject of their supposedly settled rights. This is the work of the sovereign border; because the border is sticky it follows and sticks to certain people as a tool of racialised governance. Against the many assumptions regarding borders as a tool of immigration, sticky borders are shown to stick to citizens as well as migrants. The violence of this move to dispossess is normalised and hidden because it is cast (through the logics of white nationalism) as a common-sense defence of the white family. White subjects who commit similar crimes, who travel to war zones to fight, are not stripped of their citizenship because they are not racialised as 'out of place' – they *belong*, even when committing violence.

This chapter has traced how borders stick to certain bodies, animated as this is by shifting modes of racialised sexuality. Here appeals to the white (often national) family work to constitute certain forms of violence as exceptional and monstrous. Some violence is thinkable and feelable in ways that create familial attachments – such as the 'daughters of the nation.' Such attachments I have shown both silence and but also generate other forms of violence. We are reminded of how 'family' is not only related to processes of control within colonial domestication but also dispossession. In this way, it is important to not examine the case of grooming in isolation but to probe at what this tells us about the character of borders and citizenship in postcolonial Britain more broadly – where borders go and what they do to apparently settled rights. This demands a broader analysis of the deprivation of citizenship, which I turn to in the next chapter.

Notes

1 In terms of method in this chapter, I largely drew upon Sara Ahmed's work on affect to trace the emotional circulations that different discursive utterances, images and narratives bring together and manifest. Affect is about the coalescing of emotions, moods, atmospheres, senses which are always embodied but that can be shaped by interaction with discursive and textual objects (novels, documents, images, etc.) (Ahmed 2004: 13–14). To Ahmed (2004), emotions circulate and emerge (and can be fostered) in a way that brings certain points of contact together. Using this approach, I studied thirteen novels on the subject of grooming published between 2011 and 2018 to examine what emotional impulses they shaped and directed around the racial dynamics of grooming. Here I employed discourse analysis to understand the grammar and logic of these narratives and how they connected to wider social grammars around grooming, paying attention to the way emotions are brought up and used. To map this out further, I paid attention to how I felt and the emotions stirred in me whilst reading these novels, and also examined how the novels had been reviewed by readers and linked into broader debates about grooming – for example by right-wing organisations. This involved tracing the emotional politics of whiteness and grooming.
2 Particularly the 'spread' of American 'black gang culture' into the UK through hip-hop music, but also localised genres such as garage, drill and so on.

3 Black and Asian people make up 26 per cent of the prison population in England and Wales but only represent 13 per cent of the general population (Sturge 2018: 4).
4 *Easy Meat* is published by English Review Press, a subsidiary of the World Encounter Institute, which works to propagate a project of white supremacy through a blog series and book press. It does so through claims to protect 'Western civilisation', which is often limited to just 'English-speaking democracies'. As with much of the new right, this project claims to 'speak truth to power' through protecting 'freedom of speech' and this is used to justify a clearly Islamophobic agenda. See the mission statement here: www.newenglishreview.org/World_Encounter_Institute/ (accessed 23 July 2018).
5 It may seem (as it did to me) an unattractive prospect to critically analyse the personal experience and trauma of victims of abuse through such novels. But these accounts remain a vital site in the animation of coloniality for reasons that will hopefully become clear. These texts are also brought together as part of the economies of grooming. Whilst dubbed as 'confessional' and 'autobiographical' accounts, we should remember that they are not spontaneous outpourings of trauma but are commissioned by publishers and editors as part of an industry of voyeurism that circulates and moulds such moral panics.
6 In what might be a nod at dark irony, the font and format of the books mirror that of popular teen fiction such as *The Baby-Sitters Club*.
7 The covers of the books can be seen on the Penguin website – *The End of My World*: www.penguin.co.uk/books/1083666/the-end-of-my-world/9780091930523.html; *Exploited*: www.penguin.co.uk/books/109/1095140/exploited/9780091950460.html (both accessed 31 July 2019).

5

Deprivation

In the last chapter I showed how ideas of the imperilled white family have animated the scandal of grooming and play a part in how this act is rendered exceptional, and how this conditions the exceptional act of the state depriving subjects of citizenship. Now I want to delve into more detail regarding the tactic of deprivation itself. This means teasing out how deprivation works in relation to race, sexuality and empire. In this chapter I want to explore in more detail how 'citizens' are made into 'migrants' who can then be detained, deported and made killable (for example, at the end of an RAF drone). The threat of citizenship deprivation is used to throw light on postcolonial citizenship more broadly. This follows Saskia Sassen's (2016) provocation that we should examine the 'systematic edge' because doing so reveals broader practices of border regimes, rights and the organisation of dispossession (also see Kapoor 2018: 6).

Following on from the investigation I began in the last chapter, I explore where the practice of citizenship deprivation came from and how it is used today in line with other bordering practices linked to the War on Terror. Whilst the militarisation and securitisation of the War on Terror and the hostile environment have expanded authoritarian governance through tactics such as deprivation (alongside deportation, passport removals and assassination), I show how deprivation is attuned to both the orientation and management of racial categories of empire and contemporary imperial formations. Against much of the contemporary work on citizenship deprivation, which argues that deprivation is an 'exceptional' aberration of citizenship (Joppke 2016; Choudhury

2017; Fargues 2017; Gibney 2017), I argue that de facto deprivation of rights and personhood was arguably foundational to modern citizenship. Rather than an aberration of citizenship, the racialised control we see today is better understood as an intensification of this past function. This I argue reveals a particular type of imperial family drama which rages through British citizenship.

I conclude the chapter by considering how contemporary rights and citizenship are shaped by the historical figurations of the 'indentured labourer' and the 'fanatic rebel' and/or 'slave'. These figurations, and the colonial violence that accompanies them, continue to haunt and activate British citizenship today. Importantly, the act of depriving a number of terror suspects and CSE convicts of their citizenship further intensifies and normalises the practice of deprivation. We thus need to understand how this makes *all* naturalised and dual citizens amenable to the evisceration of rights. It makes large sections of society once legally categorised as 'citizens' into 'migrants'.[1]

Deprivation and the terrorist

As I began to describe in the last chapter, the increasing use of deprivation of citizenship forms a part of wider counter-terrorism tactics in Britain, which have become bound up with the steady intensification of authoritarian immigration practices, such as detention, deportation and extradition (Kapoor 2018). Intensifying the use of legislation and royal prerogatives to dismantle citizenship forms a particular type of 'sticky border'. This is because as a practice it threatens to potentially convert *all* naturalised and dual British citizens into deportable subjects.

Contemporary scholarship on deprivation has sought to reveal how this works as an aberration of settled forms of British citizenship (Gibney 2014; Ross 2014; Sykes 2016; Webb 2017) – that is, as a particular, exceptional fusion of racialised immigration practice and security logics that have emerged out of the War on Terror (also see Kingston 2005; Bauböck 2014; Joppke 2016; Choudhury 2017; Gibney 2017). There is good evidence to support this position. Deprivation of citizenship has emerged as a tactic in Belgium, France, Canada and Australia as a direct part of counter-terrorism protocol (Choudhury 2017). Whilst it has been legally possible to deprive British subjects of their citizenship since 1918 if this was in the expressed 'public good' or for acts of 'disloyalty' (Webb 2017: 296), from 1973 to 2002 this power lay almost dormant. Whilst revamped in the wake of 9/11, it is predominantly after 2011 that we see the wide application and acceleration of this power. Until the cases of grooming it had been used almost exclusively against those suspected of involvement in terrorism or for those accessing citizenship through fraud (which has been widely interpreted).

In 2002 and then 2007 the New Labour administration made it easier to deprive both naturalised citizens and those born into British citizenship of fundamental rights, but only if it could be proved that they had *access* to another nationality. Kapoor (2018) shows how this mirrored extradition legislation that made it easier to expel terror suspects to the United States. Since 2014, in order to circumvent international law on statelessness, the Home Office has pushed the principle that a subject only 'potentially' has to have access to another nationality for deprivation to be applied (effectively anyone with a family attachment – imagined or otherwise – to 'elsewhere'). Using royal prerogatives, the Home Secretary has increasingly used cancellation of passports to avoid juridical procedures and (the albeit light) body of evidence needed to formally remove citizenship (Kapoor 2018). This also expands the population of people who can be subject to such policing. In 2018 it was reported that 115 'suspected terrorists' had their passports cancelled (Lavi 2010).

Whilst formal citizenship deprivation works towards making citizens deportable and ultimately killable (usually at the end of a drone), passport removal works towards a cruddy method of social death internalised within the UK. Those who have their passports cancelled within Britain are bound by internalised borders (Kapoor 2018), this denies them a right to movement and in doing so it restricts access to housing, the job market, welfare and healthcare (especially given accompanying immigration rules mean that access to services and shelter relies on showing a passport). As with the proliferation of mass detention and deportation for 'irregularised' migrants, this is a form of criminalisation and incarceration that bypasses the ordinary criminal justice system and expands a racialised state of exception (Hussain 1999). This use of sovereign powers not only bypasses juridical procedures but also parliamentary and civil accountability. For instance, the Special Immigration Appeals Commission (SIAC), which presides over cases of deprivation, works by limiting the information available to defendants and defence lawyers.[2]

Whilst deprivation works to contain or expel (through imprisonment, detention, deportation or exile), and passport removal to expel or contain, this also joins up with the (im)possibility of acquiring rights to settlement and citizenship. Since 2001 successive British governments have made accessing citizenship more difficult to achieve – for example, by introducing expensive citizenship tests and ceremonies, and banning people with criminal convictions (including for immigration offences) from applying. Multiple forms of structural disadvantage (poverty, involvement in criminality) are reinforced in this practice where the state reinforces the precarity of populations without settled rights by making them into 'eternal guests' (de Noronha 2016). Such hostility has been a central feature of the architecture of the hostile environment in the UK, which concerns irregularising migrants and criminalising them at the same time. Investigations into what became the 'Windrush scandal' have shown that it is not just those without settled status who can be subject to deportation and subjects of the hostile environment. Commonwealth citizens who have been unable to evidence that they have citizenship (such as with a passport) have been regularly treated as 'illegal migrants' and exiled to Jamaica (Gentleman 2018a).

This reflects increasing links between counter-insurgency practices, the criminal justice system, immigration practice and economic and social inequalities structured by race. Recent operations by the Home Office have ramped up the targeting of migrants with criminal convictions for deportation. In 2012 the Metropolitan Police and Home Office initiated 'Operation Nexus' – an information-sharing programme aimed at fast-tracking the deportation of 'foreign criminals'. The scheme not only aimed to deport people with convictions but also those 'suspected' of criminal intent and behaviour, such as involvement in 'gang activity' (Griffiths and Morgan 2017). Given how racialised the discourse of gangs is in metropolitan centres like London and Manchester, the impact of such a move is significant. On the one hand, young black and Asian youth are policed for their suspected involvement in gang activity (e.g. in practices of stop and search, or losing access to social housing due to suspected gang activity); on the other, the heavy policing of black and Asian communities means that people with informal status (who may have been born and raised in the UK, we should remember) can be detained and deported for suspected gang involvement. Operation Nexus criminalises without individuals being subject to due process or criminal prosecution. It is significant that gang activity is frequently linked to the collapse of family structures. As discussed in the previous chapter, the 'failed patriarchy' of black households is made hypervisible in cases of gang violence (Collins 1998; also see Sewell 2018).

We can see here how existing inequalities produced through racialised capitalism with regard to job prospects, housing, education, welfare and the effects of austerity on wider black and Asian communities provide a further structural context for this type of border regime. There is also a clear geopolitical-imperial dimension to this expansion of sticky borders. Deportation programmes are reliant on diplomatic agreements, such as the one pursued by the British government in 2015 when the state offered £25 million to build extra prisons in Jamaica for deported 'criminals' (BBC 2015), just as hundreds of people with distant links to the Caribbean are set on flights and abandoned in cities such as Kingston. The British state uses the structural linkages of empire to refashion and extend the carceral state overseas and to expel and contain its 'problematic' internal colonies (de Noronha 2016).

The racialised structures of criminal justice meet up in insidious and authoritarian ways with the renewed practices of deprivation and deportation (Home Office 2014b). It is important to note here that whilst the white family is protected at all costs (as demonstrated in the previous chapter), violent practices of immigration raids, detention, deportation and deprivation split up or destroy intimate relations, kinships and families. And yet this so often goes unnoticed or unchallenged. The dispossession of family and kinship ties is instead broadly accepted and normalised. The power of 'family' fails to stick to those racialised bodies and kinships 'without' value (de Noronha 2016; see, for example, the case of Kenneth Oranyendu described in Taylor 2018).

Deprivation of citizenship

Deprivation has without doubt intensified through the proliferation of counter-terror devices, closed courts and passport removals, alongside the extension of the policy of the hostile environment and the ease with which authoritarian practices are normalised through 'monstrous' security and policing concerns. Here the 'jihadi terrorist', the 'illegal migrant' and the 'grooming gang' do a lot of political work in joining up security mechanisms such as policing with the sovereign power of the immigration state – to expel, abandon and kill targeted bodies. We should consider in particular how neoliberal forms of racialised capitalism mark certain populations as surplus and without 'value'. And how particular imperial military interests of the British state in the Middle East are served in the deprivation of citizenship – such as the case with ISIS recruits. Scholars of citizenship are right to reveal this worrying trend. However, we need to consider how much this offers a radical departure or *aberration* of British citizenship. Instead, I read the proliferation of formal deprivation and its corollary practices of detention, deportation and extrajudicial killing as already tied to the violent mandate of modern citizenship. The settlement and practice of British citizenship is not only forged out of empire but remains wedded to the categories and demarcations of colonial domestication which are reworked and adapted into our contemporary moment. To trace this means thinking more broadly about how deprivation has functioned as a historical practice and how this shapes its current articulation. If *de jure* (i.e. formal, legalised, institutional) deprivation was almost dormant during most of the twentieth century then de facto (i.e. practical, structural, everyday) deprivation was alive and well.

For many colonised people, Commonwealth citizens or 'subjects of the Crown', citizenship has never 'stuck'; it has slid off and over them. We need to remember that categories of the human have failed to stick to certain bodies/populations and such categories of the human are remade through contemporary border practices. Appealing to this genealogy of colonial deprivation allows us to consider more appropriately what the relationship is between citizens who are never allowed to belong and those who are formally made deportable, and with that killable. And in turn we must consider how this structures citizenship more broadly.

This is what I turn to now, offering up some examples to remind us how citizenship functioned across the British Empire, in processes of colonial domestication, before reflecting on the reworking of deprivation and monstrousness today as an extension and readaptation of colonial rule.

Deprivations under empire

On 27 April 1888 the SS *Afghan*, a Japanese-owned ship, was stopped from disembarking in Melbourne Harbour. On board were up to sixty-seven Chinese labourers who had travelled from Hong Kong for work in Victoria. Whilst the Chinese Restriction Act of 1881 allowed authorities in Victoria to restrict the movement of indentured Chinese labourers into the state, what was significant was that the majority of those travelling on the *Afghan* were British subjects. As subjects of the Crown they retained the right to move across the British Empire, codified in the promise of imperial citizenship which London was supposed to uphold (Gorman 2007). Amidst mounting pressure from white constituencies who argued that Chinese and other Asians were 'unsuited' for life in

Australia and posed an economic threat, the local authorities kept the ship under quarantine (Crawford 2014).

As the *Afghan* remained in the harbour, the port authorities worked a sleight of hand: rather than merely outright refusing entry to those onboard, they instead worked to 'check the documents of the labourers' and found that their naturalisation papers and contracts were in fact 'not bonafide' (Campbell 1921); they were, to use a current parlance, 'illegalised'. Whilst protests were raised by both the ship's Japanese owners and elites in Hong Kong, local authorities agreed that this was enough to warrant suspicion and the ship was turned away from the state of Victoria and subsequently quarantined in Sydney (Turner 1904: 278–279). In order to avoid further incidents, the Australian government issued quarantine orders on any ships arriving from Hong Kong, forcing shipping companies to stop selling tickets to people of Chinese descent.

That the passports of around sixty British subjects could be rendered 'fake' or 'inauthentic' rests on how the body of these passport holders could never be fully translated into the authentic 'British subject'. Whilst paying lip service to the 'multiracial' Empire, the British authorities worked in union with the Australian settler state to deprive these subjects of their right to mobility. Several months after the crisis, Colonial Secretary Baron Knutsford expressed sympathy with Australian authorities, arguing that he was also 'keen on not seeing Australia swamped by Chinese labour' (Parl. Deb. 1888). Rather than being treated as British subjects, these labourers were instead translated into 'unwanted' remnants of the Empire. They could be subject to expulsion because the rights of 'imperial citizenship' could not stick.

As I demonstrated in chapter 2, this was how imperial citizenship was managed on an everyday level across the Empire: from dismantling direct shipping routes from the Indian subcontinent to settler states such as Canada, to medical inspections at the border, to the enactment of deportation and vagrancy orders. It was similarly found in the regular claims that identity papers were 'fake' or in claims that a person did not look like a spouse, partner or child of a British subject. These tactics became part of the institutional fabric of the Empire, where the claim over the right of mobility, settlement and life were made (im)possible for non-white populations. They could be moved but they never had a right to move.

In considering why those aboard the *Afghan* could be denied entry, it is worth turning to Browne's work on the early emergence of the control of movement. It is worth reminding ourselves that regulation has always been bound to distinctions over personhood. In contributing to a counter-history of the passport, Browne (2015: 52) shows how slaves were subject to extensive surveillance of mobility within and beyond the plantations of the Americas from the seventeenth century. This was regulated at ports, on slave ships, through the slave pass, in slave patrols and in 'wanted' posters. Merely not looking like a citizen (i.e. white) in many US states meant being subject to immediate and legally sanctioned violence. For instance, in 1845 a law in Georgia declared that any slave found off their master's plantation without a pass would be subject to arrest and a standard twenty lashings.

Browne goes on to explore how the figure of the black slave animated bordering practices more broadly across empire. For instance, she details the formation of *The Book of Negroes* in eighteenth-century New York (Browne 2015: 88). This was a ledger that allowed evacuation from the city aboard British ships. If former slaves could be included in the book, they were given a right of mobility out of America (as part of a claim to be a British subject). To Browne, the legal struggles over which black subjects could be included in the book, often against claims by former masters and opportunists that they were 'fugitive slaves', reveals a particular struggle over the racialised codes of personhood. It reveals a struggle over the right to be treated as a person with the *possibility* of legal and political rights, or be deprived of all personhood and translated into property.

What we can begin to see here in these brief examples is that deprivation is not only orientated towards depriving subjects of already existing rights. But deprivation follows a history of practices through which people have been categorised as political (in)humans with access to recognition, rights and dignity. Deprivation in this sense creates boundaries between who can be human or not-quite/non-human. As I have argued across this book, this was continuously shaped and resuscitated by claims to the familial. Such violent distinctions between categories of the human rebounded across the British Empire. Writing in 1879 to the Imperial Office in London, Francis Lock, Brigadier General of Aden, provided a detailed assessment of new powers to expel 'vagrants' in his province (Lock 1879). Musing over the usefulness of deportations, Lock argued that the main problem in Aden was 'African coastal migrants'. Whilst indentured labourers of 'good character' could be tolerated, he argued, Africans – who carried with them the 'essence of slavery' – merely cluttered the jail cells and lived lives of deviancy. 'They no doubt are pleased', he argued, 'to be clothed, fed and watered' (Lock 1879). Unconcerned whether the 'African coastal migrants' were British subjects, Lock proposed rounding up and expelling the whole of this idle and deviant population and barring them from re-entering the province.

Almost a decade later, the Governor General of Baluchistan, India, was outlining the best tactics to deal with the infiltration of 'trans-border rebels' into the Punjab region. Described as 'Muhammadan fanatics', the rebels were fighting a low-intensity insurgency against colonial outposts and hiding within the mountain villages (Spence 1887). Sharing a similar logic to Lock, the Governor General suggested that the penal criminal code was again inadequate to deal with these 'fanatics'. Banishment, deprivation of property rights, punishment of the wider family and tribe were all considered as possible options to deal with the rebels. However, it was proposed that the most effective deterrent to rebellion was to hang and burn the fanatic's body in front of their family and village (Archer 1887). This spectacular act of violence, it was argued, was the only way to send a message to the fanatics and the wider community. If this message was not heeded, soldiers were then ordered to burn the whole village to the ground, and force the villagers to cut and burn their own crops and trees (see the Frontier Murderous Outrages Regulation 1901, also Punjab Murderous Outrages Act XXII 1867 and Act IX 1877, which legislated forms of brutal collective punishment over the 'tribal areas' of what is now Pakistan).

As with the figuration of the 'African coastal migrant', the fanatic or rebel needed to be subject to physical and public forms of suffering. The body of the fanatic was subject to gratuitous violence both before and after death, precisely because they were considered the monstrous *remainders* of social order. Rights as subjects of the Crown did not even form part of the social calculus in either case here. Nor did the associated kinship ties and community relations they were viewed as embedded within. The wider Indian penal code was too good for them; trial and imprisonment made no sense here. The 'African migrant', the 'fanatic', and then the whole 'Muhammadan village' were already rendered outside of logics of progress, labour and thus personhood.

Colonial differentiation

These scales of deprivation structured imperial and colonial rule. Whilst some subjects could become included within modes of personhood as not-quite-human (those who could pass as 'British subjects', labourers or who could be included in *The Book of Negroes*), this rested on the categorisation of others as non-human (the fake citizen-subject, the captured slave, the rebel/fanatic, the African coastal migrant). Here we are able to dig deeper into the different racialised-sexualised subject positions of coloniality, and with this the structural positionalities which are arguably resuscitated today through modern British citizenship. For certain classifications of colonised subjects, a right to labour, settlement and family could be provisionally met and sustained, as long as it worked in equilibrium with the demands of the imperial capitalist and liberal order. We might here consider the figure of the indentured labourer as one who is temporally employed, subject to disciplinary violence but included in a modified form of wage labour and certain rights of mobility and kinship, if not full personhood. Against this, other subjects were viewed as incapable of personhood and family life – as merely flesh, property or as a threat to the reproductive circulations of empire. The exemplary figure here is that of the ungendered slave who is converted to chattel, unable to ever attain access to European ideas of personhood such as gender, sexuality and family; their work is never convertible into labour, and they can never have family – they can only reproduce (Spillers 1987).

It is worth remembering here how the figure of the black slave has underpinned the stratification of people into human/not-quite/non-human. It was the black slave who was both denied family life, had all forms of kinship dismantled and was depicted as outside of liberal time and progress. Blackness, via the position of the slave, and engendered slave body, is the defining feature of the unfamilial. To Sharpe (2016), the black body has subsequently been demarcated as the site of gratuitous violence and suffering. Wilderson (2010) further argues that what arranges both suffering and death in colonial modernity is 'anti-blackness'. Following Weheliye (2014) and Mbembe (2003), anti-blackness relates to the structuring of violence and organises treatment of individuals and populations. Here anti-blackness and the propensity towards spectacular violence, social and physical death that reached its peak under chattel slavery can also be applied to other populations who are not socially recognised as 'black'. In this way we can consider how anti-blackness and the reducing of people, bodies, populations to the position of the non-human (i.e. the slave) structures all colonial categories of people and their treatment. Those who are cast in relationship to blackness can be subject to increasingly gratuitous violence (such as the fanatic or African coastal migrant above) because of how they are positioned on scales of differentiation between white and black. However, whilst the indentured labourer could be 'useful', the slave was ultimately expendable and *killable*. Whilst the indentured labourer held the structural position of the not-quite-human, the slave (and/or the fanatic) was explicitly non-human. Violence aimed at the non-human did not have to be justified or accounted for; it was already structurally accepted and normalised.

Struggles over the deprivation of personhood have arguably structured the foundations of modern citizenship. As I have begun to sketch out, this was premised not just on who had access to full political rights, but more fundamentally on who had the right to recognition of life, body, intimacy and personhood. Bringing this discussion back into the contemporary moment, we can reflect on how modern British citizenship has been consistently shaped by the (im)possible rights claims of colonised people. If we cast our minds back to chapter 3, we can remember that the British Nationality Act 1981, which created the national definition of British citizenship, relied on an act of mass deprivation. Whilst often overlooked, this Act effectively meant that some four million people across the Commonwealth were deprived of claiming their historic rights of British citizenship. It ended the rights that colonised people had fought to maintain and the legal framework that made it possible to move and settle in the British metropole, to join family members or support communities through work and remittances. Just as British subjects were denied rights and personhood across the Empire in a de facto fashion, this legal deprivation followed and institutionalised this legacy. It did so by marking out the national space as a white family hosting long-invited guests of colour (see Dixon 1983; Kundnani 2001).

As the case of grooming suggests, when these 'guests' transgress, their right to citizenship can be removed, a practice that is not open to white subjects whose citizenship never comes into question (criminal justice is the response to transgressions, not the border). What monstrous transgressions such as grooming reveal is that citizens of colour, following the rhythm and orientations of empire, have never really had full citizenship in the first place.

Impossible rights

In February 2018 the tabloid newspaper the *Sun* published an online article explicitly celebrating the assassination of Naveed Hussain (otherwise known as Abu Usamah al-Britani) by an RAF drone in northern Syria (Akbar 2018). The headline read: 'GO TO HELL'. Hussain remained a British citizen at the time of his death. The article represents a particular theatre of racist violence and sexualised voyeurism which is relevant here. It was reported that Hussain had previously attempted to convince a Page Three model to convert to Islam and join him in Syria. The paper celebrated Hussain's death as the destruction of a monstrous deviant. And it did so by juxtaposing his death with a half-naked picture of the 'innocent' white model, who we are invited to imagine has been 'saved' by the RAF drone strike. Revealing the slippery character of the deprivation of rights/personhood in our contemporary moment, on this occasion the British state did not remove Hussain's citizenship before his death. There was no legal wrangling. He was simply killed as an 'enemy combatant'.

What was particularly noticeable in this event were the circulations of rage, hatred and glee that ran through the comments under the online article. Most commenters celebrated the act and the need for more drone strikes ('Wonderful News!' read one from Redbean, 17 February 2018, comment on Akbar 2018). Others called for this kind of spectacular violence on UK streets: 'when finished over in sand-land they can land on the target in any UK inner city' (James Soros, 17 February 2018, comment on Akbar 2018). Again, as we saw in chapter 4, war comes 'home', attached as it is to the racialised-sexualised body of the non-human terrorist/monster. Such racist nationalism could be viewed as exceptional (even monstrous) as it often is to liberal audiences, with the one rejoinder that the killing of Hussain was carried out by the British military with barely a protest in the Houses of Parliament.

That the British state did not need to deprive Hussain of his citizenship formally is significant. It was not necessary because his citizenship could never stick in the first place. One comment on the *Sun* article (Maximus Hispania, 17 February 2018, comment on Akbar 2018) was just as revealing as the actions of the state:

> British? hahaha That monster has no British cultural background, even if he s [sic] born in London. Your parents condition your real nationality. And monsters like these don't deserve British citizenship.

At Sassen's (2016) 'systematic edge' (the assassination of an enemy combatant who remains a British citizen) we learn how tightly citizenship is bound to colonial intimacies and the white family. Monsters, we should remember, and those who occupy the structural positions of the non-familial/non-human monster have no citizenship in contemporary Britain.

Deprivation as colonial violence

Through the above examples, I hoped to illustrate the persistence of deprivation of citizenship and its varied forms. Deprivation is bound to broader claims to personhood, because if humanity cannot stick to certain bodies then how can citizenship? In this context, contemporary deprivation cannot only be understood as shaped by the War on Terror or the hostile environment.

Instead, deprivation might be more keenly understood as part of the wider racialised governance which has circulated globally throughout modern empire. It is not that British citizenship has been fundamentally altered but that for certain populations citizenship has always been impossible. It has been impossible because the humanity of colonised people is constantly in question. Contemporary changes to the rules of deprivation map onto, resuscitate and are normalised by this historic impossibility. Citizenship in this sense is not only imprinted by imperial 'legacies' but is better described as 'designed' to continue and enhance hierarchies of empire (for a more detailed discussion of 'failure by design' see Tyler 2010). Here contemporary imperial interests such as carrying out colonial military operations in the Middle East, the emergence of ISIS and the rapid expansion of 'surplus' populations through contemporary racialised capitalism meet up with older logics of deprivation.

I want to conclude this chapter by suggesting that cases of deprivation, exemplified by what happened in Rotherham, reveal important things about ongoing colonial and familial hierarchies. Citizenship in contemporary Britain is structured by the afterlife of the colonial categories of the human/not-quite/non-human

The powers of deprivation we have seen develop since 2002, which were expanded in the wake of the Rotherham grooming scandal, continue to make *all* citizens who have an attachment to another state, or who are naturalised or dual citizens, into potential 'migrants'. Here possessing citizenship can longer be viewed as protection against bordering and immigration practices. What the threat of deprivation does is transform mainly non-white citizens into a structural position akin to the indentured labourer – that is, these subjects hold provisional rights, and are subject to exploitation and discipline. This exploitation, discipline and provisional regime of rights are increasingly made arbitrary with limited recourse to legal challenge. These communities are made steadily deportable as borders become stickier – that is, they can be subject to citizenship stripping, detention and deportation as their rights become conditional. We can think here of how the removal of passports works as a method of enclosure, or of how those whose citizenship appears to be brought into question are denied essential medical treatment (Gentleman 2018a), or of the high rates of incarceration of young black and Asian men (Elliott-Cooper 2016). The indentured labourer, we should remember, was at times useful: they could be temporarily 'good' and 'worthy', they held provisional recognition of kinship. But their worth and rights were always contingent. This is the realm of the not-quite-human.

What conditions the temporality, control and exploitation of the not-quite-human is the possibility and threat of being subject to state-sanctioned and gratuitous violence. The normalised violence against monsters – street groomers, terrorists, gangs – reminds us that not-quite-human populations can be quickly transformed into killable bodies and populations. Here people who are stripped of their citizenship, abandoned, killed by drone strikes or extradited (Kapoor 2018: 51–83) are arguably subjected to the remnants of anti-black violence that we saw perpetrated against slaves, fanatics and 'African coastal migrants' above. Acts such as the deprivation of citizenship, drone assassinations, torture, expelling of unwanted migrants are orientated towards the destruction and raw punishment of bodies (Richter-Montpetit 2014). We can see this death drive in the glee that runs through the celebration of the deportation of grooming convicts, the expulsion of 'foreign criminals', the drone strikes on 'terrorists'. It is a spectacle of violence which is desired and celebrated as the gratuitous deaths of the monstrously perverse. But in these acts of violence is the structuring of the vulnerability of wider racialised populations whose rights and bodies are also brought into question. What differs in terms of the subject position of the racially exploited and those of the (fanatic or) terrorist is that rather than this violence being orientated towards life, as a productive force, it is focused on death. Here we can consider this parallel violence as linked to the history of anti-blackness as a death drive (Sexton 2011). This is the realm of the non-human. Because this violence is motivated through racialised-sexualised claims to personhood, intimacy and evolutionary ideas about family, it structures the treatment of wider populations and creates further conditions for the evisceration of rights and personhood.

Conclusion

What I have demonstrated in the last three chapters is that the family is bound to economies of life and death in ways that do not appear immediately obvious. Whilst chapter 3 examined the way that appeals to family worked to manage colonised populations as shams, in chapter 4 and here the family was orientated towards protecting and sustaining whiteness, bound as this is to gratuitous forms of violence. If the modern liberal family is outwardly presented as inclusive, when we push at this, we can see how imperial, privileged whiteness is reasserted powerfully. Family thus works as control but also dispossession in our contemporary moment. For example, borders are arranged to limit the rights to those deemed shams; citizenship is restricted through the denial of inheritance. But borders are equally bound to securing the white family against its perverse others.

Recognising that deprivation of citizenship acts as a particular form of sticky border has revealed the extent to which British citizenship is already sustained by colonial orientations and racialised logics. Here it is important to further examine how bordering haunts non-white citizens, whether they were born into British citizenship or whether they were naturalised – people can be subject to an evisceration of rights and subsequently their lives. This reminds citizens racialised as non-white that not only can they never 'belong' but that their access to personhood (and with it, rights, habeas corpus, survival) is constantly in doubt. In the case of parents losing their citizenship, this effectively means that dependent children are also stripped of their rights (Woods and Ross 2013). Just as legal categories of 'slave' or 'free person' were natally transferred or how citizenship is passed on through bloodline, in modern Britain deprivation can now be inherited through women's bodies (see, for example, Embury-Dennis 2019). This is not merely a 'legacy' of empire, attuned as it is to hierarchies of imperialism, but the ongoing fabric of colonial rule which feeds off the stratification and management of populations along deeply racialised lines.

To understand the role that monstrous violence plays in contemporary bordering is to be attuned to the way that spectacular violence and suffering remains attuned to anti-blackness. Here coloniality is animated by securing the white heteronormative family and paternally managing 'tolerable' populations; but it is equally bound to the spectacle and desire to inflict punishment and suffering, orientated towards bringing certain ways of being in the world to an end. If the feminised body of the reproductive (unintegrated) woman is a threat to the nation through her fertility and failed motherhood (as we saw in the chapter 3), the masculinised monster demands more martial solutions.

If non-white citizens are rendered deportable populations, attached to the legacy of the indentured labourer, they are bound to an inevitable form of failed (or sham) citizenship. They remain positioned by liberal developmentalism as an example of underdeveloped sexuality and family life within the postmetropole. This works to legitimise forms of violent bordering that not only control but also expel people, and in so doing enhances inequalities and creates even more precarious populations and spaces of abandonment. Underpinning this, and structuring this precarity, is the ever-present possibility of being demarcated as killable; as the monstrous; as the expendable. This is the demarcation of not only failed citizenship but also failed futurity (Mbembe 2003), where bodies are rendered beyond the social calculus; that is, outside of and without a future.

Notes

1 This chapter was based on archival work undertaken in 2016 and 2017 at the National Archives, Kew, the British Library, London, and the Bristol Archives.
2 Deprivation of citizenship can be done on the basis that it is in the 'public good'. The definition of this is entirely up to the discretion of the Home Secretary. Subjects can appeal through SIAC. However, because the state has the legal right to withhold evidence if it is in the 'interest of national security', defendants and lawyers rarely have adequate material to base their case on. Equally, the Home Office regularly issues deprivation orders when a subject is out of the country, meaning that lodging an appeal may be impossible in the time frame (ten days after a letter of expulsion has been received). Courts are extremely cautious of overturning cases based on issues of security. Furthermore, the legal basis of deprivation stands on such arbitrary grounds that even suspicion of collusion with terrorist organisations can be enough for the court to rule in favour of the Home Office. This evidence-light approach is reflected in the low success rates of appeals: between 2009 and 2017, only one appeal against citizenship deprivation was successful, six were dismissed, two were struck out and three remained open (a list of decisions can be found at http://siac.decisions.tribunals.gov.uk/).

6

The good migrant

The good migrant is placid. The good migrant accepts their place. The good migrant contributes. The good migrant pays their dues. The good migrant is domesticated. The good migrant is always happy to be here, forever grateful for the tolerance and begrudging acceptance of their hosts. They change their name because it was always too hard to pronounce. It made people feel awkward. They are happy to be given their marked and cramped space at the margins of the tolerant nation. The good migrant subjects themselves to the endless gaze, compromises their history to 'pass' and pose for the camera, in the thankless yet highly visible task to be 'included'.

On 17 October 2016 a small group of child refugees arrived in the English town of Croydon under a newly devised child resettlement scheme (commonly referred to at the time as the 'Dubs amendment'). Under this scheme the government had reluctantly agreed to allow initially 480 unaccompanied children, previously based in the informal settlement or 'Jungle' camp in Calais, the right to settle in the UK.[1] Despite widespread initial support for the scheme (including from usually hostile right-wing tabloids), the fourteen minors stepping off coaches that day were doggedly hounded by the press. Almost immediately questions were raised as to whether these refugees were 'really children'. As further doubt was spread over the next few days, journalists began referring to them as 'burly lads' (Greenhill *et al.* 2016). Attention was placed on their masculinity and bodied features of age such as 'crow feet', 'eye bags' and 'facial hair'. The Conservative MP David Davies tweeted that 'they don't look like "children"' ... I hope British hospitality is not being abused' (quoted in McLaughlin 2018: 7).

Faced with what Elizabeth Brown (2011) calls 'unchildlike children', the *Daily Mail* became the first newspaper to publicly use facial recognition software to 'test' the refugees' ages (Wright and Drury 2017). The front covers of the following day's papers were full of photographic portraits of the children – now transformed into 'youth' or 'young men' – with their suspected, computer-generated ages showing them to be adults. Focus fell on the apparent risk these 'young men' would pose in British schools as a sexual threat to young girls (Wright and Drury 2017). Speaking in an interview on BBC Radio 4, Davies argued that these 'unchildlike' children should be subject to dental examinations and X-rays to prove their age (BBC 2016). Warding off arguments that this would be unethical and a violent intervention, Davies suggested that this was nothing compared to what asylum seekers (or 'economic migrants' in his lexicon) go through – a mere dental examination could not be compared to the risk of crossing the Mediterranean and surviving the conditions of the 'Jungle' camp (also see Royston and Mills 2016). If they were 'real' children after all, what did they have to hide?

This event captures a number of different bordering moves around the body of the child, the 'real' refugee and the 'good' or domesticated migrant, bordering moves which are tied up with a powerful politics of victimhood, innocence and 'deservedness' and the visual regimes of all three. The figuration of the child does a huge amount of political work in this encounter and in global politics more broadly (Faulkner 2011). As I touched upon in chapter 4, 'the child' is bound to heteronormative futurity, and with this hope, and thus is made into the ultimate vulnerable subject. But this relies equally on who can be a child and, subsequently, who can be innocent, vulnerable and a subject of empathy and protection (Crawley 2011). It makes us ask which bodies are maintained by the dominant value of childhood, and how this might structure questions of mobility, borders and belonging more broadly.

Childhood

Global regimes of humanitarianism rely upon the codification of childhood as victimhood, for example to 'save' and 'protect' refugees or vulnerable people. And yet we already know that childhood, and with that victimhood, is already racialised, gendered, sexualised in particular ways. Sharpe (2016) reminds us that childhood is never accessible to some. Consider how black children are consistently rendered as 'youth', and with this dangerous and threatening (Jackson and Pabon 2000; Duru 2004), often known only through violence, 'gang culture' or 'knife crime' (on asylum seekers see Davidson 2016), or how the above child refugees were immediately converted into a sexualised threat to white school girls. The messiness, cultural and geographical locatedness of childhood is obscured and often only made intelligible in relation to a white, Western and universalised idea of family. There is childhood, and there is sham childhood.

In the assertion by Davies that 'they don't look like "children"' we are reminded initially of how images of children work to create empathy in the context of humanitarian events and disasters; and secondly, of how this produces a grammar of 'real' suffering. Consider, for instance, the now infamous picture of Alan Kurdi, the toddler whose dead body was photographed lying face down on a beach in Bodrum, Turkey, in 2015. This picture is often upheld as a devastating and humanising moment of photojournalism (Gunter 2015). It is understood by many to have shifted the European public's perception of the 'migrant' or 'refugee crisis' and created the conditions for more liberal policy-making (including, some argue, the Dubs amendment discussed above; Bleiker 2018: 32). And yet, as Miriam Ticktin (2016) argues, this image was able to pull at Western heartstrings because the photo captured the dead child in the likeness of a Euro-American boy in holiday beach wear. It is significant that when I look at that picture now, I still see my own son. It is devastating. But this is fundamentally about who can be *imaged*, and at the same time *imagined*, as (un)worthy (see Butler 2010).

Who gets to be a 'child' – known, seen, empathised with as a 'child' – is historical, just as who gets to be seen as a refugee or 'good' migrant is historicised within particular terms and relations of who is familial. In order to be accepted as 'genuine' refugees, or even to be mourned, children must fit within the dominant account of childhood and the family (Holland 2004). Or more precisely, they must be amenable to a population who can see them as their own children – as children that can slot into a national family and be protected, cared for, or grieved for by benevolent, white, European parents.

This gaze is not only present within Western media but it also organises the everyday practice of mobility. Human traffickers, for instance, are keenly aware of the racialised politics of vision. It is well documented that lighter-skinned refugees, particularly women and children, are often arranged on the top of boats crossing the Mediterranean, whilst black and darker-skinned people are often forced into bowels of the vessel. This is a stark reminder to Sharpe (2016) of the ongoing presence of the hold for black lives. Those thought to be seeable as 'real' refugees, as victims, as more human, are placed within plain sight in order to be counted worthy of saving.

Visuality

These bordering moves rely on ideas of who is the 'real' child and the 'real' refugee or 'good' migrant. But as I have begun to sketch out, this is always bound to particular forms of visuality, or ways of seeing. As well as not fitting within regimes of childhood, the children stepping off the coaches in Croydon could be photographed and rendered 'adults' and 'unchildlike' through particular visual techniques. Photography was used here not only to represent moving bodies but also to capture and render the inner truth of suspicious movement (Amoore and Hall 2009). As discussed in chapter 3, the delineation between who is genuine/in-genuine and deserving/undeserving (in this case the refugee) demands an ever-present suspicion of the intimacies and bodies of those moving

and claiming rights. Likewise, this also relates to suspicions over relationships, kinships, age, the authenticity of identity documents and the
recognition of embodied likeness (see Turner and Vera Espinoza 2019).
As with the sham marriage, suspicion demands the use of technologies
to extract the 'truth' from migrants, where deservedness can be read
in textual evidence, images and on the body (from body language, skin
colour, scar tissue).

In this context, the attempt by newspapers to use facial recognition
software to test the age of child refugees is telling. Facial recognition
software has become a key aspect of security practices and biometric
technology which attempts to locate, categorise and capture subjects
on the move – from airport scanners and passports, to checkpoints and
police patrols. Despite huge technological problems with facial recognition software, making it almost practically useless for mass surveillance
(Dodd 2018), it still continues to proliferate. Whilst most liberal arguments against such surveillance rely upon issues of privacy, we might
consider the way this re-networks racialised codes of humanness (and
with that 'childhood', 'adulthood', 'gender' and 'sexuality'). It works by
codifying particular bodies as (ab)normal. Browne (2010) demonstrates
how this technology relies upon the recognition of key facial feature
that are attuned to a 'standardised' facial imprint of white Europeans.
The 'normal' is coded through particular appeals to white 'epidemiological'
features (Browne 2010). The use of facial recognition on child refugees
reveals the ongoing circulations of the racialised body in visual surveillance of contemporary bordering.

It is worth dwelling on a further point regarding vision and race
here. When David Davies argued that the UK government should subject
'unchildlike' refugees to dental examinations, he redeployed a key logic
of racial/colonial science, one birthed from eugenics: that the facial,
dental and bone structure of people should be compared, studied and
categorised to extract the 'truth' of their character and morality. The
supposed scientific promise to know the truth of the suspicious body
(in images, X-rays, algorithms) is conditioned by colonial epistemologies
and ways of seeing populations and bodies (Ittmann *et al.* 2010;

Nishiyama 2015). This is not so much about 'fixing identities', but rather about finding the inner purpose, morality, danger and deviancy of particular subjects (Amoore and Hall 2009).

Davies also offered up another colonial 'truth'. In arguing that dental examinations should be brought in to test refugees, he made the case that they were already exempt from ethics and rights. Presenting the idea that they had 'been through worse' recognised that they had already been dehumanised. Or, they were never properly human in the first place. The proposal to X-ray these children is a culmination of 'thingifica-tion' (Cesaire 1972: 42). They are made into 'things', not people subject to rights and ethics, but caught in the racialised trap of the not-quite/ non-human. That is, they are made into flesh to be examined.

Here, the ways of seeing and imagining who is a 'real' child and thus a 'real' refugee or 'good' migrant, becomes conditioned by technology but also by histories of the visual. Photographs are one significant practice in the codifications of humanness, attached as they are to a particular national/civilisational grammar of suffering and empathy. 'Family' here is again both the quiet remainder and energising principle of such circula-tions. Family translates the seeable, it converts and modifies those that can be human-like, through welcome, threat or expulsion.[2]

The good migrant

> Pictures are not simply of what things looked like, but how things were made visible, how things were given to be seen, how things were 'shown' to knowledge or to power – two ways in which things became seeable.
> (Rajchman 1988: 91)

Drawing upon the example of the treatment of child refugees above, I propose that if borders are intimate (chapter 3), if borders are sticky (chapters 4 and 5), then borders are also visual. This chapter further pushes at the visual regime through which contemporary bordering operates. If the last three chapters focused on the explicit violent practices of contemporary colonial bordering, this chapter aims to examine how people are made to *look* 'out of place'. It does so, perhaps counterintuitively, by tracing the contemporary rendering of the 'good' migrant in the UK and beyond. It focuses on those mobile subjects whose presence is tolerated, welcomed, even 'celebrated' in the UK. Off the back of the contemporary governing promise that 'real' child refugees can be welcomed, that 'genuine' marriages can allow settlement, that the good, 'integrated', minority citizen deserves rights, I want to ask: what does this domesticated subject look like? Or to put it differently, how is the 'good', familial and integrated migrant imaged/imagined? That is, on what visual terms, and on what cultural codes and intimate relations, are moving bodies 'included', allowed to belong or at least 'pass' in contemporary Britain? It explores these questions by investigating the role of images and photography in both reproducing and contesting borders.

In the last two chapters I focused on how bordering/borders are energised by threats and dangers, from 'suspicious' to 'monstrous' intimacies. This arguably has led to reinforcing precarity, vulnerability and the abandonment of racialised settled and migrant communities alike. If the figure of the monster (terrorist, groomer, gang member) and the sham drives this bordering, so too does the figure of the 'good' migrant – the one who can be welcomed and included. Domestication, we should remember, is a liberal strategy: it includes to exclude. Borders need to be constantly redrawn around who is (un)domesticated, who is familial, who can move/settle, who is 'out of place'. It is from the potentiality of improvement, inclusion, progress that liberal government is re-energised. And with it, the violence that underpins domestication is equally rationalised and silenced. What I want to probe at here is how the promise of the 'good' migrant can also work to hide and remake the colonial hierarchies that dominate mobility and citizenship.

Consider, for instance, how the depiction of the 'good' child refugee – vulnerable, innocent, victim – conditions the unchildlike 'burly youth' or 'bogus asylum seeker'. Or how sympathy for victims of what became known as the 'Windrush scandal' in the UK have been used to justify the continued deportation of 'illegal' migrants (de Noronha 2018, 2019). Or how a fixation on women and men who have 'escaped' Islamic communities and joined 'mainstream society' (Razack 2007; Casey 2016) is used to justify the surveillance and discipline of Muslim populations more broadly. Who can be a subject of empathy conditions who can be forgotten or silenced, and who is unworthy. In exploring how 'good' migrants are imagined, and by this I mean made *thinkable* and *seeable*, I tease out how this creates further bordering moves. Delineations around who is 'good' are also key sites for colonial duress.

In this chapter I turn to the role that photography and exhibitions play in the making of the 'good' and, equally, 'familial' migrant. I first explore the role of photography in colonial domestication and in particular the place of family portraits in the ordering of intimate relations across empire. I investigate how photographs played a significant role in limiting who could be part of a family. I then bring this analysis up to date by considering the role of photography and vision in contemporary border-ing both in the UK and Europe. This pays attention to the exhibiting of the 'good' migrant, which occurred during the 'refugee crisis' that came to prominence from 2015. I pay special attention to exhibitions and projects that claim to contest or challenge the dominant negative representation of immigration, mobility and settlement, and produce a positive account of migration. To analyse this in more detail, I focus on the photographic exhibition *Arrivals: Making Sheffield Home* as one example of how positive stories and imaginaries are formed around migration, through appeals to local/global ideas about humanitarianism, as well as multicultural and civic nationalism. I thus explore what is contested and reproduced in these visual practices of inclusion and in making migrants familial, and more significantly, what the limits are to a politics of humanitarian or compassionate nationalistic welcome and inclusion.

Photography and looking back

Throughout this chapter, photography is treated as a key but ultimately part component of visuality – which is what Gregory (2012a) refers to as culturally contingent vision or way of seeing. In the use of 'visual regime' throughout the chapter, I refer to a series of components which work in a relatively autonomous but interconnected manner to make up a dominant way of visualising and constituting social reality. To refer to a visual regime is to consider both how things are seen and represented but also the ways that things are rendered historically seeable and unseeable (through techno-cultural processes). So, for instance, there is a visual regime of childhood. This is made up of different components (discourses, ideas, past images, visual techniques) and histories (heteronormative socialisation, Eurocentric ideas of the superior white family, commodification, racialised capitalism, gendering) that align to make, for example, one body look like a 'helpless child' and another a 'burly lad'. In discussing the 'gaze', I refer more specifically to a dominant visual regime that is tied to particular formations of social control and power relations. Mostly I speak, via bell hooks's (1992) seminal work, of the 'colonial masculine gaze'. This gaze was central to imperial and colonial government and continues to proscribe and haunt contemporary imaginaries and ways of seeing.

In studying how the 'good' migrant is imagined/imaged, this chapter engages with the politics of photography itself. Photography has historically been a key resource and product of the colonial masculine gaze, even as a creative and artistic enterprise. That photography has been relatively democratised (Bleiker 2018: 27) does not negate its role in empire-making. This is also reflected in humanist projects of modernity, where photography has been central to regimes of extractive truth telling, or used in practices of security and biopolitical management (Meek 2016). The legacy of these histories continues in bordering today, for example in the use of facial recognition software, security scanners at airports or biometrics in the control of mobility. As I demonstrate, photography also plays a key role in normalising and reproducing borders in everyday and mundane places like newspapers or art exhibitions, particularly in celebrations of whiteness (or in the case I examine, progressive/humanitarian whiteness).

However, images – and photographic images in particular – also hold the power to disrupt. If photography remains a site of colonial domestication, this power is relational; it is constantly resisted and shaped by numerous social forces. Visuality and aesthetics play an important role in resisting bordering. Such analysis has been largely absent in this book and I attempt to introduce some of these questions here before expanding on them in the penultimate chapter.

Photography as domestication

Photographs are a powerful force because of how they relate to the claims of Western knowledge to access unmediated and scientific truths (Debrix and Weber 2003). Imperial and colonial rule was shaped by technological possibility of knowing, capturing and recording the 'reality' of territories, populations and movement (Jay and Ramaswamy 2014). From the inception of photography in 1839, the medium was tied into other practices such as cartography and demography in the governance of colonised people and lands. Photography could provide detailed records of lands, infrastructure and natural resources central to military strategy, surveillance or accumulation. We know that the power to see 'at a distance' was vital to the development of modern military power (Virilio 1989; Collins 2017). This was as true with the violent pacification and aerial bombardment of Iraqi civilians throughout the 1920s, as it was with the invasion of Iraq in 2003 and again in the expanding drone war that continues over the Middle East today (Gregory 2012a). Rendering territories and populations as seeable through still (and then moving) images is central to the art of colonial war and extraction (for more on this see Barkawi and Stanski 2012).

Movement again was constituted as both problematic and controllable within particular visual regimes. As we may remember from chapter 3, visual identifiers were used by colonial states to mark out and categorise criminals, suspects or those moving bodies thought to be 'troublesome'. Branding was central to the control of slaves in the American South and the West Indies, tattooing and then fingerprinting was developed in India to make criminals categorisable and visible prior to the creation of photographic recognition and 'mug shots'. Photographic recognition would eventually be established in the passport and identity card systems of the late nineteenth and early twentieth centuries, but these were predated by practices such as slave ledgers and 'wanted' posters (Pegler-Gordon 2009: 11; Browne 2015). The recorded image shaped how the labourer, the rebel or the slave could be made knowable and classified (Thapar 2015), just as it made it possible to make lands and people primed for penetration and extraction – such as in the feminised images of the Orient as a space of sexual promiscuity and decadence (figure 1).

Said (1978) proposed that orientalism was a visual as well as textual regime. Colonial power required the construction 'of a sort of Benthamite panopticon' from whose watch-towers 'the Orientalist surveys the Orient

1   'In the harem', Lehnert & Landrock postcard, 1900s–1910s

from above, with the aim of getting hold of the whole sprawling panorama before him' in every 'dizzying detail' (quoted in Gregory 2012b: 152). This unidirectional and centralised analysis of vision has been contested (see Jay and Ramaswamy 2014). But we should remember how colonial administrators pursued photography as a means to visualise and thus make territory and people amenable to being governed. This worked both in terms of representing absences and producing places as familiar. The means of capturing still images as 'objective truths' could be used to reduce the complexity of social life into simple generalisations. To Mitchell (2000: 6–10), the colonial gaze was not always about taking pictures of the 'East' but instead making the East *into a picture*. Photography was a vital aspect of the cultural economy of imperialism, from travelogues and commercial photojournalism to postcards and exhibitions, which circulated images and imaginaries of the exotic/ erotic to populations across metroimperial space who were ready to consume the visual production of empire (on animals, imperialism and visuality see Margulies 2019).

The state of the photo album

The production and consumption of images also worked to manage racialised social relations. Colonial photography played a powerful role in constituting and distributing scientific racism. Coco Fusco (2003: 16) has argued that 'rather than recording the existence of race, photography produced race as a visualizable fact'. Photography provided anthropologists with an 'objective lens' to record and sensationalise ideas of human difference, progress and civilisation. European exhibitions often provided a space for such a spectacle, just as imperial and settler state archives held thousands of images of 'native' subjects for education, inspection and often entertainment (Maxwell 2000). Images provided 'evidence' of colonised people as savage and primitive, and as ethnographic records rather than people (consider the *Savage South Africa* exhibition described in chapter 1).

In the 1870s ethnographers Henry Huxley and J. H. Lamprey devised a systematic way of photographing aboriginal people across the British Empire. Their subjects were stripped naked and photographed in front of measuring apparatus, including a cross sectional mesh, so to compare anatomical characteristics. Huxley saw this as useful for racial categorisation but also to make judgements about the suitability of populations for coerced labour and other types of work in mind of moral 'uplift' (Maxwell 2000: 42–43). This ethnographic approach was contrasted with later cultural relativistic photography and more 'benevolent' methods of study where indigenous people were cast as bearers of unique and fast-disappearing cultures. In this way, colonised people were photographed as a mode of extractive racial categorisation, as a means of knowledge production for empire, for the benefits of imperial capitalism and as a spectacle to confirm European progress and development, which meant that images were produced and consumed as both for 'scientific' study and for titillation and desire.

Commercial and ethnographic photography was a key optic of the domesticating state, but equally artefacts such as family photo albums or portraits provided an intimate site for the production of coloniality, race-making and the scripting of the white self. Exploring the archives of colonial administrators reveals how colonised people were invariably conditioned as the observed – for example as 'house boy', 'labourer' or 'farm hand', 'native', 'criminal' – or as ethnographic remnants. The camera lens both provided a means of objectification but equally a technology through which the myriad of white colonial selves were performed – the adventurer, entrepreneur, philanthropist, home-maker, artist, socialite. Here it is important to recognise how this blurs (if not totally eviscerates) the line between what we might consider 'private' and 'public' photography – photographs are always public, even if meant for private consumption (such as those that find their way into official state archives – see the Bristol Archives British Empire & Commonwealth Collection collection, for example).

The most striking example of this is the family album or portrait. Lalvani (1996) argues that photography did not merely reflect bourgeois colonial family values but was part of its architecture. Portraits, for instance, arranged particular codes of the white bourgeois European family – father, mother, children arranged in hierarchical order. According to Lalvani (1996: 65):

> The family album is both a document of social assertion and a sentimental register ... The regulation of images, in providing for 'a common sexual and economic goal' and in enabling ideological oversight to permeate the private realm, plays 'a central role in the development in the ... ideology of the family.'

Drawing on Lalvani, we can consider how an artefact such as a hanging photograph becomes a means of shaping and producing 'family' and 'family memories' as regulatory ideals (Wexler 2000). This is significant because of the way photography works to frame normative ways of being but also because the aesthetic of the family photograph produces excesses and conditions who can be seen as 'out of place'. This is about what and who is permissible to photograph but also about how a photographic type relays continual 'truths', in this case intimate truths to be stored, displayed and treasured.

Just as photography was an intimate site of family-making in Europe, this was used in different social relationship across empire. Colonial administrators often focused on photographing domestic spaces as a means of showing how colonised land could be tamed and pacified, such as with fencing, gardening, the building of European style homes or bungalows (Mills 2008: 102–136). Colonised subjects were brought in to reproduce settler households within shifting codes of gendered and racialised stratification – as 'workers', 'gardeners', 'house boys', 'nannies', 'milk maids', or as 'lovers'. Importantly, colonised subjects could be partially included in the household but they could not be sustained or photographed as 'family' (see, for example, Stoler 2002 112–140). Whilst intimately connected, they remained subordinated and racialised labourers (as presented in figures 2 and 3).

This intimate inclusion/exclusion is important. The partial inclusion of 'good' colonised subjects within the settler household firstly reveals the racialised inequality of who worked for who under white supremacist capitalism, but equally this partial, often intimate, 'inclusion' in the household (such as the being viewed as the 'good house boy' or 'ayah'; see figure 2) works to obscure the dispossessive violence of wider colonial structures. It hid this violence by the appearance of intimate 'inclusion'.

The intimate dehumanisation of African bodies was often obscured in the complex 'inclusion' within colonial settler houses. But such pictures remind us of how easily black bodies were turned into objects, com-modities or used as a spectacle of white pleasure and entertainment, such as in one infamous image of the African Oil Nut factory workers (see figure 3). It is significant that Badagry was a major Atlantic slave point, home to Gberefu Island – 'the point of no return'. As this photograph demonstrates, abolition did very little to alter such social relations.

The structure of the white colonial household and the family album was equally paralleled in the everyday experiences and visual registers of colonised subjects who travelled to the metropole, as British subjects, or after 1947 as Commonwealth citizens. Black and Asian photographers grew in number during the nineteenth and twentieth centuries. Their work often troubled dominant modes of visuality, for example by examining and representing kinship and belonging in alternative ways (see, for example, Gilroy and Hall 2007). Despite this, however, dominant forms of photography and popular visual culture in the UK focused on framing black and Asian subjects and communities as both inferior and 'out of place'. Consider how images circulated to reveal the problem of 'race relations' or orientalist codifications of exoticism (Tolia-Kelly 2016), of ungoverned domesticity and poor motherhood (Webster 1998), or inversely fixated on nostalgic images of a 'lost' whiteness, contaminated by decolonisation and the movement of black and brown bodies and intimacies. Reconstituting the colonial masculine gaze, Commonwealth citizen migrants were rendered visible along an axis of assimilable subjects who could be civilised into the marked space of the 'good', domesticated migrant, and those deemed unassimilable, who needed to be contained and expunged.

2   'My house boys', taken in Badagry, Nigeria, 1922, by 'Mr Verdin',
manager of the African Oil Nut Company. He annotated the photograph
'My house boys… Godrey, James and Godrey's wife'. Godrey and James's
subjugation within the colonial settler house is equally marked by the
evisceration of Godrey's wife's name.

3 The Verdins' idea of a Christmas card (same photographer as figure 2), again taken in Badagry, 1923

The family portrait

If empire is always bound to family, as this book argues, then how could we think of colonial photography in relation to the family album or family portrait? If the family portrait was shaped by who could be photographed in relation to the family (settler household, white national family), we need to consider how photography worked to remake and normalise the treatment of colonised people: it demarcated who could be viewed as living outside modern time (ethnographic photography), or as an object of white consumption and subjugation (the family portrait), or as the primitive 'native' to be examined and preserved, or as a problem population 'out of place' (such as the presentation of Commonwealth citizens as migrants). Colonial photography worked to reduce personhood into bodies or things, as a subordinate to white personhood. In all of this, colonised people are materialised as in excess of proper familial relations with their appropriate gendered and sexualised codes of civilisation, nation, family.

Here the family portrait becomes the absent presence in photographs of colonised peoples and then people on the move. That is, it works to reveal what is missing or lost, figuratively or literally. As Wexler (2000) has argued, whilst colonised subjects and freed slaves took up photography, almost from its inception, not only did they face issues of resources and access but what could be recognisable as people and kinship within those photographs was shaped by the dominant white order. The colonial visual regime relates to how close one is able to perform European bourgeois domesticity. So, whilst some colonised populations were and continue to be cast as 'without family' – such as indigenous people or the enslaved – others are deemed as progressing towards heteronormative personhood. This is often revealed in how people were photographed or made seeable in relation to the (white) family portrait.

Photography, control and mobility

What I hope to highlight here is not just that pictures have symbolic power but that they also do things. It means thinking about how images are already placed within particular colonial power relations, bound to processes of domestication which circulate within imperial capitalism. Consider, for instance, how the portrait photograph became institutionalised into bordering practices through the emergence of identity cards and passports. The passport works through immigration law to constitute the individual subject as the holder of rights, but this is bound to how a subject resembles a photographic portrait – in other words, how they are 'seen' (see Torpey 2009). At the turn of the twentieth century, 'looking' like a passport photograph became one of the primary means for states to organise the movement of people, distinguishing between worthy/unworthy, the genuine/in-genuine (Browne 2015). This supplemented other visual practices such as medical inspections, and would eventually be proliferated in practices such as immigrant identity cards, police inspections and registration. Resembling a photograph became a dominant means of accessing rights of mobility and settlement and for authorities to expunge and control. How one is seen and made seeable matters.

As I touched upon in the introduction to this chapter, visuality plays an ever-expanding role in the government of mobility in contemporary states – from drone images and naval mapping, to heat tracing and facial recognition. Whilst northern states propagate these regimes, tracking, surveillance and imaging of 'events' such as the 'refugee crisis' in Europe is also done by international organisations, NGOs, militaries, corporate media and private security contractors, as well as by subjects on the move themselves (Tazzioli and Walters 2016). For instance, the United Nations Refugee Agency (UNHCR) uses visual recognition software called ProGres to profile asylum seekers, to manage their claims for refugee status, but also in the distribution of resources such as food and increasingly as a tool used indirectly in the push to deport those with 'failed' claims. The EU similarly relies on the Eurodac system to monitor the arrival of mobile people into the EU through fingerprint tracing as well as facial images – this data is explicitly used to track, contain and deport those back to country of entry or origin (*The Economist* 2017; for a long discussion of borders and biometrics see Scheel 2019).

Who is made invisible, who is pictured, who is imaged as a problem, who is imaged as in need of saving or as a 'good' or 'bad' migrant runs through these technologies and shapes the contemporary politics of mobility. But perhaps, as importantly, such a regime of visibility is also about *in*visiblity – who can avoid detection, who can escape or dodge the camera or the scanner. To Tazzioli and Walters (2016: 453), the governing of mobility is not merely enacted through the camera, but the 'dynamics which the camera imparts profoundly shapes' how bordering functions. This includes the possibility of not being pictured.

Whilst this regime of visuality is expanding technologically, photographs remain key to how state actors make judgements over suitability for the right to move and settle. Think again of how the UK regulates the movement of people by claiming that kinship ties or 'romantic' relations between subjects are invalid or in-genuine (chapter 3). This works beyond surveillance and the passport photo. Those moving on the basis of kinship, dependency or love often have to demonstrate 'family relations' through paper identification but also visual recognition (see Shah 2012). Here a 'family portrait' can quite literally become a legal document to evidence proof of intimate relations or be used as a justification for state officials to deny entry (White 2014). In the UK family migration visa application, for example, photographs are used to make claims over the subsisting and genuine nature of a relationship (Turner and Vera Espinoza 2019). This means that photographs are read for signs of love and intimacy by state agents suspicious of sham marriages (D'Aoust 2018). This raises questions about who has access to photographic technology (which is still overstated even in the era of mobile camera phones) but also the cultural history of how socio-sexual intimacy is made intelligible. It relays a history of who can be recognised as 'familial' within the specific colonial terms of the (white) family portrait.

If borders are visual, we need to be attentive to the ways that mobility is seen and how migrants and mobility are imagined. In the next section I want to examine in more detail how particular bodies and populations are made to look not only 'out of place' but 'welcomable' – as subjects of 'inclusion' into the national or family space. Visual bordering works to distinguish the 'familial' and 'unfamilial', the 'worthy' and 'unworthy', the 'good' and 'bad'. Reflecting on how colonial photography was preoccupied with making colonised populations categorisable as exotic and/ or domesticable, I now turn to contemporary strategies to imagine the 'good' migrant.

Imaging and imagining the 'good' migrant

On November 2017 the *Arrivals: Making Sheffield Home* photographic exhibition opened in Weston Park Museum in the northern English city of Sheffield. To the collection's photographer, Jeremy Abrahams, this set of curated images offered an explicit 'counter-narrative' to the way that immigration and migrants were represented in the mainstream media in the UK (interview with the author 2017). In the context of the proliferation of dehumanising images of the 'refugee crisis' (Bleiker *et al.* 2013), of drone images relaying depictions of 'swarms' and 'flows' of people crossing into Europe in the summer of 2016, of nationalistic anxiety about 'foreign others' and 'cultural difference' and explicit policies designed to create a hostile environment, the exhibition and wider campaign was intended to display a positive visual story about migration. In this context, the exhibition sought to ameliorate the conditions of different people from across the world who were 'making Sheffield home' (Abrahams 2016).

This relied on the curating of seventy-two portrait photographs of people who had made Sheffield 'home', creating, it was hoped, a 'joyous and uplifting portrait of a creative and diverse city' (Abrahams 2016: 1). Reflecting international photo campaigns such as the International Organisation for Migration's (IOM) 'I am a migrant', each portrait was underpinned by a textual narrative of the subject's journey to the UK and practices of home-making. What was promised in the exhibition was that the portrait could be a frame through which someone stopped being a 'migrant' and became a 'Sheffielder', and in the civic terms of 'inclusion' could be viewed as a human (or at least *more human*). It is equally noteworthy that Sheffield is the next city over from Rotherham, the town that's name became a byword for grooming scandals and the scene of accompanied anti-Muslim (state) racism which I covered in chapter 4.

I want to linger on this exhibition because it offers an everyday site for what are both global and colonial logics surrounding the humanitarian 'welcome' of migrants and particular visual registers of 'good' migrants, 'integration' and multicultural nationalism in the UK. Furthermore, I am intimately entangled with this exhibition and campaign. The Weston Park Museum lies directly behind the department I worked in during the research and writing of this book. I would often walk through the exhibition space on my way to work or on breaks. After the exhibition closed, the photographs were displayed across the city and throughout the university. Several of the photographs now hang in the City of Sanctuary community centre, which aims to support and welcome refugees, asylum seekers and migrants to the city. Furthermore, the circulating politics of the images were invested in and claimed within the global and local struggle to welcome people on the move. This joins other campaigns by IOM, UNHCR, international art exhibitions and activist groups to provide a humanitarian response to moving people, in which refugees and migrants are made welcomable.

The dominant visual regime of contemporary migration often found in the news media is preoccupied with images of boats, masses, camps and imperilled victims. It is often organised around both the dangerousness of black and brown men and also the hypervisibility of what Enloe (2018) calls 'womenandchildren'. This visual regime has been revealed as dehumanising and orientalist by numerous scholarly accounts (Johnson 2011; Bleiker *et al.* 2013; Philo *et al.* 2013). What is less obvious is how positive and humanising visual regimes may have similar effects.

The visual terms of who can be welcomed and included in the UK are thus important for how we understand the politics of bordering and its ongoing colonial orientations. Not only do such exhibitions energise bordering but they also connect up with and reproduce a broader visual regime which makes particular moving bodies 'out of place'. Exhibitions such as *Arrivals* are not isolated events; they render often very explicitly what are wider logics and circulations of ways of seeing people. Here I want to consider questions of *visibility* with regard to the exhibition and construction of the 'good' migrant – that is, who is viewed as welcomable and how this welcome is made intelligible. But I also want to explore *invisibility* – who, or what, is obscured and *unseeable* in these campaigns. The exhibition is not read here to responsibilise anyone, but rather to understand the logics, assumptions, silences that shape and are reproduced across the both the photographs, the narrative of the exhibition and the local and global discourse of the 'good' migrant more broadly (see, for example, Shukla 2016).

In utilising the medium of portrait photography, the *Arrivals* exhibition partakes in a wider global push to 'humanise' migrants and redraw borders in relation to more cosmopolitan and liberal logics. The intention of Abrahams's (2016) campaign was to 'remove immigration from the zone of contention … and to humanise it through images and stories of people who have migrated from around the world'. This connects up with humanitarian approaches to contemporary mobility, where the assumption is that if only northern publics could *see* migrants as *equally* human – or more precisely, as individuals and people – they could empathise with their plight (see Johnson 2011). The stress here is on how the deaths of people crossing the Mediterranean in particular are ungrievable (Butler 2010) because of the way they are dehumanised as collectives and though animalistic metaphors – as 'swarms', 'hordes', 'cockroaches' and so forth.

Portrait photography has become the go-to medium for the visual counter-practice of humanisation.[3] Rather than focusing on mobility, collectivities or masses – a focus which is viewed as dehumanising and replicating a racist field of vision – the portrait photograph is supposed to show to the audience the humanity of the migrant. This follows social-scientific research which has evidenced how pictures of individuals and particularly images of faces tend to energise feelings of empathy and compassion in audiences (Bleiker *et al.* 2013). Jenny Edkins (2015) reminds us of how the history of the portrait is always concerned with the biography of the liberal self and its quest for wholeness as a symbol of the human. *Arrivals* relays this logic in the composition of images which foreground the face and body of its subjects. Rather than situating the 'migrant in peril', the stress of these pictures is on the inclusion and home-making capacity of its subjects, who are pictured as embedded within the urban fabric of Sheffield. Differing from the humanitarian images of disaster, it is not suffering that is supposed to humanise the migrant in *Arrivals* but rather their capacity to function within the cultural and productive economy of the city and nation. This is the visual cue of their relatability and the promise to 'become human'.

4 Pedro Fuentes, photographed by Jeremy Abrahams (2016)

Take, for example, the photograph that opened the *Arrivals* exhibition and campaign: Pedro Fuentes is pictured in Sheffield Forgemasters, perhaps the city's most famous steelworks (figure 4). The hard hat and goggles worn by Fuentes relate to his role in the steel industry, just as he is positioned in front of the kinetic sparks of the furnace. Fuentes is captured in the very symbolic heart of the city, which prides itself on its industrial past (and steel-making in particular). We should note here how the foreign body is rendered as 'integrated' and made 'useful' in relation to both the city's and nation's industry of production. The terms on which Fuentes has made a 'home' and is made 'welcomable' is depicted through the masculinised role of his labour. This is key to the substance and renewal of the city's economy as well as nostalgia for its place in the circuits of imperial capital and wealth. The terms on which Fuentes can be viewed as 'at home' in Sheffield, as a masculinised labourer – contributing by producing steel – is tied to the wider role that 'contribution' has in the politics of mobility in the UK and beyond. 'Contribution' has become key to figuring who is a 'good' and worthy migrant, and equally who is redundant, 'illegalised' or deportable.

'Contribution' (i.e. through work and labour) is superficially econo-mistic. But this understanding of economic value is bound to circulations of heteronormativity and with it racialised accounts of the nation. As I have previously argued, the liberal account of nationhood relies on making distinctions over who produces economic and cultural value, tied as this is to inclusion in the labour market, principles of self-government and progressive familial intimacy. As I showed in chapter 3, this is how multicultural difference is pacified and presented as deracialised in liberal discourse. Contributing is to be forward-facing, modern and to reproduce for the nation (Berlant 1997: 83–85). Fuentes can be welcomed because his body is rendered central to the reproduction of the city's (and thus the nation's) symbolic and economic value.

In this way, the question running through the *Arrivals* exhibition could have been: what have migrants contributed to Sheffield and the UK? What are they 'giving back'? Or as Ahmed (2010) reinterprets it – they are merely 'giving back what they owe'. These photographs reveal subjects embedded in the city's urban space but also as tied to key economic and civic institutions: the town hall, cathedral, city parks and universities. This visual narrative of place and value is intended to trouble the outwardly hostile depiction of the migrants as a 'drain on resources', as social and economic 'parasites' or as an unintegratable subject of 'cultural difference' (think back to chapter 3). Instead, the 'good' migrants – those who can tell a positive story about migration – are rendered as both normal participants in the city's/nation's economy of value but also exceptional, 'gifted' and talented contributors.[4]

Contribution is not only visualised in economic and civic terms in the *Arrivals* collection but it is also codified through love as a circulation of value and progress. Just as I examined love to function in relation to the white family or nation in chapters 3 and 4, love here brings together different points of contact. Whilst many of the portraits capture individualised subjects, a number focus on heteronormative and familial love as key aspects of home-making – as anchoring proper belonging (see below). Starting a family and especially having children is central to the exhibition's attempt to explore what a 'good' migrant is and what

a domesticated subject looks like. What is emphasised across the exhibition is how people either 'travelled for love' or 'found love' in the city.
Heteronormative (and to a far lesser extent homonormative) familial
love circulates across the photographs, such as in the focus on close
body contact, holding hands, touching on a sofa, hugging children.
Here 'proper' familial intimacy is offered as the solution to the challenge
of mobility and belonging.

But love is also projected onto the people of Sheffield and the city.
The 'good' migrants are not only shown as embedded within the urban/
national space and within heteronormative domesticity but their contribution (what makes them 'good') is also found in their expression of
love to those who welcomed and 'hosted' them. This love is orientated
towards both the people of Sheffield and correspondingly the nation.
'We love Sheffield, its friendliness, trees and parks, its civic culture', is a
common sentiment expressed through the exhibition. Here the migrant
story is presented as one of displaced violence which is fixed by the
love of the host nation. This is particularly the case for those who have
claimed asylum or been guaranteed refugee status. Here violence and
state oppression are rendered a 'nightmare' – spatially and temporally
positioned elsewhere, far away from the city in past lives and foreign
lands – whilst the transfer of love, welcome, tolerance is grounded in
Sheffield and Britain.

The visualisation of love throughout the portraits is not only found
in examples of heteronormative intimacy and domesticity but also in
the relationship to productive activities – such as gardening, painting,
civil society activities and paid labour – and in emotional appeals to
codes of happiness such as smiling and laughter. Here the contribution
of the migrant works to ameliorate their difficult presence. Their difference
and potential for diasporic melancholy (Brah 1996) can be diffused by
appropriate intimacy and the expression of grateful love and happiness
at being 'here' rather than 'there'. This is given away in the promise of
the exhibition, which is to provide a 'joyous and uplifting portrait of
the city' (Abrahams 2016: 1). Love is not only to build heteronormative
relations to secure the future of the multicultural nation but also to be

happy, to commit to and to love the new home. We come to know that the 'good' migrant is the 'loving' migrant.

Love thus works in this context to make certain migrants 'good' and familial. But love has another function: it equally works to obscure and make 'difficult' experiences of racism and the 'imperial grooves' of mobility unseeable (and forgettable), even when accounts of racism are explicitly raised in the exhibition. In juxtaposition to his smiling portrait, Abdi Aziz Suleiman describes in his story how the racism he experienced in the UK 'was like a grenade thrown at the foundations of our carefully constructed confidence' (Abrahams 2016). This is a powerful intervention. And yet despite several contributors raising the issue of racism in their stories, the visual regime of the exhibition is figured towards the celebration of joy and positivity and love of the city. This means it is unable to explore the poetry of Suleiman's words. Instead, the images of 'good', civic (and often white European) migrants feeling love/lovingly functions to smooth over these cracks and difficulties, or works to push racism into being a thing of the past. Racism is something that could occur in the 1950s, goes the refrain, but not *now*. Through a focus on joyous love, struggling against institutional racism is rendered unrepresentative of the 'good' migrant experience. It does not fit within the register of being happy and loving one's host society. Ahmed (2010: 144) reminds us that the 'melancholic' migrant who holds on to racism and struggles with it is always an obstacle to the happy and loving nation. Thus, to be a 'good' migrant is to let go of race and learn to love. Love not only smoothes over the force of institutional and structural racism and violence in the UK but it does so to pacify and make certain migrants look 'familial'.

Here it is worth considering which bodies are presented as indicative of the 'migrant experience'. The *Arrivals* exhibition works to create a visual register where EU migrants speak from the same position as non-European migrants and subjects who travelled from ex-colonies – often as Commonwealth citizens. This is also a common liberal strategy in global campaigns (IOM, for example) because, after all, moving is viewed as 'universal'. This firstly eviscerates different positionalities and global-colonial inequalities. It secondly works to hide racialised, sexualised, classed and gendered structures and experiences. Whilst people of colour in the exhibition attempt to raise the issue of race and a more complex claim to belonging, white European migrants empathetic appeal to the love of the city and place allows them to speak for all migrant experiences, and to whitewash the experience of others through their happiness and joy. We are reminded here that the good migrant of colour must overcome injury and prejudice for the future endurance of the multicultural nation into which they can (partially) 'belong' (Fortier 2008).

Visual borders

What we learn from such exhibitions and the wider logics they shore up and distribute is that the 'good' migrant 'contributes'. This contribution is materialised as different types of value: love, individualism, heteronormative family, domesticity, happiness, forgiveness are all terms on which the migrant is visualised as good, included and thus domesticated within 'multicultural' Britain. The visual regime of the *Arrivals* exhibition works because it reproduces wider local/global registers of recognition, such as humanitarianism and multiculturalism, but codifies this in local/national terms. Here 'family' works as a developmental logic, revealing and demonstrating humanity and progress, and making migrants welcomable.

Elena Fiddian-Qasmiyeh (2016) argues that the promise of the contributing migrant has come to dominate the treatment of mobility globally. Following on from the logic of contribution that we saw with *Arrivals*, she highlights the expansion of the 'super-refugee' (e.g. the Olympian swimmer who has overcome obstacles to achieve herculean feats, the hypersuccessful entrepreneur, the genius who changed the world). To be welcomable, the refugee must evidence being an 'exceptional person' or an exceptional contributor to humanity and nation. In parallel, this motivates the exceptional act of welcoming refugees and migrants by European publics (Fiddian-Qasmiyeh 2018). Whilst expressively about welcoming and revelling in difference, these examples remain orientated towards both a global humanitarianism and a local 'compassionate' nationalism, which draws borders around who can be empathised with and who cannot, translated as who can contribute to and benefit the civilisation and/or the nation and who cannot. In this way, the reification and materialising of the 'good' migrant, such as in the exhibition *Arrivals*, can be thought of as a site of bordering. Here it is important to recognise that sites such as exhibitions matter because of the way they benignly reproduce broader local and global logics, and they do so whilst appearing to be 'unpolitical' and merely about 'humanity' or 'art'.

But I do not want to just leave this here. Such sites normalise ideas about the good/bad, worthy/unworthy. But they also do work to comple-ment and energise powerful modes of domestication. We need to remember the significant role photographs and images play in the control of mobility in the codification of who can have rights, move, settle. Sites such as the *Arrivals* exhibition can be viewed as part of a connected visual regime which actively materialises who looks 'out of place' and who 'belongs'. We can think here of how bordering criss-crosses such a set of images, reifying certain figurations (the 'good', familial migrant) at the same time as producing other absent presences (the unintegratable woman, the rebel, the terrorist, the illegal, the monster, the melancholic and angry migrant or citizen of colour, the sham family – those who love and inclusion cannot be extended to, who cannot be imagined as familial). If welcome can be extended to those who fulfil the criteria of the 'good' migrant, this redraws borders around those who remain risky and those who need to be expunged.

Within the wider construction of humanitarianism and the visual regime of migration, this set of images does further political work and bordering. To Abrahams (2016, my emphasis), the exhibiting of these images proves that that '*they* have indeed become part of *our* community'. *They* have proved to *us* their inclusion and thus their worth. As with wider humanitarian visual regimes of migration, the exhibition is orientated towards proving both the national value but also humanity of the photographic subject. As with wider humanitarian visual regimes of migration, the exhibition is orientated towards proving both the national value but also humanity of the photographic subject. This form of humanitarianism works to coax empathy and compassion out of a 'host' society – which is imagined to be nationalised, settled and pre-dominantly white. Not only are migrants imagined to be exceptional contributors and benefactors for the host community – in other words, they can be included because they are good families, good workers, good civic leaders – but they are also expected to be forever grateful for the benevolence of the host nation.

Arguably, what is hidden through the intimacy of the portrait photograph is not only the institutional racism suffered by black and Asian migrants but also the colossal architecture of bordering which traps, contains and excludes racialised and mobile subjects. As with humanitarian appeals to help those suffering, this works to hide the violent architecture of borders and the complicity of the white audience in these structures. As with the inclusion of colonised subjects within the domestic space of the colonial household, the 'good' migrant is not only subordinate but their presence is only 'good' when their lives are put in service of the economic, social and cultural renewal of the postcolonial nation and family. We might consider a parallel here with the colonised subject who was intimately included or excluded from the settler household. In this way, the 'good' migrant is haunted by the image of the colonial 'house boy' whose subordinated presence and proximity both reveal and hide dispossessive violence. This parallel to the colonial 'house boy' works to hide how racialised populations are contained and continually interpolated as not-quite/non-human.

Humanitarianism, and its accomplice compassionate nationalism, ignores the intimate violence of bordering, which as I have discussed in this book is far from 'elsewhere' but in fact is intimately bound to racialised governance in Britain. My point here though, is that these images matter because of how they map onto and reproduce wider local and global visual regimes and how this feeds into other border sites. Images of who is a 'good' migrant circulate and feed into a wider landscape where decisions over who can move, settle and claim rights are taken. The happy, loving, heteronormative/homonormative and contributing migrant has social power.

Given how authorities work to distinguish who looks suspicious, a sham or a monster, the figure of the 'good' migrant circulates and energises distinctions over who looks welcomable and who looks dangerous. Consider how refugee resettlement schemes prioritise protection to 'children' and 'families' in camps across the Middle East, or visa regimes are orientated towards productive individuals through the UK tier system, or how moving as a dependent of a settled person is conditional upon looking like a spouse/partner or dependent child. In all of these sites, authorities make distinctions over who can be included premised on clear visual registers of who could be a 'good' migrant. This is more than an issue of (mis)representation. Instead we need to recognise that because borders are visual, the imaginary of the 'good' migrant helps play a part in creating the conditions of who can move, who can be given rights and who can be expelled. In light of this, consider the figures for the scheme for the resettlement of unaccompanied refugee children to the UK which we began this chapter with (of which the Dubs amendment provides one particular route to settlement). It was widely publicised in 2018, in the wake of the 'unchildlike' child refugee scandal, that only twenty child refugees had been resettled from camps in the Middle East (out of three thousand places initially promised). It was also noted that resettlement from informal camps in Calais has almost ground to a halt (Townsend 2018). Who can be imaged/imagined as a refugee or a 'good' and welcomable migrant matters.

Humanising migrants

As I noted above, portrait photography (such as illustrated in the *Arrivals* exhibition) is frequently offered as a solution to the explicitly racist representation of migration in the mainstream media – from the drone images and biometric scans, to the photography of crowded boats. This reflects broader ideological principles and assumptions that run through the politics of liberal inclusion and humanitarian welcome more generally. This means that we should ask what assumptions run through the 'humanising' promise of the portrait photograph and its focus on the 'human face'.

It is telling that in her discussion of colonial photography, Maxwell (2000: 44–45) argues that portrait photography offered more dignity to colonised people. It was 'humanising', regardless of who was taking the photograph or for what purpose. Against older practices of ethnographic recording, the portrait is viewed as empowering subjects, because those subjects could meet the colonialist gaze and be given 'equal' status as a nameable subject. However, Maxwell's argument and the liberal humanism that dominates the welcome of people, locally and globally, arguably falls into the trap of wishing away the power relations of photography, its cultural location and the visual regime and hierarchies it helps to maintain.

Through the proliferation of the masculine colonial gaze, acceptance and inclusion into personhood has been premised on being able to be imagined (if never included) as part of a family portrait, as a series of gendered and sexualised relations within the family home. The examples of child refugees, or the imaginary of the 'good', contributing migrant, demonstrate how the very conditions of personhood are mediated by who is, or can be imagined to be, part of the national/civilised family. Just as the family portrait was the frame through which colonised subjects were offered claims to their humanity (by whether they were able to look like a family), the portrait does similar work to obscure and hide who gets to be viewed as human.

In appealing to a humanitarian logic of empathy and compassion, or a joyous celebration of diversity, migration is viewed through portrait photography as a universal human journey. This has become exemplified in focus on the human face as universalising. The structural conditions and imperial grooves that continue to move people, and move people to the UK, are unseeable in this apparently universal story. Take, for example, the historical conditions such as transnational diasporas, connections through imperial language or ongoing forms of neocolonial warfare, capital accumulation, global inequality, kinship ties. This humanitarianism is repeated in similar naive cosmopolitan claims such as 'we are all migrants' or 'all refugees', a position which obscures the history of colonial violence and inequality that both created borders and sustains the movement of people to the Global North.

In viewing the portrait as humanising, this also firstly assumes that the humanity of migrants must be evidenced. This is problematic on its own terms, but even more so here because being photographed is the medium through which the migrant is supposedly transformed into the human, as an individual subject who is complete and thus relatable to as 'human'. As problematically, this equally assumes that humanity is judged by the spectator. Under this logic, the person of colour and the migrant can only be included as human once they have been made visible through the dominant techniques of portrait photography, and by the visual codes and relatability of the 'good', contributing/familial migrant. Ultimately, the migrant awaits to be transformed into human by being pictured and then being witnessed and accepted by a pre-dominantly white audience.

What I want to stress here in this reading is that rather than breaking free or challenging violent borders, the universal appeal to the human, compassion and empathy found in the imaging/imagining of the 'good' migrant' not only obscures but reproduces colonial bordering. In idealising the 'good' migrant, this hardens the boundaries around the 'bad' migrant. This equally works to conceal and hide the violence of bordering. It does so by reproducing the patronising and paternal but also intimate offer to be included within the family/national home that we witnessed with the treatment of the colonial 'house boy'.

Whiteness and compassionate nationalism

Whilst contesting explicitly racist and nativist accounts of migration, such as from the far right, the visual regime of the 'good' migrant and leftist-liberal humanitarianism also arguably reproduces many of the assumptions of the white nationalism it supposedly contests. This is because this visual regime is geared towards satisfying an audience that people rendered 'different' (often encoded racially) can be pacified, made like 'us' or can even be 'good for us' (i.e. they can love 'us' or contribute for 'us'). But also, because this works to praise the tolerant understanding and even 'love' of the host community, white spectators are invited to imagine themselves as benefactors, compassionate and ethical subjects. The working of racism, and with it gendered and sexualised inequality, is concealed in this appeal to a tolerant community, just as (neo)colonialism and the questions of what continues to move people are completely erased.

What I argue is manifest in the imagining of the 'good' migrant is in fact a re-scripting of colonial whiteness (also see Danewid 2017 for a comparative argument). It is the outward rejection of a xenophobic-racist nationalism and the reformulation of a supposedly compassionate and humanitarian nationalism. But what haunts both accounts are appeals to white innocence (Wekker 2016). Compassionate nationalist accounts have particular traction on the liberal left in the UK – where the 'civic nation' is reimagined alongside an appeal to British values of democracy, equality, tolerance and 'postracialism' (Fortier 2008). We see its inflections in the commitment to integrate Muslim women out of their troubled domesticity, or in attempts to work in solidarity with refugees, or in the push to protect the rights of 'Windrush generation' citizens who are threatened with deportation. This humanitarian leaning and often multiculturalist nationalism 'includes' and even celebrates diverse others, whilst constituting them as 'welcomed' guests of the original (unmarked but white) nation.

Ida Danewid (2017: 1682) argues that this compassionate nationalism is concerned with a re-scripting of the white national and civilisational self around ideas of tolerance and solidarity. It involves a reimagining of the white self, who is now bound to multiculturalism, migrant solidarity and liberal hospitality – values which in themselves seem appealing to a progressive audience. In this setting the reaction to the approach of the migrant 'stranger' is one of empathetic welcome rather than hate and vilification. On the surface, this seems resoundingly positive. However, such a position of empathy fails entirely to produce a critique of the colonial masculine gaze and instead merely reinvigorates it. Just as with the *Arrivals* exhibition, under humanitarian and compassionate nationalism the migrant other is consumed and included, but only to renew the white national self and to evidence and celebrate the tolerance and benevolence of those who identify with it. Consider, for instance, how contribution is viewed in terms of the economic benefits the migrant brings to the nation, or the 'love' and thankfulness they demonstrate towards their 'hosts'. Or equally, how the 'good' migrant is made welcomable by evidencing their exceptionalism. Such 'cannibalisation of the other masquerading as care' (Hemmings 2012: 152) is made possible by historical amnesia and the erasure of colonial dispossession, violence and the visual regime of 'humanity'. It involves an active forgetting of the connecting tissue that moves people to Europe and the UK and the violence and exploitation that did and still accompanies this relationship. These tissues have been created through formal colonialism, the accumulation and dispossession of imperial capitalism and in ongoing colonial war in the Middle East. This position of humanitarian/compassionate nationalism may not be explicitly nostalgic for empire, but it only works by hiding this history and by promising to offer the migrant their humanity back as a part of their inclusion in the national family. However, as I discussed in chapters 4 and 5, inclusion in British citizenship for the once colonised is always a failed promise.

Not only are the boundaries between 'good' and 'bad' migrants re-established in this discourse but this type of humanitarian and compassionate nationalism is a complex work of resuscitating white social relations on the terms of empathy and progressivism (Danewid 2017). Firstly, this works to dehumanise migrants by 'offering' them their humanity through the spectacle of being welcomable. Secondly, it renews what Wekker (2016) has called 'white innocence', which works not only to silence colonial histories and presents but also actively works to preserve the unjust structure of the status quo and its visual hierarchy of the human (also see Mills 2017). The imaginary of the good migrant not only structures bordering around who can be included or excluded but it is also used to reproduce and renew the very structures of white nationalism that deny migrants humanity in the first place.

To consider the visual regime of the 'good' migrant we have to consider how it is connected to a celebration of the white family portrait. Recognising this is important for understanding the distinct limits and silences of attempts to 'humanise' people on the move, which has become so central to contemporary logics and counter-visual practices of humanitarian and compassionate nationalism.

Conclusion

I started this chapter by demonstrating how mobility is regulated around who can be imagined as a 'good' migrant. Child refugees can be transformed into 'burly lads' by a visual regime of childhood which makes certain bodies 'unchildlike' and subsequently undeserving of rights. This helps us understand how borders are visual, as they are 'sticky' and 'intimate'. Being made 'out of place' is also a product of being made visible as 'out of place'. This follows the increasing way that borders rely upon visual technologies to distinguish and categorise people, to track movement and manage access to rights. Imagining who belongs, who can be welcomed and who can also be expendable is also about who can be *imaged* as such. But this imagining/imaging is constantly wrapped up in the politics of family, who can look domesticated, who can look familial – as 'wife', 'husband', 'partner', 'child', and we might extend this to 'good neighbour', 'civic actor', 'citizen'.

This, I argue, relates to a wider interlinking history of colonialism and visuality of which photography is an important part. In exploring the role of photography under wider empire I demonstrated how images were central to race-making and presenting people as objects, commodities or other. Photography was central to the regulation of populations through warfare and anthropology, just as it was in organising the intimate relations of the colonial household. Family portraits, for example, stand as a key means of arranging who could be counted as worthy of family and who could only *work for* the family (as 'house boy'/'labourer'/'ayah'). Photography helped arrange often-intimate hierarchies within households where colonised subjects could be 'included' but only as subordinate and never as properly familial. This point is more than about symbolism. With the networking of photographs into the global regulation of movement, through identity cards, passports, surveillance technologies and visa applications, images (and with them ways of seeing people) have become powerful sites of bordering.

In pushing this book's argument that borders are dispersed and networked through more than immigration law, I turned to how activist campaigns and art exhibitions play an important role in the imagining of 'good' and familial migrants. Rather than focusing on delineations of sham or monstrous others, I explored examples of where migrants are celebrated and 'humanised'. Using the exhibition *Arrivals*, I revealed how humanitarian logics of 'welcome' fail not only to contest right-wing and explicitly racist depictions of immigration (that is, as disembodied hordes, dangers, deviants) but also reproduce heteronormative whiteness and a forgetting of colonial violence. Rather than an endless imperilled victim, the 'good' migrant here is presented as the contributing, loving, familial migrant. 'Family' here works as a developmental logic. It shapes claims over who is worthy/unworthy. It is on these terms that they can be 'included' and offered 'humanity'. This again is far from being only symbolic. Just as with the example of the child refugees, who is made seeable as the 'good' migrant is central to how mobility is regulated and how colonial sensibilities are reformed and reworked. Bordering in sites as distant as family visa applications, refugee resettlement programmes, points-based immigration systems, works to offer rights, mobility and settlement based upon fulfilling the terms of the 'good' migrant.

Whilst a celebration of the progressive white self who can welcome distant others, the humanitarian and compassionate nationalist logic we can see circulating in northern states is both limited and paternalistic. The welcome of the 'good' migrant can be treated as a recycling of the position of the colonised 'house boy' who was offered an intimate place subordinated within the colonial household, only ever to work for the good of the 'real' family/national home. This does nothing to alter the terms under which bordering continues to make people 'out of place', nor does it work to challenge the way that structural logics of racialised violence continue to drive government in the UK.

If, as I have argued, the colonial masculine gaze still dominates ways of seeing, what of hooks's (1992: 115–116) provocation of how colonised and enslaved people look back? If humanitarian logics merely replicate colonial ways of seeing, what other alternatives, what other ways of looking have worked to resist and look away from this visual regime, and with it, colonial borders and the power of family? It is to this question of other counter-visual practices and resistance to bordering that I now turn.

Notes

1 Although it was hoped this might make way for wider scheme of up to three thousand resettled children.
2 This chapter is based on archival work undertaken in 2017 and 2018 at the Bristol Archives, which holds the Commonwealth Photography archives. It also draws upon ethnographic and observational field work conducted at several exhibition sites – the Weston Park Museum, Sheffield, the Bristol Museum, the British Library, the Migration Museum, London, and interviews with photographers, artists and participants. I visited galleries, exhibition spaces and museums that hosted events and exhibitions on mobility, empire and family across an eighteen-month period (2016–2018) At the core of this chapter is an engagement with visual analysis (Bleiker 2018) which aims to investigate what Gregory (2012a) calls the techno-cultural history of photography, mobility, race and borders. Rather than focusing purely on visual methods as a form of representational practice, I consider how visuals (photography in the main) emerged within the history of colonial expansion and warfare and how the very technology we tend to consider as neutral and objective is culturally and politically located within colonial modernity (also see Virilio 1989). This involved examining common themes and styles of photography across archival photographs, moving images, family portraits in the late nineteenth and early twentieth centuries (predominantly in the British Empire & Commonwealth Collection in the Bristol Archives), investigating visual methods and surveillance during this time, such as the rise of the passport, and examining the styles, representational

practices and techniques used in photography exhibitions on human mobility in 2016–2018 (in exhibitions across Britain, as noted above).

3 For similar themes, see National Geographic, 'The New Europeans', available at www.nationalgeographic.com/magazine/2016/10/europe-immigration-muslim-refugees-portraits/; the Joint Council for the Welfare of Immigrants' 'I am an immigrant' campaign, available at www.iamanimmigrant.net/i-am-immigrant-poster-campaign; IOM's 'I am a migrant' project, available at http://iamamigrant.org (all accessed 11 September 2019).

4 The full collection of photographs from the *Arrivals* exhibition can be viewed at www.jeremyabrahams.co.uk/arrivals_sheffield (accessed 17 September 2019). I would like to take this opportunity to thank the artist Jeremy Abrahams for taking the time to speak to me about the project and for sharing his images in the spirit of productive engagement and critique.

7

Looking back

Seven young and adolescent children sit with an older man, eating melon in a working field in Jamaica, around 1860. They are wearing the working clothes of the agricultural poor. It is likely that they are indentured labourers, bound to both the land and white settler farms by indenture contracts which dominated the imperial economy in Jamaica after the abolition of slavery. This photo, entitled 'These water melons' (figure 5), captures a particular intimate moment of the British Empire.

Kate Anderson and Graham Mortimer Evelyn (2019) remind us that the photograph would have taken over fifteen minutes to compose. It is worth imagining the intimate racial dynamics of those fifteen minutes: the white photographer lining up the shot, fixing the children in the line of sight of the camera, the shuffling, tiredness, boredom, the potential bafflement, indifference or quiet resilience to the gaze of the camera and imperialist. When I first stumbled across this photo in the British Empire & Commonwealth Collection (Bristol Archives), I 'saw it' and 'read it' as another example of the colonial masculine gaze. The fixation on these labourers eating melon, sheltering from the sun, replicates multiple colonial stereotypes: of 'idle' black labourers gorging on water melon, or undomesticated, unchildlike children or youth. They are 'reduced to caricatures set in the Jamaican landscape' (Anderson and Mortimer Evelyn 2019). The caricatured 'joke' (i.e. that Jamaicans just eat melon, a stereotype which begat the phrase 'watermelon smile') strips these subjects of their humanity. As did their subjuga-tion and exploitation at the behest of the colonial state and imperial economy.

Water Melons

5 'These water melons', *c*.1860.

The second time I encountered the image was in the Bristol Museum
gallery in a display on *Empire through the Lens,* a display of twenty-seven
images describing the impact of the British Empire. This time, the image
was accompanied by a reading by Anderson and Mortimer Evelyn (2019).
They highlight the racist composition of the image but also argue that
in these labourers 'look' is a recognition that they are being caricatured.
Within this look, they argue, 'resides a testament to endurance'. The
children's stare, which could be tiredness and exhaustion – as in my
reading – is posed instead as oppositional. There is a *knowing* in this
reading, one that suggests a subversion of the colonial masculine gaze
and an excess of this regime of visuality which I initially saw as dominating and dehumanising.

Visuality and contestation

This raises a number of questions for how we are to understand the duress of empire, race, the colonial masculine gaze and the possibilities of other intimacies, kinships and ways of being in the world (that 'look back' and 'endure'). It also raises questions over how my own structural positionality and the power of whiteness obscures and shapes my own analysis (such as in my reading that overemphasised the subjugation and dehumanisation of the labourers in ignorance of practices of subversion and agency).

If the colonial masculine gaze is co-opting in its ability to reform and translate into new and 'progressive' forms – such as the tolerant, multicultural nationalism and humanitarianism – we must also consider the proliferations of ways of 'looking back', contesting and enduring. There are many ways of 'looking back' which struggle within and against historic and contemporary regimes of bordering, and with it visuality. As hooks (1992: 115–116) reminds us, within any power relations there are always counter, oppositional and subversive ways of seeing and being seen. Under slavery, hooks argues, looking was not only a means of control over the slave but a form of resilience, a slave was expected to look down in encounters with the master so looking back or away was a primary strategy of defiance (also see Browne 2015). According to hooks (1992: 115–133), black women have developed particular strategies of looking which have flourished after abolition, Jim Crow, decolonisation, the civil rights era and diasporic migration. We can see these ways of looking as cracks, openings, alternatives that capture, renew and refuse the bordering of the domesticating state. Alternatives can be co-opted, or can replicate the terms of coloniality – such as local/global humanitarianism and compassionate nationalism – others provide for and recover more critical sensibilities and orientations.

In this penultimate chapter, I examine three strategies of struggle over contemporary visuality which are also in turn struggles over borders, mobility and hierarchical claims to family. What mark these practices apart from the plethora of other forms of resistance, is the way they attempt to renew and recover mobile and (post)colonial personhood which have been enacted globally from anti-colonial struggles and decolonisation. In doing so, they can work to (in)directly challenge and deconstruct the politics of the 'good' migrant and liberal promises of 'inclusive citizenship', and with this challenge and disrupt codes of intimacy, family and domestication which animate the exclusion of people racialised as non-white from humanity.

The three strategies and forms of struggle I expand upon are: 1) *inversions*, the inverting of the colonial gaze and its patterns of seeing against itself – this can be through forms of counter-surveillance or through practices of visual empowerment; 2) *escape* – that is, modes of becoming invisible and refusing to work within dominant ways of seeing; and lastly, 3) *decolonial aesthesis*, a political and ethical orientation used both to show the violence of colonial rule and recover and forge new expressions of being in the world.

Inversions

In diverse environments, from migrant camp dispersals, to police stop and search, to protest movements, the use of photography to hold the state and its agents and international organisations to account has become increasingly powerful. Whether this is filming police violence (Wall and Linnemann 2014), or illegal detention practices, or physical and sexual abuse, photography is increasingly used to put pressure on states or to attempt to persecute individuals, companies and governments. The proliferation of images taken by people on the move to and across Europe, or into the UK, has revealed the danger of moving and the conditions people are subjected to. We should consider these means of documenting and revealing the deep violence of borders, from the reporting of drone strikes, to deaths of migrants in the Mediterranean, to resistance against counter-terrorism practices. I call such strategies 'inversions' because they invert the gaze of the domesticating state by revealing its violence. Smartphones, for example, have become central to the contemporary migrant experience. Not only do phones provide a lifeline and a survival strategy (Stierl 2016, 2019) but they also provide a means of photographing deaths, destitution and abandonment that would otherwise go unnoticed.

Such strategies of visibility have been deployed historically by numerous social movements and in artistic and activist experiments to recognise and render violence, and the subjects of violence, worthy of seeing. In the UK the United Families and Friends Campaign (UFFC) uses photographs to make visible those who have died at different border sites – at the hands of the police, in prison or psychiatric custody. UFFC use photographs of the dead to reveal these forgotten victims of state brutality and have increasingly done so by linking to international movements such as Black Lives Matter and anti-detention protestors (Elliott-Cooper 2016). In their annual procession in London, UFFC members wear T-shirts with the faces of the dead 'so they are not forgotten' (Picture Capital 2016). Whilst speaking for 'everyone' who has died in police custody, the movement was born out of black communities' experience with the police and reminds us that it is young black men who are most likely not only to be subject to police harassment throughout their lives but also to die at the hands of the police (see Andrews 2018). UFFC often appeal to themselves as a 'family'. Significantly for us, this is a 'family' bound not by European heteronormativity but by the historic experience of the colonial state and police oppression which forms a series of intimate political bonds (for a longer discussion of gender and race in the context of anti-police struggles see Elliott-Cooper 2019). Such an appeal to a wider networked and historical appeal to family is about producing solidarities for survival. Such inversions are a refusal to remain invisible (also see Sancto 2018). In the case of the UFFC, visuality is used to call upon the state to recognise and act by making visible what state authorities and white audiences want to forget – the institutional racial violence of law enforcement and the criminal justice system (Perera 2019).

Another very different and less explicit example of inversions might
be those who use techniques such as sham marriages to gain rights.
Playing off the suspicions of inappropriate intimacies created by the
colonial state, subjects can facilitate the appearance of love and 'familialness' with others who the state would not normally deem a 'couple' or
a 'family' (friends, short-term partners, acquaintances, non-biological
dependents) to move and make claims to settle in northern states. They
do this by emulating and forging intimacies with subjects to gain rights
and settlement through looking like a 'genuine' heteronormative/
homonormative couple (see White 2014; also Turner and Vera Espinoza
2019). A performance of love – such as providing evidence of 'looking
like' a romantic couple – can be a way of accomplishing political needs
at the behest of a state that can only recognise particular affective
relationships over others. Because it is deemed evidence by the state,
photography can be utilised to perform the sham of the heteronormative/
homonormative couple.

What inversions have in common, and what distinguishes them from
humanitarian/compassionate nationalist approaches, is that they focus
on calling out the violent inequality of bordering/borders. They can
also be attuned to the racial violence of the domesticating state. Rather
than offering themselves as 'good', domesticated, 'familial' migrants or
happy multicultural citizens, these movements and practices of resistance
appeal to a collective demand to be recognised on the terms of past
and present exclusions (see Butler and Athanasiou 2013). This is not a
strategy that demands that people be viewed as 'contributing' in the
eyes of a white audience; it is instead born out of the historical experience
of being excluded by the domesticating state.

These strategies, which recognise and make visible histories of
exclusion, also work to foster bonds and affective relations that are *in
excess* of heteronormative/homonormative and nationalist appeals of
'belonging'. Examples include UFFC's appeal to family as a disparate
connection of those who have suffered police oppression, or the inverting
of the genuine family by performing a sham marriage to gain rights.
These types of affective relations can be compatible with other ways of

being together which are politically and socially significant but equally troubling to an account of 'family' (see the decolonial approaches I offer below). In the examples above, what bonds people together is rooted in historical experiences of movement, of bodied violence and the racialised sexuality of modern citizenship. Inversions stare the state down on its own terms without necessarily rejecting it, its visual regime or the function of national liberal citizenship as the dominant way to be seen and recognised.

Escape

If inversions use the visual regime of portraits and images to empower subjects and/or build communities then this is still built on the promise of visibility and, with it, *recognition* – that is, recognition of deaths or of being 'couple-like'. Holding the colonial state to account by asking to be recognised can be effective in challenging certain border practices and claiming limited liberal rights. However, this is ultimately a limited political project. Such strategies are limited because they fail to explore the wider issue of who is *seeable* and the terms under which someone is humanised in local and global racial-colonial hierarchies. Calling for migrants, colonised and racialised communities and the violence to which they are subjected to be made *more visible* is ultimately a call for recognition (see Coulthard 2014). Recognition is performed on the terms set out by the beholder, the colonial masculine gaze and the domesticating state. Whilst often a necessary project, this risks a scenario in which visibility remains conditioned by colonial hierarchies of human/ not-quite/non-human.

Glen Coulthard (2014) argues that recognition will always remain a limited strategy when groups are asking for recognition from (settler) colonial states. Rather than working towards freedom and dignity outside of liberal claims to citizenship it ultimately leaves the subject position of the colonised/colonialist in place. If being recognised is to be made visible and amenable to 'equal rights', then it risks limiting this strategy to a demand to be included and accepted as a citizen within the confines of the colonial domesticating state. Strategies of inversion can either work by using the tools of the state to gain rights (e.g. performing a sham marriage) or asking to be seen and given due process (the UFFC). These tools do little to challenge the more fundamental problem of the way the colonial state reproduces the distinctions of empire through citizenship, a citizenship which, as I have demonstrated, replicates people as human/not-quite/non-human.

In realising that the system of citizenship and bordering in the UK (and we can offer a parallel to other European and northern states here) is always set up to fail them, at the expense of their humanity, mobile subjects are sometimes forced to become 'invisible'. People moving to and within the Global North often practice what Papadopoulos *et al.* (2008) call modes of 'escape'. Disfiguring fingerprints, burning passports and identity papers, smashing smartphones, running away from sheltered housing or social services, ignoring asylum interviews – the very visual cues and strategies of 'managed migration' – are used as means to refuse and to disappear from methods of domestication and the orderly rhythms and humiliations of 'legal' migration (Tazzioli 2014). In the context of the asylum system in the UK, this can be called 'going ghost' (also see British Red Cross 2018).

Given the increasing fragility that settled rights such as citizenship offer (after the extension of deprivation, deportation, precarity and state-sanctioned death), this reflects the dismantling of the myth of liberal inclusion. Often born out of desperation and fatigue but also displaying in-depth knowledge of border techniques and surveillance, these strategies subvert through dismantling forms of visibility and recognition (see Tazzioli 2014: 150–153). They rely on the promise, perhaps quite a radical promise, to become 'unseeable'. If borders are intimate, sticky and visible, refusing to be seen appears to offer a powerful way to contest the domesticating power of the contemporary state.

Eduardo Glissant's (1997: 189) appeal to a 'right to opacity' is useful to consider here. If dominant modes of visuality are bound to colonial power, and rest on hierarchies of the human, then Glissant makes a political and ethical demand to be 'unseeable' and thus 'unknowable' to the modern state and its adjunct authorities – that is, to refuse the terms under which one is seen and made 'transparent' (made meaningful and categorised in Western thought). An increasing body of scholarship has taken up this politics of (in)visibility by arguing that refusing to be visualised within the terms of the 'good' migrant, citizen or family, such as with the destruction of paper identity and in countering legalised routes of mobility and rights, offers transformative potential. To many scholars (see, for example, De Genova 2017) such acts represent the forgings of hybrid ethical and political subjectivities which push up against, escape and reform liberal codes of domestication, bordering, intimacy and liberal labour commodification (also see Papadopoulos *et al.* 2008; Mezzadra and Neilson 2013). Here invisibility is treated as an ambiguous process (i.e. can anyone ever become entirely 'invisible'?) but part of a broader struggle over imperial capitalist relations and hetero- or homonormative citizenship, and with it, dominant claims of 'family'.

Invisibility may not only be a form of abandonment but a strategy to forge alternative political and social spaces through movement, and in doing so produce other ways of relating to each other. Agathengelou's (2004) work, for instance, examines how the rejection of the managed migration of domestic workers has led to informal solidarity movements and the creation of women-only communities of care and support. Escaping the legal regime and visibility of domestic work and the border regimes that shape this precarious work, offers to these women (temporal) bonds of affection. These communities of affection are not arranged around the intimacies of the heteronormative family and its gender relations. Such communities provide forms of material survival which mean that subjects are not reduced to working as 'domestic help' for the social reproduction of bourgeois households (Agathangelou 2004: 153–178). They are bonds of alternative modes of care, sexuality and intimacy in excess of the family.

If inversions rely on recognition, as I noted above, then strategies of escape help question whether *all* political subjects are seeking citizenship, even if citizenship still remains the dominant mode of being recognised as politically human. To Papadopoulos and Tsianos (2008), practices of invisibility, such as passport burning, involve a splitting of *the name* and *the body*. It is a strategy that 'deliberately abandons the humanist regime of rights' that is so central to local and global forms of outwardly xenophobic but also liberal nationalism and humanitarianism (Papadopoulos and Tsianos 2008). It is a rejection of the terms under which someone is seeable as politically human. The 'right to opacity' can be brought into being through escaping regimes of surveillance and a refusal (intentional or otherwise) to be subject to the imaginary of the 'good' migrant and claims to heteronormative citizenship and family that go with it. Connecting back to hooks (1992), we might say that escape is about 'looking away' from the colonial masculine gaze and the domesticating state.

Decolonial aesthesis

If inversions rely on recognition, and escape relies on strategies of invisibility then decolonial aesthesis (Lockwood 2013; Mignolo and Vazquez 2013) offers a further way of 'looking back' and a different politics of struggle. Inversions contest borders by highlighting the violence of the colonial state. But, as I have suggested, this is often done on its own terms of visuality and intelligibility – through legal recourse and state recognition of violence. Strategies of escape can instead be understood as forging 'alternatives' which subvert dominant forms of domestication such as problematising the idea that everyone seeks citizenship and with it heteronormative family by refusing to be recognised or claim rights of asylum or citizenship.

However, it is worth asking how far a strategy of escape can go to challenge the domesticating state, colonial hierarchies of the human and with it bordering. After all, irregularisation and invisibility (that is, denying mobile and racialised subjects recognition) are both ways in which the state manages populations, and makes them amenable to exploitation and forms of abandonment and expulsion. 'Looking away', whilst often a strategic necessity, remains limited when it is so conditioned by the very rhythms, orientations and violence of colonial bordering. To put it simply, if inversions are too concerned with recognition and visibility, then escape lacks the promise of a future transformation and ultimate escape from coloniality and imperial capitalism. Is escape not the underbelly of colonial borders rather than an alternative? In this context, decolonial aesthesis offers a further form of contestation which explores both the problem of recognition found in forms of *inversion* and the absence of being able to critically engage with colonial violence found in forms of *escape*.

Decolonial aesthesis is an explicit creative and artistic project (see Lockwood 2013) that is bound to the wider social movement of decoloniality. This is the assertion that decolonisation is not 'over' and so nor is coloniality. As its starting point, decolonial aesthesis is a critique of the plethora of ways that colonial power is bound to knowledge and, with this, ways of seeing and being seen (Mignolo and Vazquez 2013). Visuality was central to colonial power, but equally, contemporary Western art and aesthetics (ways of appreciating artistic form) have remained tied to more or less explicit forms of orientalism and the degradation of colonised peoples as inferior and/or exoticised. In this way, decolonial aesthesis (rather than aesthetics; see Mignolo and Vazquez 2013) is invested in producing activistic and creative projects which call out the ongoing legacies of colonialism, including borders, citizenship and the bourgeois claim to (white) family. But equally, as Alanna Lockwood has argued, the movement is not limited to revealing colonial violence but is attuned to the production and embrace of forms of immunity 'healing' (Lockwood 2013, but also see Mignolo and Vazquez 2013) – that is, rediscovering, reorienting, curating ways of seeing colonised people which are in excess of the colonial masculine gaze.

To Shilliam (2013), this is a project of 'retrieving and redeeming aesthetes that have been dismissed by colonial masters as superstitious, irrational, ugly, and primitive'. Examples include forms of indigenous knowledge, diasporic connections, religious and spiritual practices, artistic forms of the Global South, which work in parallel with, not separately from, colonial modernity. It is also about re-establishing the connectivity of histories outside of the assumption of national/civilisation ideas of colonial states (Bhambra 2014). For example, the term 'Afropean' shows the unresolvable connections between Europe and Africa, which are bound by the history of slavery and direct colonial control, as well as extraction of wealth and resources (Hansen and Jonsson 2014). This directly shapes contemporary imperial capitalism as well as the movement and death of people crossing the Mediterranean (see Black Europe Body Politics 2013). This recognises the intimate bonds that bind people to each other through the ongoing experiences of global patterns of imperial/ colonial dispossession.

The orientation in this work, which has evolved within artistic exhibitions, moving/still images and sculptures, or soundscapes (Weheliye 2005), is not about demonstrating the humanity of the colonised, mobile or postcolonial subjects and communities. It is instead a refusal to be 'familial' to a predominantly white audience and white gaze (and we might think of whiteness here as epistemic as well as bodied). It is instead about reasserting forms of personhood that have run alongside or been extinguished by colonial violence and with this the development, control and dispossession of 'family'. To Alanna Lockwood (2013), this project is directly linked to the contemporary politics of mobility, citizen- ship and borders. It begins with a rejection of having to account for yourself as someone 'out of place' within colonial ideas of time and space. It is a refusal to have to account for yourself (and be recognised) in the terms of liberal inclusion, national citizenship and the structures of the (white) family. Instead, Lockwood (2013) asserts the primacy of colonial exploitation to the presence of black and colonised people in Britain today: 'we have always been here as the hidden side of modernity, therefore our presence is self-explanatory'. We might think of this in relation to Ambalavaner Sivanandan's famous provocation to 'the English' in explaining the imperial grooves of migration: 'we are here because you were there' (Sivanandan 1989).

Rather than needing to be recognised or humanised, and thus tolerated, the movement of people to postmetropoles is directly tied to the
global/colonial histories of exploitation and violence, from the slave
trade, to the forced mobility of indentured labourers, to the use of
Commonwealth citizens to rebuild the British economy after the Second
World War. The problem of the border and being seen as 'out of place'
no longer rests with the migrant or the citizen of colour; it is instead
the structure of white ignorance that fails to understand the historical
conditions of mobility that is the problem. Slavery, abolition, colonial
dispossession, underdevelopment, the racialised control of movement,
mass deprivation of rights become the loci for thinking about mobility.
In his scathing critique of the actions of the British state in deporting
'irregularised migrants' and those without 'bona fide' citizenship claims
to Jamaica, the campaigner Burt Samuels argues for a reorientation
towards this history:

> 'The legacy of slavery is why we are so impoverished and why so many
> of us have had to leave Jamaica for greener pastures, to send remittances
> home,' he says. 'We were British subjects until 1962. We fought in two
> world wars, we sent our soldiers who shed their blood for Britain. Then
> all of a sudden it became a policy that we had to apply for a visa to go
> to a country that used us for three centuries. We felt discarded. It is
> widely accepted in Jamaica that Britain has used us and refused us.'
> (Quoted in Gentleman 2018b)

It is not the failure of migrants to integrate, or modernise, or contribute,
but the historical terms on which colonial ideas of humanity, structural
violence and the creation and perpetuation of local/global inequalities
that need to be examined under such a project.

An important aspect of the project of decolonial aesthesis is directed
at the particular racialised-sexualised codes of intimacy and the
heteronormative family, for instance the historic and contemporary
degradation of black women's bodies, which as we have seen is frequently
orchestrated through depictions of failed motherhood/womanhood, as

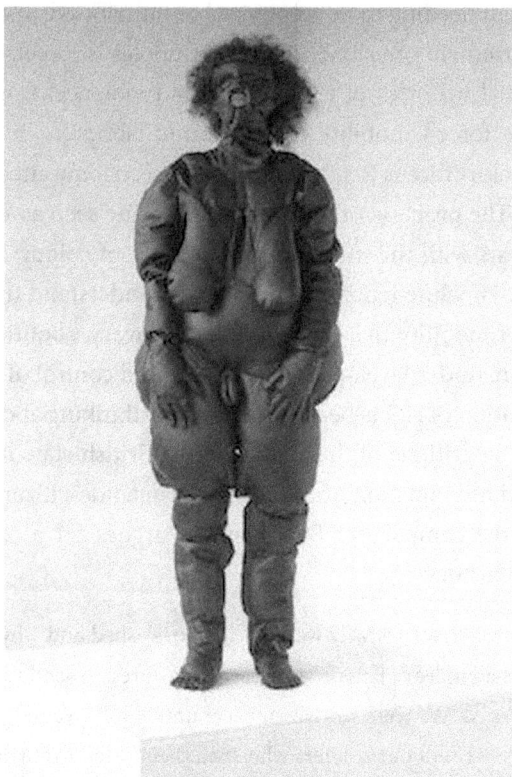

6   Teresa María Díaz Nerio's performance of *Hommage à Sara Bartman*,
2012.

outside of love and appropriate intimacy. This continues to be reinvented
across numerous social sites from international sports (Nittle 2018)
to the treatment of MPs (Elgot 2017b). Artistic activist projects have
sought to reclaim the position of black womanhood (also see Morrison
2014), such as in Teresa María Díaz Nerio's performance of *Hommage à
Sara Bartman* re-exhibited at the *Black Europe Body Politics* exhibition
in 2012 (figure 6). This installation aimed to directly capture, sustain
and trouble the sexualised-gendered 'failures' of the enslaved black
woman.

Nerio's performance in the disfigured and grotesquely sexualised
body suit directly reasserts the contemporary relevance of the figure

of Saartjie Baartman. Baartman was a Khoikhoi woman from South Africa who was exhibited as a typified 'Hottentot' woman throughout Europe, and was frequently photographed as a subject of imperial fascination, desire and eroticism/exoticism during the early nineteenth century. As Dalia Gebrial (2017) reminds us: 'even in her death she was not spared the racialised misogyny of the European gaze; her brain, skeleton and sexual organs remained on display in a Paris museum until 1974, more than 150 years after her death in 1815'. As a symbol of the commodification of anti-black racism and its visuality, Nerio's performance calls out the degradation and ungendering of black womanhood. It does so by revealing the apparent absences of feminised blackness which have always been fixed on ideas of failed womanhood, motherhood and improper intimacy/domesticity, but primarily rooted in hypersexuality (such as the grotesque enlargements of the suit).

Nerio's performance is a troubling assertion of the continuity of the colonial masculine gaze. What this performance does not ask for is for Baartman to be recognised and included as a 'real woman' on the terms of either the 'good' migrant, citizenship or family. This performance instead refuses to make colonial violence comfortable or historicised as 'a thing of the past'. It instead forces us to wrestle with the way that black women's bodies have been used to create degrading hierarchies of intimacy, kinship and the human, whether as impossible mothers (chapters 1 and 2), conducting suspicious intimacies (chapter 3) or reproducing youth/gang violence (chapter 4). At the same time, it reminds us that whilst violence against colonised women's bodies was normalised – unless suiting the interest of the colonial state – violence against white women could energise and justify spectacular displays of violence (such as deprivation of rights and personhood). Thus, such a performance can be directly contrasted with attempts to imagine the 'good' migrant, who is always orientated towards proving the benevolence, toleration and goodness of the white national subject.

In confronting the installation and Nerio's performance, Shilliam (2013) recalls the affective and embodied experience of witnessing this colonial violence and the ethical/political orientation it calls upon. He recounts how this emerged 'like a cadence of scream(s) and grunt(s)' as he walked through the exhibition space. He recollects:

> At first, a horror of being racially interpolated; the second, a gut response to these caricatures of violence visited upon the self through dehumanization. Similar to Fanon's famous experience of being challenged by 'Look, a Negro!', these art works invoke what I would call an aestheSis of outrage. This aestheSis is often mobilized to challenge the sanctioned ignorance of white publics and to compel them to recognize their complicity in the coloniality of power. (Shilliam 2013)

Here colonial violence is front and centre. As Shilliam recollects, this involves a double bind of both the experience of being 'racially interpolated' but equally a calling out of white publics for their ignorance and complicity. Through such a disturbance this rejects the figuration of the would-be included 'good' migrant just as it rejects the renewal of the white self that we see in projects of compassionate nationalism and humanitarianism. It refuses the progressive promise of domestication and liberal order by centring racialised sexuality and familial absence at the heart of the performance. It is a rejection of fitting within the frame of the colonial family portrait.

As Shilliam (2013) reveals, this works in excess of a humanitarianism which offers humanity back to colonised and racialised populations at the behest of compassion and empathy. Decolonial aesthesis is an outright refusal 'to engage the coloniality of power in its own public space' but it equally 'defends black publics wherein the sensibilities of personhoods can be cultivated other-wise' (Shilliam 2013). This is an outward rejection of recognition and its codes of heteronormative citizenship that I have illustrated dominate the politics of family and borders in contemporary Britain. Exposing colonial wounds and making them visible does not equate in this strategy to an asking for recognition and accountability by the colonial state (although this can be useful). It is instead orientated towards the cultivation of personhood that is bound to coloniality but is always in excess of it.

Artistic practice here is not only an end in itself but a means to heal wounds and create space for energising further struggle. The material effects of colonialism must be made visible to be dismantled, whilst cultivating alternative ways of being in the world (Coulthard 2014: 144).

Decolonial struggle and intimacy

I lingered on Nerio's work because it demonstrates a rupture/continuity with ways of seeing and thinking about intimacy that I have explored in this book. To take decolonial aesthesis seriously involves an overhaul of the orientations, structural conditions and imaginations that still dominate the seeable/unseeable, sayable/unsayable in contemporary postmetropoles, and retracing the imperial orientations of governance in Britain and other postmetropoles and settler states alike. In calling upon decolonial aesthesis as a different way of seeing/being, I want to stress that this is not an abstract, 'artistic' reorientation, but rather one that is grounded in everyday experiences of communities in ongoing anti-colonial and anti-imperial struggles. This feeds across numerous sites of historical resistance to empire, some of which we have already encountered: from the Morant Bay rebellion, the Indian War of Independence and black community organisers defending sailors in Liverpool in 1919, to the refusal to accept police oppression and brutality in Southall in 1979, Toxteth or Brixton in 1980, the resistance to the criminalisation of forced marriage by Asian, Islamic and black women's groups, or the demands of Black Lives Matter, and renewed calls from Commonwealth countries for colonial reparations (for more global circulations of violence/solidarity see Davis 2016). Coulthard (2014: 131) points to how creative and artistic endeavours have always been central to such anti-colonial struggles, from the Francophone cultural and literary critique often called 'negritude', which came to prominence in the 1930s, to contemporary movements such as Black Europe Body Politics. Creative and cultivating ways of seeing are not indulgences but have been central to the dismantling and challenging of colonial rule and colonial duress.

Family, borders and decolonisation

We should consider these sites of struggle in respect of the dual forces of family and borders/bordering that run through this book. It is arguably within anti-colonial and decolonial struggles that we need to situate the movement of people from the Global South into Europe – for example, in the 'refugee crisis' of 2015, or the multicultural realities of contemporary Britain (Gilroy 2006; Modood 2007). Despite efforts to the contrary, the mobility of people continues to escape the management of international organisations, states and the violent practices of bordering that aim to subdue and order people (Plonksi 2018). Colonial control, as I have argued throughout this book, was premised on the domestication of movement through primitive accumulation, dispossession and the regulation of dangerous populations and bodies; movement continues to shape neo-imperialism and colonial bordering in northern states. Part of this movement is born out of desperate circumstances of colonial war and inequalities; but at the same time this movement is a demand and refusal to be ordered by colonial categories of worthy or unworthy movement. The biggest shift in our current moment is to orientate ourselves towards thinking about the (de)coloniality of movement, through orientations offered by decolonial thought and decolonial aesthesis.

The whole way that mobility and settlement has been made thinkable is shaped by colonial hierarchies, claims to civilisation and the normalised idea that spaces like Britain have been timeless, white domestic nations. How mobility is made seeable and thinkable is bound by these categories. This both silences colonial histories, historical patterns of movement and imperially mandated global inequality that bring people to post-metropoles (even in compassionate versions such as the humanitarianism I discussed in the last chapter). Such histories are central to the orientations of black community and feminist movements (such as the Southall

Black Sisters and Imkaan), or in radical black politics, or Pan Africanism inspired by figures such as Marcus Garvey (also see Andrews 2018: 94–99; Rodney 2018). Such connections remain intimately experienced by many communities in places like the UK, but almost unseeable and unthinkable to wider white publics. This is perhaps best evidenced in the discipline of migration and refugee studies, which whilst promising to offer insights into the politics of contemporary movement too often reiterates forms of colonial amnesia (for accounts of this see Wekker 2016; Bhambra 2017a; Mayblin 2017).

But what of family? As this book has argued, what has energised – and continues to energise – bordering and colonial domestication is 'family', and with it, hierarchical claims to intimacy, love and domesticity that are hidden as 'universal'. Decolonial aesthesis, as I sketched out above, directly works to disrupt and unsettle the apparent universalism of 'family' and put it into its colonial context. This can work as a critical stance towards heteronormativity but also an affirmative stance in cultivating and emphasising the myriad of affective, intimate relations and kinships that exceed the recognition of the white bourgeois family. Here we might consider how mobility can in itself constantly disturb the connections of citizenship, nation and family that the modern state rests on. Firstly, patterns of dependencies stretch both transnationally and through relations that would not be termed 'familial' – friends, lovers, partners, polygamous relationships, acquaintances, even pets. These relations exceed and refuse to be domesticated. Secondly, mobility itself creates intimate encounters and forges new connections, dependencies and sensibilities. These forms of kinship are not merely the excess of 'family' but can be a different way of orientating social relations.

An example of such forms of kinship could also be the case of the UFFC, claiming familial connections through a history of oppression, or the case highlighted by Agathangelou (2004) of communal solidarity formed by irregular domestic and sex workers. If decolonial struggles can be supplemented by forging new ways of being and living *otherwise*, then we can see how mobility forms part of these political struggles. We can consider how people on the move often dismantle and disrupt

heteronormativity and patriarchal gender relations, and forge alternatives
in the act of movement. But thinking and claiming intimacy otherwise
does not have to lead here to recognition by the state. Likewise, the
objective of such a struggle is not exclusively securing citizenship or
rights for a dependent (although that might be useful or practical in
certain struggles). Instead, I would link this being otherwise to the
forging of a non-colonial future; that is what a decolonial aesthesis
orientates us towards.

The role that family has come to play in modes of race-making
necessitates not merely that we shift how we think about affective relations
within socio-sexual relationships, or their recognition by the state.
Gebrial (2017) argues that to 'decolonise the family and love' we need
to think of how the weight of race works both *within* and beyond
intimate relationships. It is not simply enough to change how we relate
to each other through relationship etiquette or more pluralised forms
of household labour and sex, whilst keeping colonial structures intact.
Instead, resisting colonial bordering is about orientating ourselves towards
collective endeavours to alter the material and representational forms
of the colonial present (Gebrial 2017), a colonial present which is able
to hide behind a politics of family (which again so often works to
resuscitate forms of white/colonial amnesia highlighted above). It is
about working towards dismantling the relational forces that condition
who gets to be family, who gets to love and be properly intimate in the
first place. This is a key part of 'looking back'.

Conclusions

In this chapter I have considered different ways of looking back: practices,
sites, struggles over the visual bordering practices of the domesticating
state. Exploring three different political orientations to looking back,
which I called *recognition*, *escape* and *decolonial aesthesis*, I argued that
the last orientation provides a more vital form of contestation. This is
primarily because it is able to deal with colonial histories and presents

in ways that the two former forms of resistance are unable to. A decolonial and decolonial aesthesis approach contests contemporary accounts of family and borders in ways that are both alive to the ongoing structural conditions of race and orientated towards moving both within and beyond these historical processes. I have shown how far from being an abstract or artistic exercise, decolonial aesthesis is already bound to existing struggles which directly link to anti-colonial struggles globally, and in doing so help us put contemporary mobility and the politics of family in their rightful place.

Conclusion: pasts and presents

This book began as an investigation into the relationship between family and borders; however, it became increasingly apparent that this makes no sense outside of the history and legacy of empire. Government and the organisation of violence continue to be shaped by imperial and colonial histories and the ongoing remaking of liberal empire within and beyond postcolonial states like Britain.

In this context, borders and bordering are better understood as modes of colonial rule brought 'home' to metropoles, energised and legitimated through appeals to family. This meant first understanding how the regulation of mobility and borders/bordering emerged as an imperial/ colonial project and how this continues to shape the function and character of borders today. We see this in the orientation of borders – who they keep out, contain or include, such as people marked as not-quite/non-human from ex-colonies and peripherised parts of the globe – but also in where such practices of control came from. These practices, for example deprivation of citizenship, intimate surveillance of migrants, deportation regimes and visual registers of normality, emerged as experiments of colonial management.

Central to the continuity of colonial borders has been the way that 'family' works as a transit point for colonial taxonomies of perversion and the human – that is, in categorising who should be subject to borders, who can move, who can settle, who is dangerous. From sham marriages, to monstrous intimacies, to the 'good', domesticated migrant, I have shown the work that the normative power of family does in making certain people appear normal, domesticated, familial – and others abnormal, undomesticated, unfamilial, and in this way subject to different modes of bordering and violence. This is about placing bordering/borders and colonial rule within a complex system of racialised-sexualised ordering, or what I call domestication.

Here I propose that rather than 'family' not being treated with enough respect, or rights within current bordering regimes, instead the problem is that dominant conceptions of the family continue to produce exclusions and organise violence and dispossession. The problem is that through colonial histories, certain populations and groups are continuously rendered as bereft of family and familialness. This provides a powerful means for the readaptation and resuscitation of colonial and racial violence in the present.

Tracing the varied work that family does to make empire in our contemporary moment means examining how micro governing practices and logics, from the family unification visa, social work safeguarding, to criminal prosecutions and even photographic exhibitions, work to reproduce borders/bordering – that is, how they both govern and align social groups as 'out of place', unfamilial and how this makes people privy to cruddy, everyday and sometimes spectacular forms of violence. Bordering emerges as a complex network of practices which govern racialised mobility and this book has examined three overlapping forms of borders. The first, 'intimate borders', police and govern intimacies of migrant families as shams but also other populations deemed suspicious. In the current moment, and with the expansion of counter-terrorism practices, intimate borders focus on Muslim households, but there are historical precedents littered throughout social work and welfare interventions in black and Asian families. 'Sticky borders' are the emergence of borders that 'stick' to some subjects and fall off others. In the case of deprivation of citizenship specifically, sticky borders dismantle previously settled rights claims of British citizens and can make them stateless and killable. This further reveals not only the legacy of colonial borders but also how citizenship remains organised less around rights than about claims to personhood. Lastly, the book examined 'visual borders', which work to interrogate migrants/citizens for their 'genuineness' and in doing so produce who looks 'out of place' and who looks like they belong. If borders/bordering have been understood as orientated towards the regulation of racialised populations moving from the Global South, the imperial orientation of this regulation is matched by the way that colonial bordering also regulates people within Britain. This is to recognise, as Walia (2013: 41) argues, that 'large-scale displacements and precarious conditions … are not coincidental but rather foundational to the structuring of border imperialism'.

In considering the power of heteronormative family in contemporary liberalism, the book has set out the case that colonial taxonomies continue to uphold white bourgeois domesticity as the model of family life. 'Family' remains a means of developing, controlling and even dispossessing subjects and communities who are cast as 'backwards' and in need of domestication. I have shown how being cast as unfamilial, so not doing family properly, or endangering the normative and intimate relations of family, can lead to material violence: social work intervention in households; being separated from loved ones by visa requirements; becoming subject to intimate surveillance; stripping of citizenship; passport removals; deportation. These practices are far from simply being remnants of empire but are intensified in contemporary projects of security which flow from the Global War on Terror, the resurrection of anti-Muslim racism and anti-immigration projects such as the hostile environment.

In exploring borders as more than immigration law and attached to broader forms of bordering, the book has pushed at the often-false dichotomy presented between 'citizens' and 'migrants'. Whilst citizenship is often considered to be about settled rights, this distinction hides more than it reveals. Taking borders and bordering as modes of racial governance, borders are not solely confined to the policing of migrants but also orientated towards abandoning and making precarious settled citizens of colour. This reveals the extent to which spaces of the not-quite/non-human continue to expand within postmetropoles like Britain, tied not to divisions over formal citizenship but the making and unmaking of personhood.

In this context, teasing out how love and family make empire means showing where continuities with formal empire are grounded. But it also means revealing how this is constantly and subtly remade through liberalism as colonial *duress*. Colonial racism and its attachments to family may have changed but they have far from disappeared. Whilst seemingly postracial, advanced liberal claims to worth, value, contribution and belonging still demarcate people as backwards or modern. This relies on the incorporation of people into a liberal political economy, but also the demonstration of properly intimate and familial relations. In our contemporary moment, forward-facing, 'progressive', liberal types of love are deemed of value, against those who are bound to tradition, culture and kinship, which are without value. Far from being postracial, this involves a remaking of nineteenth-century anthropological categories of perversion which work in tune with claims to the modern/progressive family and ideas of liberal love to make distinctions over value. For instance, the sham marriage debate in the UK and the legislation imposed to police shams relies upon codifying certain Asian and then Muslim communities as practising 'traditional' and hyperpatriarchal forms of marriage and domesticity (arranged marriage, forced marriage and honour killings are all hypervisible here). Such marriages and kinships are deemed perverse and 'without value' compared against the normative template of the 'romantic love' marriage idealised by liberalism. Not only have the kinship practices of Muslim communities been cast as perverse but they are presented as endangering Muslim women and the order of British society more broadly (through, for example, the reproduction of terrorism).

What this tells us is that whilst categories of the modern family have begun to include homonormative couples and rich (whiter) migrants, this produces numerous categories of perverse others who are categorised as not only without value but also not human enough to have a right to family life in the UK. The power of liberal categories of love is to produce racialised perversions but also cover this up. We should remember, for instance, how the work to police migrant families and Muslim households is all done in the name of 'safeguarding children' or to ensure that all couples claiming rights are merely 'genuine'. This works to equally hide the racist and misogynistic violence committed against Muslim women (Al-Shamahi and Lkaderi 2019) normalised by state policies such as Prevent.

Whilst advanced liberal categories complicate and rework the imperial mapping of people into backwards or modern, the modern family remains bound to both whiteness and anti-blackness. This is structured around the continual threat of black and brown masculinity and hypersexuality – that which is deemed monstrous violence. White nationalism has long appealed to the ideals of family as a space of femininity and white purity – manifest historically in fears over interracial sex, proximity, marriage. What contemporary events, such as the ones I traced in Rotherham and the national debate around grooming and deprivation of citizenship of those convicted, reveal is that the liberal state is also energised through such appeals to the white family. Not only is the exceptional act of stripping those convicted of grooming of their citizenship highly racialised (i.e. white citizen sexual criminals are not subject to deprivation) but these crimes are only able to be viewed as exceptional because they rely on the sexual threat of race. Quite simply, other equally violent and horrific cases of grooming and CSE (see, for example, Independent Inquiry Child Sexual Abuse 2019) do not produce the same practices of deprivation and martial solutions.

It is not progressive ideals of the modern family that the state seeks to defend in such cases but instead the compulsion to protect the white family from attacks from racialised others (in this case specifically bound to anti-Muslim racism). The point I have tried to make here is not about the rights and wrongs of the case of grooming per se, which remains an abhorrent crime, but how the responses to this crime play into the broader ideas about citizenship and belonging in modern Britain. What I have been interested in exploring is how citizenship is ultimately bound to whiteness and the white family. And in turn, what this does to (un)make the citizenship and, with this, the personhood of people of colour living in postcolonial northern states like Britain.

This points to the powerful way that family *makes* and *unmakes*. Dominant claims to family can work to organise who is excluded, abandoned and killed, but also those who need to be protected. Family here can produce bodies and relations that can be empathised with, addressed and cared for in ways that demand sustenance and protection (from the state and related authorities). In the example of grooming, what becomes apparent is how much the whiteness of the family matters here. But this also stratifies others who can look more or less familial: for example, the real refugee is structured through the victimhood of 'womenandchildren', and resettlement schemes focus on resettling real families. Equally, the 'good', domesticated migrant is promised inclusion by producing heteronormative family relations, upholding European forms of domesticity.

But of course, the sustaining and fostering of 'real' family also necessitates the violence towards those who threaten the family; towards subjects who can be eviscerated in ways that reveal the authoritarian power of the liberal state (through being deported, or killed at the end of a drone). Equally, violence can be directed towards those who cannot be seen and recognised as family (that is, as 'real' family) and are subject to abandonment: the families subject to intimate surveillance through the Prevent strategy, families suffering immigration raids, families split up by visa requirements, or through deportation and detention (see Corporate Watch 2018: 65–96). Such kinship, intimacies and affective relations are not registered as families; they barely stir the emotional register of anything like the reaction to grooming scandals that accompanies the white family. These families are not mourned. More often than not, such violence is rationalised and made unthinkable precisely because they do not fit within the dominant codes of who is family.

In light of the discussions that have run through this book, the place of whiteness and family must also be understood with regard to its contingency and flexibility. Liberalism remains a violent project of domestication but it is also one of inclusion. Borders include and exclude. We should think here of the imagining of the 'good' migrant who can be familial, empathised with and even celebrated (such as in the *Arrivals: Making Sheffield Home* exhibition). Humanitarian and civic nationalist appeals to show solidarity with, humanise and defend migrants reveal that there is more going on in liberal states than a relentless politics of dispossession and violence towards people on the move. There are attempts here to contest borders in ways that are attuned to valuing multiculturalism and thinking nationalism and internationalism otherwise.

However, in exploring who gets to be empathised with, celebrated or *humanised*, this also reveals the risk of such projects when they consider inclusion outside of the terms of colonial/imperial histories and the context of racism. In the forgetting of why people move, where they move from and to, and the histories of dispossession and inequality that structure this movement, it is often the case that humanitarian and civic multiculturalist projects end up repeating a form of colonial paternalism and benevolence. Because of this active colonial amnesia, such projects end up valorising white 'host' communities for their apparent tolerance and goodness and authentic domesticity and indigeneity. The further risk is that this not only produces whiteness as tolerant and progressive and silences colonialisation (of the past and of today), but it further dehumanises those communities who have been subject to colonial rule (both in the Global North and South). It normalises the violence that is endemic to contemporary colonial borders and the reproduction of not-quite/non-humans by the pretence that white societies are welcoming and ultimately tolerant. Rather than overtly justifying anti-black violence, this uses the figure of the migrant to ask questions of the extent of the 'goodness' of British (and with that European) society, thus again revealing that the humanity of migrants from the Global South and citizens of colour is continually up for debate.

The debates running through this book have focused on the mandate of colonial dominations. But this is not done in a vacuum or without resistance. This is not to diminish the struggles that black, Asian and migrant communities and other social movements have made in contesting colonial borders, to gain legal redress against forms of racism and in the limited achievements of a politics of multiculturalism and recognition.

Instead, it is to suggest that without being attuned to the histories of empire such contestations can only go so far. And in the orientations to recognise the colonial character of borders and government we also need to recognise the role of family here, as one of the sites were empire is constantly made and unmade. Heteronormativity is bound to colonial racism and whiteness as much as it is to heterosexuality, so a decolonial politics must equally be attuned to this. In following this lesson, the contestation of normative intimacies to include differ-ent affective relations, kinships, dependencies, is far from an issue of private orientations or about who can be intimate with whom; instead it is about how worth, value and with that humanity continues to be organised – that is, made and unmade – in postcolonial societies like Britain and beyond.

This book has demonstrated some of the reach, embeddedness and everyday character of colonial rule in contemporary Britain, and how it both conditions political possibilities and the broader social landscape, and also structures the more detailed work of immigration policy, social work, policing, citizenship law and so on. Exploring different sites and processes around family and borders/bordering from exhibitions, to counter-terrorism strategies, to novels, to deprivation practices, shows some of the intractability of these processes. Surveying different yet connected sites shows the reach and normalisation of these processes bordering into the fabric of both the colonial domesticating state and cultural and social life. It was to show some of the continuities that are often flattened out when we examine 'migrants' and 'citizenship' as separate dichotomous categories. And yet in following such an approach there have been notable absences and silences, for example the role of family in the organisation of detention regimes, immigration raids, the evisceration of asylum seeker rights, the deportation of undocumented migrants and the levels of destitution and dehumanisation of refugee communities. This of course deserves further examination (for other examples see Mayblin 2017; Davies and Isakjee 2018; De Genova 2018). And any account is always far from exhaustive. What the book instead has provided are points of connections and illustrations of broader trends

– both of how borders and bordering continue to organise racialised colonial governance and the way that family energises, rationalises and hides these processes. But there is always more to do.

One way of considering absences is to consider how Britain acts as a site for wider global processes. This is more than just saying that there are parallels with other (post)colonial states (which of course there are); how government and, with it, borders are configured in the UK is determined by Britain's place as a postmetropole and a site of empire. Whilst I have chosen Britain as a case, the idea here has always been to forgo any methodological nationalism and instead to explore the global nature of colonial rule that has materialised in Britain. Borders emerged across European empires in the management of undomesticated mobility; these were imperially and colonially orientated experiments that have become embedded within the British state. Today, immigration law is a localised manifestation of global processes. The white bourgeois family was not solely born out of European social change and the emergence of capitalism in the West. Instead this social relation was a product of imperial and colonial encounters, including the discovery of 'undomesticated' populations and the accumulation of resources and peoples. In this context, the ideal of the family was needed to justify dispossession of land, kinships and communities.

Further to this, the reshaping of heteronormativity, liberal love, the anti-Muslim racism of the War on Terror are equally global (or at least international) in orientation and manifest in particular ways within Britain. Imperial formations, colonial domestication and racialised capitalism are always contingent. Whilst studying Britain, the relationship between family and borders that I have presented here is a wider story about the way that empire continues to organise liberal international order and the distribution of violence. This works between more overt forms of empire such as in overseas military interventions and colonial war but also in the ongoing structuring of forms of everyday and often more mundane internal colonisation and the structuring through race of inequalities (housing, education, labour market access, criminal justice).

The point I make here, is that it should not be possible to study the politics of either borders or family, or government within northern states such as Britain without first recognising the role of empire, not as a past but also as a present.

Pasts and futures

The historical orientation of this book and the focus on continuities from formal empire should not dim our concern at the scale and intensity of bordering and borders today. The danger here is the normalisation of strategies of government which are inherently violent. Certain forms of state force appear acceptable because of the apparent necessity of borders. This necessity of borders and the violence attached to them is constantly naturalised by claims of 'family'/'family values'/'family life'. Claims to uphold the family continue not only to organise but also hide the violence of bordering. For example, that we have come to a point where it is widely accepted that there are such things as sham marriages that need policing, reveals the extent to which evermore restrictive racialising border policies can be enacted and overtly supported by northern publics. Or the absence of attention given to the evisceration of family rights of unification of refugees by the mainstream media. This reveals both a complete amnesia, or instead a worrying delight, in the types of violence done in the name of, say, policing sham marriages, in ignoring the affective relations and kinships of dehumanised populations.

Tied into such concerns, we need to recognise that we are increasingly witnessing the normalisation of authoritarian forms of rule, borrowed from colonial experiments in the policing and bordering of racialised communities. These relate to both colonial experiments of the past and present – such as in the adoption of counter-insurgency strategies honed during wars in the Middle East, in the use of RAF drones to assassinate 'problem' citizens, or in the use of closed courts (such as SIAC). We should also be concerned that this authoritarianism is normalised and extended through the colonial stratification of people. We can see this in the surveillance of extremism and radicalisation through the Prevent programme, which has rapidly expanded into every public service sector since 2015. Or, in the extension of detention and deportation practices to all categories of irregularised migrants and the development of the detention estate throughout the UK (Tyler 2013). Furthermore, it is also evident in in the stripping of citizenship, the use of closed courts to hear cases regarding terrorism offences, extradition orders, passport removals, targeted assassinations of former British citizens by drone. These are not merely policies and practices of the hostile environment created by the Conservative administration since 2010, but developments which cross the political spectrum. Many of the most draconian of border practices, such as detention and deportation, began under New Labour (and of course have much older lineages). But they are expanded and accepted through the threat of race that energises them.

Whilst such authoritarianism can begin to target 'exceptional' populations, for example the small number of extremists or violent grooming gangs, the normalisation of such forms of rule should point to worrying trends for everyone. We can note, for instance, the increased use of powers to strip people of citizenship enacted since 2002. Whilst there were only eleven people deprived of their citizenship up until 2011 this blossomed to eighty-four by 2015 and in 2019 Home Secretary Sajid Javid claimed that hundreds may have their citizenship deprived (Javid 2019). This does not include passport removals – a de facto removal of rights – and those who have had application for citizenship denied often on the basis of granting of such being deemed not in the 'public good'. The removal of citizenship is enacted by the Home Office, with the only juridical oversight being SIAC. This is a closed court which, as Kapoor (2018: 83–113) argues, functions like a colonial court – there is no jury, just a panel of judges who make decisions on evidence that is frequently withheld from the defendant and their legal team on grounds of 'national security'. We should remember that citizenship deprivation was used (and used rarely) to punish treason offences throughout much of the twentieth century. It was then expanded to deprive those charged with terror offences after 2002 (albeit again rarely), but it has been further expanded after 2010 to cover association with terrorists, involvement in gang activity, grooming and other cases where granting of citizenship rights is deemed not to be in the interest of the public good. Such a normalisation of this authoritarian practice of bordering works to expand those populations who can be subject to deprivation of citizenship. As I argued earlier, it makes all those citizens with kinship links to, migration histories and secondary passports from other states subject to deprivation and deportation. Such power may reflect deep trends shaped by empire but it should not stop us attending to this violence now. What this demonstrates is the potential for the broadening of authoritarian powers over any 'troublesome' social group.

Here we might consider how border practices and the racialised government of mobility provide a perspective or a lens through which to view other modes of government. We should note the violence done to communities and how this is often silenced (through the workings of race and, with this, claims to family). But we should also recognise that borders expand and grow and filter through different populations and enact violence on different people, possibly not always on those first intended. For example, we would do well to remember that the emergent regulation of mobility was experimented with in the slave trade, on plantations, in the regulation of vagrants. Emergent immigration law was trialled in settler states to manage the movement of indentured and 'Asiatic' labour. Immigration law in the UK grew in relation to restricting 'coloured immigration' from the newer parts of the Commonwealth. This was then expanded to include *all* migrants from non-EU states (not just those from former colonies). In the wake of a possible Brexit in 2019 it is likely that immigration rules will now apply broadly to all non-British citizens. Whilst deportation historically has targeted non-EU citizens and often people from former colonies (de Noronha

2019), it is striking that in 2017 a total of 5,301 EU citizens were deported
from the UK (Young 2017). The normalisation of borders has a dragnet
effect of pulling people in and spitting them out.

Equally, we might consider the recent concern about the criminalisation of democratic protest in Britain as part of these issues of
normalisation of authoritarian bordering. With high-profile cases such
as the arrest and prosecution of fracking protestors in Lancashire, or
the Stansted 15,[1] or cases such as the heavy-handed tactics of the police
in student fees protests, or in the clearing and eviction of the Occupy
movement, questions have been raised as to how the police suppress
democratic protest in the interests of elites and particularly those of
international capital. However, we should bear in mind the lineage of
these authoritarian tactics of policing (Iqbal 2018). The violent policing
and suppression of 'mobs' was honed in colonies (e.g. the 1919 Amritsar
massacre; Morant Bay in Jamaica; the 'Mao Mao' rebellion in Kenya;
the Troubles in Northern Ireland); this was translated into the relentless
policing of black and Asian communities in Britain (exemplified in
practices like stop and search and the suppressive violence used in
the 1919 Liverpool 'race riots'; Nottingham in the 1950s; Southall
in 1979; Brixton in 1980; London in 2011). This has since been expanded
to the treatment of other anti-systematic protests and unruly groups.
We should remember who is subject to this and where these practices
came from.

Understanding what borders do, where they go and how racialised
governance is enacted also tells us about the broader government of
everyone. To put this back into terms of family and domestication, we
can think about the expanding terms of who begins to be recognised
as unfamilial and undomesticated. It concerns the expansion of the
definition of those that threaten the familial nation and the narrowing
of the definition of those whose lives are deemed 'family life'. This
sentiment returns in the language around 'hard-working families' as
well as 'illegal migrants', constructs that have grown in use to normalise who is (un)deserving in austerity/Brexit Britain. If we take such
authoritarianism as a general trend, further elicited by the War on

Terror and the intensification of the hostile environment in Britain, then colonial histories do not just point to the past, they also point to the future.

Notes

1 The Stansted 15 were a group of anti-deportation activists who were charged using anti-terrorism legislation after they successfully attempted to stop a deportation charter flight scheduled to depart from Stansted Airport on 28 March 2017 (for more on the case see de Noronha and Chowdhury 2018).

References

Abrahams, J. 2016. *Arrivals: Making Sheffield Home*. Sheffield: Northend Creative Print Solutions.

Agathangelou, A. 2004. *The Global Political Economy of Sex: Desire, Violence, and Insecurity in Mediterranean Nation States*. London: Palgrave.

Agathangelou, A. and Killian, K., eds. 2016. *Time, Temporality and Violence in IR: Defatalising the Present, Forging Radical Alternatives*. Abingdon: Routledge.

Ahmed, S. 2000. *Strange Encounter: Embodied Others in Postcoloniality*. London: Routledge.

Ahmed, S. 2004. *The Cultural Politics of Emotion*. Edinburgh: Edinburgh University Press.

Ahmed, S. 2010. *The Promise of Happiness*. Durham, NC: Duke University Press.

Ahmed, S. 2016. 'Bogus', *Feministkilljoys* [blog], 27 October. Available at: https://feministkilljoys.com/2016/10/27/bogus (accessed 3 June 2017).

Akbar, J. 2018. 'Go to hell: British ISIS thug planning attacks on home soil is killed in US drone strike in Syria on the orders of the RAF', *Sun*, 17 February. Available at: www.thesun.co.uk/news/5599267/british-isis-thug-planning-attacks-on-home-soil-is-killed-in-us-drone-strike-in-syria-on-the-orders-of-the-raf (accessed 11 June 2019).

Alexander, J. 2006. *Pedagogies of Crossing: Meditations on Feminism, Sexual Politics, Memory, and the Sacred*. Durham, NC: Duke University Press.

Allen, R. 2008. 'Capital, illegal slaves, indentured labourers and the creation of a sugar plantation economy in Mauritius, 1810–60', *Journal of Imperial and Commonwealth History*, 36(2): 151–170.

Al-Shamahi, A. and Lkaderi, S. 2019. 'What is gendered Islamophobia', *Middle East Eye*, 10 June. Available at: www.middleeasteye.net/video/what-gendered-islamophobia (accessed 11 June 2019).

Amadiume, I. 1987. *Male Daughters, Female Husbands: Gender and Sex in an African Society*. London: Zed.

Amoore, L. and Hall, A. 2009. 'Taking people apart: digitised dissection and the body at the border', *Environment and Planning D: Society and Space*, 27(3): 444–464.

Amos, V. and Parmar, P. 1984. 'Challenging imperial feminism', *Feminist Review*, 17(1), 3–19.

Anderson, B. 2013. *Us and Them: The Dangerous Politics of Immigration Control.* Oxford: Oxford University Press.

Anderson, D. 2016. *Citizenship Removal Resulting into Statelessness.* London: Independent Reviewer of Counter Terrorism Legislation.

Andrews, K. 2018. *Back to Black: Retelling Black Radicalism for the 21st Century.* London: Zed Books.

Anderson, K. and Mortimer Evelyn, G. 2019. 'These water melons', *Empire Through the Lens* [photographic exhibition]. Available at: https://exhibitions.bristolmuseums.org.uk/empire-through-the-lens/?utm_source=referral&utm_medium=event&utm_campaign=empire (accessed 24 April 2019).

Andrews, K. and Palmer, L. 2016. *Blackness in Britain.* Abingdon: Routledge.

Anievas, A., Manchanda N. and Shilliam, R., eds. 2015. *Race and Racism in International Relations: Confronting the Global Colour Line.* Abingdon: Routledge.

Anonymous (Girl A). 2013. *Girl A: The Truth about the Rochdale Sex Ring by the Victim Who Stopped Them.* London: Ebury Press.

Apna Haq. 2018. 'Our research'. Available at: http://138.68.147.29/about-us/our-research (accessed 10 July 2019).

Archer, C. Captain. 1887. 'Note on burning the bodies of Muhammadan fanatics after execution', Political Agent Thal-Chotiali, Colonial Record India, British Library, IOR/L/MIL/17/13/21.

Arondekar, A. 2005. 'Without a trace: sexuality and the colonial archive', *Journal of the History of Sexuality*, 14(1/2): 10–27.

Arvin, M., Tuck, E. and Morrill, A. 2013. 'Decolonizing feminism: challenging connections between settler colonialism and heteropatriarchy', *Feminist Formations*, 25(1): 8–34.

Attorney General Dar Es Salaam. 1951. 'Telegram to Dr Rusford: African Marriage Survey', November 1st. Colonial Record: National Archives Kew. Ref: H451

Ballantyne, T. 2005. 'Putting the nation in its place?: world history and C. A. Bayly's *The Birth of the Modern World*', in *Connected Worlds: History in Transnational Perspective*, edited by A. Curthoys and M. Lake, pp. 23–44. Canberra: Australian National University Press.

Ballantyne, T. and Burton, A. 2009. 'Introduction: the politics of intimacy in an age of empire', in *Moving Subjects: Gender, Mobility, and Intimacy in an Age of Global Empire*, edited by T. Ballantyne and A. Burton, 1–30. Urbana: University of Illinois Press.

Barder, A. 2015. *Empire Within: International Hierarchy and Its Imperial Laboratories of Governance.* Abingdon: Routledge.

Barkawi T. and Stanski, K., eds. 2012. *Orientalism and War.* London: Hurst.

Barrett, M. and McIntosh, M. 1991. *The Anti-Social Family.* London: Verso.

Bauböck, R. 2014. *The Return of Banishment: Whose Bad Guys Are Terrorists?* Florence: EUDO Observatory on Citizenship.

BBC, 1999. 'Fighting arranged marriage abuse', BBC News, 12 July. Available at: http://news.bbc.co.uk/1/hi/uk/392619.stm (accessed 3 September 2019).

BBC. 2002a. 'Blunkett "wrong on arranged marriages"', BBC News, 8 February. Available at: http://news.bbc.co.uk/1/hi/uk/1809791.stm (accessed 1 November 2017).

BBC. 2002b. 'Blunkett defends marriage comments', BBC News, 8 February. Available at: http://news.bbc.co.uk/1/hi/uk_politics/1807885.stm (accessed 10 July 2019).

BBC. 2011. 'Jack Straw criticised for "easy meat" comments on abuse', BBC News, 8 January. Available at: www.bbc.co.uk/news/uk-12142177 (accessed 6 November 2018).

BBC. 2015. 'UK to build £25m Jamaican prison', BBC News, 30 September. Available at: www.bbc.co.uk/news/uk-34398014 (accessed 6 November 2018).

BBC. 2016. *Today,* BBC Radio 4, 19 October. Available at: www.bbc.co.uk/programmes/b07zx6k7 (accessed 20 October 2016).

BBC, 2017. 'Who are Britain's jihadists?', BBC News, 12 October. Available at: www.bbc.co.uk/news/uk-32026985 (accessed 6 November 2018).

BBC. 2018a. *Today,* BBC Radio 4, 18 September. Available at: www.bbc.co.uk/programmes/b0bk12j8 (accessed 6 November 2018).

BBC. 2018b. 'Human rights groups call for children to be taken off Nauru', BBC News, 20 August. Available at: www.bbc.co.uk/news/world-australia-45244149 (accessed 6 November 2018).

Beattie, A. R. 2016. 'Between safety and vulnerability: the exiled other of international relations', *Citizenship Studies,* 20(2): 228–242.

Beckles-Raymond, G. 2019. 'Revisiting the home as a site of freedom and resistance', in *To Exist is to Resist Black Feminism in Europe,* edited by A. Emejulu and F. Sobande, pp. 91–103. London: Pluto Press.

Bell, D. and Binnie, J. 2000. *The Sexual Citizen: Queer Politics and Beyond.* Cambridge: Polity Press.

Benedict, R. 1935. *Patterns of Culture.* London: Routledge.

Berlant, L. 1997. *The Queen of America Goes to Washington City: Essays on Sex and Citizenship*. Durham, NC: Duke University Press.

Bhambra, G. 2014. *Connected Sociologies*. London: Bloomsbury.

Bhambra, G. 2016. 'Comparative historical sociology and the state: problems of method', *Cultural Sociology*, 10(3): 335–351.

Bhambra, G. 2017a. 'Brexit, Trump, and "methodological whiteness": on the misrecognition of race and class', *British Journal of Sociology*, 68: 214–232.

Bhambra, G. 2017b. 'The current crisis of Europe: refugees, colonialism, and the limits of cosmopolitanism', *European Law Journal*, 23(5): 395–405.

Bigo, D. 2006. 'Internal and external aspects of security', *European Security*, 15(4): 405–422.

Black Europe Body Politics. 2013. 'Be.Bop 2013' [website]. Available at: https://blackeuropebodypolitics.wordpress.com/2012/07/09/be-bop-2013/ (accessed 17 October 2016).

Blaney, D. and Inayatullah, N. 2010. *Savage Economics: Wealth, Poverty and the Temporal Walls of Capitalism*. London: Routledge.

Bleiker, R., Campbell, D., Hutchison, E. and Nicholson, X. 2013. 'The visual dehumanisation of refugees', *Australian Journal of Political Science*, 48(3): 398–416.

Bleiker, R. 2018. 'Mapping visual global politics', in *Visual Global Politics*, edited by R. Bleiker, pp. 1–29. Abingdon: Routledge.

Blinder, S. 2017. 'Non-European migration to the UK: family unification and dependents', The Migration Observatory (briefing). Available at: https://migrationobservatory.ox.ac.uk/resources/briefings/non-european-migration-to-the-uk-family-unification-dependents/ (accessed 3 July 2018).

Bonjour, S. and Block, L. 2016. 'Ethnicizing citizenship, questioning membership. Explaining the decreasing family migration rights of citizens in Europe', *Citizenship Studies*, 20(6–7): 779–794.

Bonjour, S. and Hart, B. 2013. 'A proper wife, a proper marriage: constructions of "us" and "them" in Dutch family migration policy', *European Journal of Women's Studies*, 20(1): 61–76.

Brah, A. 1996. *Cartographies of Diaspora: Contesting Identities*. London: Routledge.

British Red Cross. 2018. 'UK asylum system leaving thousands of people in poverty', 20 February. Available at: www.redcross.org.uk/about-us/news-and-media/media-centre/press-releases/press-release-uk-asylum-system-leaving-thousands-of-people-in-poverty (accessed 8 March 2018).

Bronte, C. [1846] 1992. *Jane Eyre*. London: Wordsworth Editions.

Brown, E. 2011. 'The "unchildlike child": making and marking the child/adult divide in the juvenile court', *Children's Geographies*, 9(3): 361–377.

Browne, S. 2010. 'Digital epidermalization: race, identity and biometrics', *Critical Sociology*, 36(1): 131–150.

Browne, S. 2015. *Dark Matter: On the Surveillance of Blackness*. Durham, NC: Duke University.

Burnham M. A. 1987. 'An impossible marriage: slave law and family law', *Law and Inequality: A Journal of Theory and Practice*, 5(2): 187–225.

Burridge, A., Gill, N., Kocher, A. and Martin, L. 2017. 'Polymorphic borders', *Territory, Politics, Governance*, 5(3): 239–251.

Burton, A. 1998. *At the Heart of the Empire: Indians and the Colonial Encounter in Late-Victorian Britain*. Berkley: University of California Press.

Burton, A. 2009. *Gender, Sexuality and Colonial Modernities*. London: Routledge.

Butler, J. and Athanasiou, A. 2013. *Dispossession: The Performative in the Political*. Cambridge: Polity.

Butler, J. 2010. *Frames of War*. London: Verso.

Campbell, P. 1921. 'Asiatic immigration to Australia', *Economica*, 1: 52–61.

Cantle, T. 2002. *Community Cohesion: Report of the Independent Review Team – The 'Cantle Report'*. London: Home Office.

Carver, N. 2016. 'For her protection and benefit: the regulation of marriage-related migration to the UK', *Ethnic and Racial Studies*, 39(15): 2758–2776.

Casey, L. 2012. 'Listening to troubled families'. London: Department for Communities and Local Government.

Casey, L. 2015. 'Report of inspection of Rotherham Metropolitan Borough Council'. London: Department for Communities and Local Government.

Casey, L. 2016. 'The Casey Review: a review into opportunity and integration'. London: Department for Communities and Local Government.

Cesaire, A. 1972. *Discourse on Colonialism*. London: Monthly Review Press.

Chambre, A. 2016. 'Home Office "planning to strip foreign criminals of British citizenship"', PoliticsHome, 26 February. Available at: www.politicshome.com/news/uk/home-affairs/news/58683/home-office-'planning-strip-foreign-criminals-british-citizenship' (accessed 11 September 2019).

Chamney, M. 1915. 'Confidential memorandum on illicit immigration of Asiatics to the Transvaal: the alleged minor sons of registered Indians', Colonial Record India, British Library, IOR/L/PJ/6/1235, File 1398. Document: 14/E/6849/4.

Charsley, K. and Benson, M. 2012. 'Marriages of convenience or inconvenient marriages: regulating spousal migration to Britain', *Journal of Immigration, Asylum and Nationality Law*, 26(1): 10–26.

Chatterjee, N. 2010. 'English law, Brahmo "marriage", and the problem of religious difference: civil "marriage" laws in Britain and India', *Comparative Studies in Society and History*, 52(3): 524–552.

Choudhury T. 2017. 'The radicalization of citizenship deprivation', *Critical Social Policy*, 37(2): 225–244.

Closs Stephens, A. 2016. 'The affective atmospheres of nationalism', *Cultural Geographies*, 23: 181–198.

Cockbain, E. 2013. 'Grooming and the "Asian sex gang predator": the construction of a racial crime threat', *Race and Class*, 54(4): 22–32.

Collins, M. 2017. 'A technocratic vision of empire: Lord Montagu and the origins of British air power', *Journal of Imperial and Commonwealth History*, 45(4): 652–671.

Collins, P. 1998. 'It's all in the family: intersections of gender, race, and nation', *Hypatia*, 13(3): 62–82.

Colonial Film Project. 2018. 'Landing of savage South Africa and Southampton' [video]. Available at: www.colonialfilm.org.uk/node/1186 (accessed 6 November 2018).

Corporate Watch. 2018. *The UK Border Regime: A Critical Guide*. London: Freedom Press.

Cott, N. 2000. *Public Vows: A History of Marriage and the Nation*. Harvard: Harvard University Press.

Coulthard, G. S. 2014. *Red Skin White Masks: Rejecting the Colonial Politics of Recognition*. Minneapolis: University of Minnesota Press.

Cowen, D. and Gilbert, E., eds. 2008. *War, Citizenship, Territory*. London: Routledge.

Crawford, S. 2014. 'Forgotten 19th century flashpoint between Chinese immigrants and Sydney colonials that sparked the White Australia policy', *Daily Telegraph*, 12 August. Available at: www.dailytelegraph.com.au/news/nsw/forgotten-19th-century-flashpoint-between-chinese-immigrants-and-sydney-colonials-that-sparked-the-white-australia-policy/news-story/304ed6b269785603bbcb890fd6437f99 (accessed 10 July 2019).

Crawley, H. 2011. '"Asexual, apolitical beings": the interpretation of children's identities and experiences in the UK asylum system', *Journal of Ethnic and Migration Studies*, 37(8): 1171–1184.

Crossley, S. 2016. 'Realising the (troubled) family', 'crafting the neoliberal state', *Families, Relationships and Societies*, 5(2): 263–279.

Cusick, J. 2016. 'Asian sex abusers to be stripped of UK citizenship and deported', *Independent*, 25 February. Available at: www.independent.co.uk/news/uk/crime/asian-sex-abusers-to-be-stripped-of-uk-citizenship-and-deported-a6896051.html (accessed 6 November 2018).

D'Aoust, A. M. 2014. 'Love as project of (im)mobility: love, sovereignty, and governmentality in marriage migration management practices', *Global Society*, 28(3): 317–336.

D'Aoust, A. M. 2018. 'A moral economy of suspicion: love and marriage migration management practices in the United Kingdom', *Environment and Planning. D*, 36(1): 40–59.

Danewid, I. 2017. 'White innocence in the black Mediterranean: hospitality and the erasure of history', *Third World Quarterly*, 38(7): 1674–1689.

Danewid, I. 2019. 'The fire this time: Grenfell, racial capitalism and the urbanisation of empire', *European Journal of International Relations*, online first, 25 June. https://doi.org/10.1177/1354066119858388.

Davidson, Lynn. 2016. 'Asylum seekers pretending to be kids attack their host families', *Sun*, 20 February. Available at: www.thesun.co.uk/archives/news/209265/asylum-seekers-pretending-to-be-kids-attack-their-host-families/ (accessed 6 November 2018).

Davies, T. and Isakjee A., 2018. 'Ruins of empire: refugees, race and the postcolonial geographies of European migrant camps', *Geoforum*, online first, 5 October. https://doi.org/10.1016/j.geoforum.2018.09.031.

Davin, A. 1978. 'Imperialism and motherhood', *History Workshop Journal*, 5(1): 9–66.

Davis, A. 2016. *Freedom Is a Constant Struggle: Ferguson, Palestine, and the Foundations of a Movement*. Chicago: Haymarket Books.

Dayan, C. 2011. *The Law Is a White Dog: How Legal Rituals Make and Unmake Persons*. Princeton: Princeton University Press.

Debrix, F. and Weber, C. 2003. *Rituals of Mediation: International Politics and Social Meaning*. Minneapolis: University of Minnesota Press.

De Genova, N. 2002. 'Migrant "illegality" and deportability in everyday life', *Annual Review of Anthropology*, 31: 419–447.

De Genova, N., ed. 2017. *The Borders of 'Europe': Autonomy of Migration, Tactics of Bordering*. Durham, NC: Duke University Press.

De Genova, N. 2018. 'The "migrant crisis" as racial crisis: do Black Lives Matter in Europe?', *Ethnic and Racial Studies*, 41(10): 1765–1782.

Dei, G. J. S. 2017. *Reframing Blackness and Black Solidarities through Anti-colonial and Decolonial Prisms*. London: Springer.

De Noronha, L. 2016. 'Deportation and multi-status Britain,' *Discover Society*, Available at: https://discoversociety.org/2016/10/04/deportation-and-multi-status-britain/ (accessed 6 September 2018).

De Noronha, L. 2018. 'Race, class and Brexit: thinking from detention,' *Verso Blog*. Available at: www.versobooks.com/blogs?post_author=353841 (accessed 16 September 2018).

De Noronha, L. 2019. 'Deportation, racism and multi-status Britain: immigration control and the production of race in the present,' *Ethnic and Racial Studies*, online first, 20 March. https://doi.org/10.1080/01419870.2019.1585559.

De Noronha, L. and Chowdhury, T. 2018. 'Stansted 15 and the terror of law,' *Verso* [blog], 12 December. Available at: www.versobooks.com/blogs/4171-the-stansted-15-and-the-terror-of-law (accessed 17 September 2019).

Dixon, D. 1983. 'Thatcher's people: the British Nationality Act 1981,' *Journal of Law and Society*, 10(2): 161–180.

Dodd, V. 2018. 'UK police use of facial recognition technology a failure, says report,' *Guardian*, 15 May. Available at: www.theguardian.com/uk-news/2018/may/15/uk-police-use-of-facial-recognition-technology-failure (accessed 1 September 2018).

Drew, J. 2016. 'An independent review of South Yorkshire Police's handling of child sexual exploitation 1997–2016.' Police and Crime Commissioner for South Yorkshire. Available at: www.drewreview.uk/wp-content/uploads/2016/03/SYP030-Final-report.pdf (accessed 8 November 2018).

Duff, B. 1915. 'Letter to Secretary of State of India, Austin Chamberlain.' Simla, Government of India. Department of Commerce and Industry: Emigration. No. 41, 15 October. 1–15. British Library, IOR/L/PJ/6/1051, File 4522.

Duggan, L. 2003. *The Twilight of Equality?: Neoliberalism, Cultural Politics, and the Attack on Democracy*. Boston: Beacon Press.

Duru, N. J. 2004. 'The Central Park Five, the Scottsboro Boys, and the myth of the bestial black man,' *Cardozo Law Review*, 25(4): 1315–1366.

Eddo-Lodge, R. 2017. *Why I'm No Longer Talking to White People about Race*. London: Bloomsbury.

Edelman, L. 2004. *No Future: Queer Theory and the Death Drive*. Durham, NC: Duke University Press.

Edkins, J. 2015. *Face Politics*. Abingdon: Routledge.

EDL. 2016. 'The dynamics of Muslim grooming gangs – speech in Newcastle by "Bill Sir William"', English Defence League website, 24 September. Available at: www.englishdefenceleague.org.uk/the-dynamics-of-muslim-grooming-gangs-speech-in-newcastle/ (accessed 23 September 2018).

EDL. 2019. 'Muslim grooming gangs and other rape jihad convictions', English Defence League website. Available at: http://www.englishdefenceleague.org.uk/islam/grooming-gangs/ (accessed 4 January 2019).

El-Enany, N. 2016. 'Brexit as nostalgia for empire', *Critical Legal Thinking*, 19 June. Available at: http://critictallegalthinking.com/2016/06/19/brexit-nostalgia-empire (accessed 23 October 2018).

El-Enany, N. 2017. 'The colonial logic of Grenfell', *Verso* [blog], 3 July. Available at: www.versobooks.com/blogs/3306-the-colonial-logic-of-grenfell (accessed 23 October 2018).

El-Enany, N. 2020. *(B)ordering Britain: Law, Race and Empire*. Manchester: Manchester University Press.

Elgot, J. 2017a. 'British fighters should be hunted down and killed says Defence Secretary Gavin Williamson', *Guardian*, 7 December. Available at: www.theguardian.com/politics/2017/dec/07/british-isis-fighters-should-be-hunted-down-and-killed-says-defence-secretary-gavin-williamson (accessed 10 July 2019).

Elgot, J. 2017b. 'Diane Abbott more abused than any other MPs during election', *Guardian*, 5 September. Available at: www.theguardian.com/politics/2017/sep/05/diane-abbott-more-abused-than-any-other-mps-during-election (accessed 30 October 2018).

Elliott-Cooper, A. 2016. 'State violence from old to new: from slavery to Serco', in *Blackness in Britain*, edited by K. Andrews and L. Palmer, pp. 64–75. Abingdon: Routledge.

Elliott-Cooper, A. 2019. '"Our life is a struggle": respectable gender norms and black resistance to policing', *Antipode*, 51: 539–557.

Elshtain, J. 1987. *Women and War*. Chicago: University of Chicago Press.

Elvin, H. L. 1959. 'Inaugural address by the Chairman', the Colonial Office, Social Development and the Family Conference, Oxford, 7–25 September. London: HMSO.

Embury-Dennis, T. 2019. 'Shamima Begum: Isis bride and baby son "move refugee camps after death threats"', *Independent*, 1 March. Available at: www.independent.co.uk/news/world/middle-east/shamima-begum-isis-baby-refugee-camp-syria-threats-a8802416.html (accessed 7 March 2019).

Emmer, P. C. 1986. 'The meek Hindu; the recruitment of Indian indentured labourers for service overseas, 1870–1916', in *Colonialism and Migration; Indentured Labour Before and After Slavery*, edited by P. C. Emmer, pp. 187–207. London: Springer.

Enloe, C. 1990. *Bananas, Beaches and Bases: Making Feminist Sense of International Politics*. Berkley: University of California Press.

Enloe, C. 2018. *The Big Push: Exposing and Challenging the Persistence of Patriarchy*. Berkley: University of California Press.

Eyre, E. 1865. 'Speech to the House of Assembly, Kingstown, Jamaica, 7 November', National Archives, CO 137/396/41, File 11611/65/564.

Fanon, F. 1961. *The Wretched of the Earth*. London: Penguin.

Fanon, F. 1986. *Black Skin, White Masks*. Pluto: London.

Fargues, E. 2017. 'The revival of citizenship deprivation in France and the UK as an instance of citizenship renationalisation', *Citizenship Studies*, online first, 13 September. https://doi.org/10.1080/13621025.2017.1377152.

Farris, S. 2017. *In the Name of Women's Rights: The Rise of Femonationalism*. Durham, NC: Duke University Press.

Faulkner, J. 2011. *The Importance of Being Innocent: Why We Worry about Children*. Melbourne: Cambridge University Press.

Feder, E. K. 2007. *Family Bonds: Genealogies of Race and Gender*. Oxford: Oxford University Press.

Federici, S. 2004. *The Caliban and the Witch: Women, the Body and Primitive Accumulation*. New York: Autonomedia.

Ferguson, R. 2003. *Aberrations in Black: Toward a Queer of Color Critique*. Minnesota: University of Minneapolis.

Fiddian-Qasmiyeh, E. 2016. 'Representations of displacement in the Middle East', *Public Culture*, 28(3): 457–473.

Fiddian-Qasmiyeh, E. 2018. 'Disrupting humanitarian narratives', *Refugee Hosts* [blog]. Available at: https://refugeehosts.org/representations-of-displacement-series (accessed 13 September 2018).

Foreign Office. 1933. 'Consultation: Foreign Office to the Law Officers of the Crown', Foreign Office, 17 March. Declassified File. National Archives, FO 834. 3126/695/376/1933.

Fortier, A. M. 2008. *Multicultural Horizons: Diversity and the Limits of the Civil Nation*. London: Routledge.

Foucault, M. 1984. 'Nietzsche, genealogy and history', in *The Foucault Reader*, edited by P. Rabinow, pp. 77–120. London: Penguin.

Foucault, M. 1991. *The History of Sexuality 1: The Will to Knowledge.* London: Penguin.

Friis, S. M. 2017. '"Behead, burn, crucify, crush": theorizing the Islamic State's public displays of violence', *European Journal of International Relations*, online first, 19 June. https://doi.org/10.1177/1354066117714416.

Fusco, C. 2003. 'Racial time, racial marks, racial metaphors', in *Only Skin Deep: Changing Visions of the American self*, edited by C. Fusco and B. Wallis, pp. 13–48. New York: International Centre of Photography.

Gebrial, D. 2017. 'Decolonising desire: the politics of love', *Verso* [blog], 13 February. Available at: www.versobooks.com/blogs/3094-decolonising-desire-the-politics-of-love (accessed 10 July 2019).

Gedalof, I. 2007. 'Unhomely homes: women, family and belonging in UK discourses of migration and asylum', *Journal of Ethnic and Migration Studies*, 33(1): 77–94.

Gentleman, A. 2018a. 'The week that took Windrush from low profile investigation to national scandal', *Guardian*, 20 April. Available at: www.theguardian.com/uk-news/2018/apr/20/the-week-that-took-windrush-from-low-profile-investigation-to-national-scandal (accessed 11 September 2019).

Gentleman, A. 2018b. '"My life is in ruins": wrongly deported Windrush people facing fresh indignity', *Guardian*, 10 September. Available at: www.theguardian.com/uk-news/2018/sep/10/windrush-people-wrongly-deported-jamaica-criminal-offence?fbclid=IwAR3wRODWLkGelUhR0ldD2FvkPABzct41fenUTPseFykiaf50KbDXd5WL_VY (accessed 17 September 2019).

Ghosh, D. 2006. *Sex and the Family in Colonial India: The Making of Empire.* Cambridge: Cambridge University Press.

Gibney, M. 2014. 'The deprivation of citizenship in the United Kingdom: a brief history', *Journal of Immigration Asylum and Nationality Law*, 28(4): 326–335.

Gibney, M. 2017. 'Denaturalisation', in *The Oxford Handbook of Citizenship*, edited by A. Shachar, R. Bauböck, I. Bloemraad and M. Vink, pp. 358–383. Oxford: Oxford University Press.

Gidwani, V. and Reddy, R. 2011. 'The afterlives of "waste": notes from India for a minor history of capitalist surplus', *Antipode*, 43(5): 1625–1658.

Gilbert, S. and Gubar. S. (2000). *The Madwoman in the Attic: The Woman Writer and the Nineteenth-Century Literary Imagination.* New Haven: Yale University Press.

Gill, A. and Mitra-Kahn, T. 2012. 'Modernising the *other*: assessing the ideological underpinnings of the policy discourse on forced marriage in the UK', *Policy and Politics*, 40(1): 104–119.

Gilroy, P. 1992. *There Ain't No Black in the Union Jack*. London: Routledge.

Gilroy, P. 2006. *Postcolonial Melancholia*. New York: Columbia University Press.

Gilroy, P. and Hall, S. 2007. *Black Britain: A Photographic History*. London: Saqi Books.

Glissant, E. 1997. *Poetics of relation*. Ann Arbor: University of Michigan Press.

Gohir, S. 2013. *Unheard Voices: The Sexual Exploitation of Asian Girls and Young Women*. Birmingham: Muslim Women's Network.

Goldberg, D. T. 2008. *The Threat of Race*. Oxford: Wiley.

Goody, J. 1990. *The Oriental, the Ancient and the Primitive: Systems of 'Marriage' and the Family in the Pre-Industrial Societies of Eurasia*. Cambridge: Cambridge University Press.

Gopinath, G. 2005. *Impossible Desires: Queer Diasporas and South Asian Public Cultures*. Durham, NC, and London: Duke University Press.

Gowans, G. 2003. 'Imperial geographies of home: memsahibs and miss-sahibs in India and Britain, 1915–1947', *Cultural Geographies*, 10(4): 424–441.

Gorman, D. 2007. *Imperial Citizenship: Empire and the Question of Belonging*. Oxford: Oxford University Press.

Greenhill, S. 2016. '"The first thing they do is ask for a razor": couple who have fostered child refugees warn the UK is being exploited by GROWN MEN masquerading as youngsters', *Daily Mail*, 21 October. Available at: www.dailymail.co.uk/news/article-3860790/The-thing-ask-razor-s-dead-giveaway-Couple-fostered-child-refugees-warn-UK-exploited-grown-men-masquerading-youngsters.html (accessed 7 November 2018).

Greenhill, S., Gysin, C. and Sinmaz, E. 2016. 'Give "child migrants" age tests, says Straw: ex-home secretary leads calls for checks ... as Home Office minister says 400 may come here', *Daily Mail*, 20 October. Available at: www.dailymail.co.uk/news/article-3850564/Home-Office-admits-figures-two-three-child-refugees-lying-age-actually-adults.html (accessed 19 October 2018).

Gregory, D. 2004. *The Colonial Present*. Oxford: Wiley.

Gregory, D. 2012a. 'From a view to a kill: drones and late modern war', *Theory, Culture and Society*, 28(7–8): 188–215.

Gregory, D. 2012b. 'Dis/ordering the Orient: scopic regimes and modern war', in *Orientalism and War*, edited by T. Barkawi and K. Stanski, pp. 151–177. London: Hurst.

Grewal, I. 1996. *Home and Harem: Nation, Gender, Empire and the Cultures of Travel.* Durham, NC: Duke University Press.

Griffiths, M. and Morgan, C. 2017. 'Deporting high harm foreign criminals: Operation Nexus', *Policy Bristol: Policy Briefing* 50, October. Available at: www.bristol.ac.uk/media-library/sites/policybristol/briefings-and-reports-pdfs/2017-briefings–reports-pdfs/PolicyBristol_Briefing_October_2017_operation_nexus_web.pdf (accessed 23 September 2019).

Grosfoguel, R., Oso, L. and Christou, A. 2015. '"Racism", intersectionality and migration studies: framing some theoretical reflections', *Identities: Global Studies in Culture and Power*, 22(6): 635–652.

Guardian. 2017. 'UK has stripped 150 jihadists and criminals of citizenship', 30 July. Available at: www.theguardian.com/uk-news/2017/jul/30/uk-has-stripped-150-jihadists-and-criminals-of-citizenship (accessed 7 November 2018).

Guillaume, X. 2011. 'The international as an everyday practice', *International Political Sociology*, 5(4): 446–462.

Gunter, J. 2015. 'Alan Kurdi: why one picture cut through', BBC News, 4 September. Available at: www.bbc.com/news/world-europe-34150419 (accessed 7 September 2017).

Gupta, M. D. 2014. '"Don't deport our daddies": gendering state deportation practices and immigrant organizing', *Gender and Society*, 28(1): 83–109.

Gutiérrez Rodríguez, E. 2018. 'The coloniality of migration and the "refugee crisis": on the asylum-migration nexus, the transatlantic white European settler colonialism-migration and racial capitalism', *Refuge*, 34(1): 16–28.

Hage, G. 1996. 'The spatial imaginary of national practices: dwelling–domesticating/being–exterminating', *Environment and Planning D: Society and Space*, 14(4): 463–485.

Halberstam, J. 1995. *Skin Shows: Gothic Horror and the Technology of Monsters.* Durham, NC: Duke University Press.

Hall, C. 2002. *Civilising Subjects: Metropole and Colony in the English Imagination 1830–1867.* Cambridge: Polity Press.

Hall, C. 2013. 'Britain's debt to slavery made public', *Guardian*, 27 February. Available at: www.theguardian.com/commentisfree/2013/feb/27/britain-debt-slavery-made-public (accessed 3 October 2018).

Hansard. 1961. 'Commonwealth Immigration Bill: Committee Stage, MP Judith Hart', HC vol. 650, cols 1279–1330, 5 December.

Hansard. 2007. 'Debate on Forced Marriage Bill', HL vol. 668, col. 1321, 26 January.

Hansard. 2018. 'British Jihadis (Iraq and Syria)', HC vol. 635, cols 941–948, 31 January.

Hansen, P. and Jonsson, S. 2014. *Eurafrica: The Untold History of European Integration and Colonialism*. London: Bloomsbury.

Hansen, R. 2000. *Citizenship and Immigration in Post-war Britain: The Institutional Origins of a Multicultural Nation*. Oxford: Oxford University Press.

Harrington, J. 2012. 'Orientalism, political subjectivity and the birth of citizenship between 1780 and 1830', *Citizenship Studies*, 16(5–6): 573–586.

Hartman, S. 1997. *Scenes of Subjection: Terror, Slavery, and Self-Making in Nineteenth-Century America*. Oxford: Oxford University Press.

Head, M. 2017. *Emergency Powers in Theory and Practice: The Long Shadow of Carl Schmitt*. Farnham: Ashgate.

Hemmings, C. 2012. 'Affective solidarity: feminist reflexivity and political transformation', *Feminist Theory*, 13(2): 147–161.

HM Government. 2006. Immigration, Asylum and Nationality Act 2006, section 56. Available at: www.legislation.gov.uk/ukpga/2006/13/section/5621 (accessed 10 September 2019).

HM Government (2015). *Prevent duty guidance for England and Wales*. London: HMSO.

Hoad, N. 2000. 'Arrested development or the queerness of savages: resisting evolutionary narratives of difference', *Postcolonial Studies: Culture, Politics, Economy*, 3(2): 133–158.

Hoad, N. 2007. *African Intimacies: Race, Homosexuality and Globalization*. Minneapolis: University of Minnesota Press.

Holland, P. 2004. *Picturing Childhood: The Myth of the Child in Popular Imagery*. London: I. B. Tauris.

Home Affairs Select Committee, 2014. 'The work of the immigration directorates: question 4' [video]. *Parliament TV*, 24 June. Available at: https://parliamentlive.tv/event/index/a3327f45-d56c-4622-acd7-adf27ce3a001 (accessed 5 September 2019).

Home Office. 1962. Commonwealth Immigration Act. Instructions to Immigration Officers. Presented to Parliament by the Home Secretary, 11 May 1962. London: HMSO.

Home Office. 2002. *Secure Borders, Safe Haven: Integration with Diversity in Modern Britain*. London: TSO.

Home Office. 2007. *Marriage to Partners from Overseas*. London: Home Office.

Home Office. 2011a. *Family Migration: A Consultation*. London: HMSO.

Home Office. 2011b. *Family Migration: Evidence and Analysis*. London: HMSO.

Home Office. 2013a. *Immigration Bill: Overarching Documents.* London: HMSO.

Home Office. 2013b. *Sham Marriages and Civil Partnerships.* London: HMSO.

Home Office. 2014a. *Inspection report on Immigration Enforcement.* London: HMSO. Available at: www.gov.uk/government/publications/inspection-report-on-immigration-enforcement-activity-december-2014 (accessed 10 July 2019).

Home Office. 2014b. Immigration Bill – European Convention on Human Rights: Supplementary Memorandum by the Home Office. Available at: www.gov.uk/government/publications/immigration-bill-overarching-documents (accessed 10 September 2019).

Home Office. 2015. Immigration Act 2014. Marriage and Civil Partnership Referral and Investigation Scheme: Statutory Guidance for Home Office Staff. London: Home Office.

Home Office. 2016. Immigration statistics, October to December 2016. London. Home Office.

Hook, D. 2005. 'Affecting whiteness: racism as technology of affect', *International Journal of Critical Psychology,* 16: 74–99.

hooks, b. 1992. *Black Looks: Race and Representation.* Boston: South End Press.

hooks, b. 1999. *Yearning: Race, Gender and Cultural Politics.* Boston: South End Press.

hooks, b. 2008. *Belonging.* Abingdon: London.

Horsfall P. 1915. 'Letter to Governor General Pretoria on illegal entry of Indians into the Union', 21 June, British Library, IOR/L/PJ/6/1235, File 1398, Document 55/77.

Howell, A., and Richter-Montpetit, M. 2019. 'Racism in Foucauldian security studies: biopolitics, liberal war, and the whitewashing of colonial and racial violence', *International Political Sociology,* 13(1): 2–19.

Hussain, N. 1999. 'Towards a jurisprudence of emergency: colonialism and the rule of law', *Law and Critique,* 10: 93–115.

Imkaan. 2019. 'Research'. Available at: www.imkaan.org.uk/research (accessed 24 July 2019).

Independent Inquiry Child Sexual Abuse. 2019. *Child Sexual Abuse in the Roman Catholic Church.* Available at: www.iicsa.org.uk/investigations/investigation-into-failings-by-the-catholic-church?tab=summary (accessed 8 March 2019).

Institute of Race Relations. 2018. 'The embedding of state hostility: a background paper on the Windrush scandal'. Briefing paper 11. London: Institute of Race Relations.

Innes, A. 2019. *Colonial Citizenship and Everyday Transnationalism: An Immigrant's Story*. Abingdon: Routledge.

Iqbal, N. 2018. 'Stansted 15: "We are not terrorists, no lives were at risk. We have no regrets"', *Guardian*, 16 December. Available at: www.theguardian.com/world/2018/dec/16/migrants-deportation-stansted-actvists (accessed 8 March 2019).

Ittmann, K., Cordell, D. and Maddox, G., eds. 2010. *The Demographics of Empire: The Colonial Order and the Creation of Knowledge*. Athens, OH: Ohio University Press.

Jackson, M. J. 1865. 'Letter to the Governor of Jamaica, Edward Eyre', 31 October, National Archives, CO 137/396/41, File 11611/65/264.

Jackson, N. 2015. '"A nigger in the new England": "Sus", the Brixton riot, and citizenship', *African and Black Diaspora: An International Journal*, 8(2): 158–170.

Jackson, R. and Pabon, E. 2000. 'Race and treating other people's children as adults', *Journal of Criminal Justice*, 28(6): 507–515.

Javid, S. 2019. 'If you run away to join Isis, like Shamima Begum, I will use all my power to stop you coming back', *The Times*, 17 February. Available at: www.thetimes.co.uk/article/if-you-run-away-to-join-isis-like-shamima-begum-i-will-use-all-my-power-to-stop-you-coming-back-8r2lpkfnn (accessed 6 March 2019).

Jay, A. 2014. 'Independent inquiry into child sexual exploitation in Rotherham 1997–2013'. Rotherham: Rotherham Metropolitan Borough Council.

Jay, M. and Ramaswamy, S. 2014. *Empires of Vision: A Reader*. Durham, NC: Duke University Press.

Johnson, H. 2011. 'Click to donate: visual images, constructing victims and imagining the female refugee', *Third World Quarterly*, 32(6): 1015–1037.

Johnson, J. 2017. 'Beyond a politics of recrimination: scandal, ethics and the rehabilitation of violence', *European Journal of International Relations*, 23(3): 703–726.

Jones, R. 2016. *Violent Borders: Refugees and the Right to Move*. London: Verso.

Joppke, C. 2016. 'Terror and the Loss of Citizenship', *Citizenship Studies*, 20(6–7): 728–748.

Kaplan, A. 2005. *The Anarchy of Empire in the Making of U.S. Culture*. Harvard: Harvard University Press.

Kapoor N. 2018. *Deport, Deprive, Extradite: 21st Century State Extremism*. London: Verso.

Kapoor, N. and Narkowicz, K. 2019. 'Unmaking citizens: passport removals, pre-emptive policing and the reimagining of colonial governmentalities', *Ethnic and Racial Studies*, 42(16): 45–62.

Karatani, R. 2002. *Defining British Citizenship*. London: Routledge.

Kearney, R. 2003. *Strangers, Gods and Monsters*. Abingdon: Routledge.

Kilkey, M. and Palenga-Möllenbeck, E., eds. 2016. *Family Life in an Age of Migration and Mobility: Global Perspectives through the Life Course*. London: Palgrave Macmillan.

Kingston, R. 2005. 'The unmaking of citizens: banishment and the modern citizenship regime in France', *Citizenship Studies*, 9(1): 23–40.

Kofman, E. 2018. 'Family migration as a class matter', *International Migration*, 56(4): 33–46.

Kotef, H. 2015. *Movement and the Ordering of Freedom: On Liberal Governances of Mobility*. Durham, NC: Duke University Press.

Lake, M. and Reynolds, H. 2008. *Drawing the Global Colour Line: White Men's Countries and the International Challenge of Racial Equality*. Cambridge: Cambridge University Press.

Kundnani, A. (2001). 'In a foreign land: the new popular racism', *Race and Class*, 43(2): 41–60.

Lalvani, S. 1996. *Photography, Vision, and the Production of Modern Bodies*. New York: State University of New York Press.

Larasi, M., Imkaan and Roy, S., Tweedale, R. 2014. 'This is not my destiny: reflecting on responses to forced marriage in England and Wales', Imkaan and Rights of Women Report. London: HM Government Forced Marriage Unit.

Lavi, S. 2010. 'Punishment and the revocation of citizenship in the United Kingdom, United States, and Israel', *New Criminal Law Review: An International and Interdisciplinary Journal*, 13(2): 404–426.

Legg, S. 2007. *Spaces of Colonialism: Delhi's Urban Governmentalities*. Oxford: Blackwell.

Legg, S. 2010. 'An intimate and imperial feminism: Meliscent Shephard and the regulation of prostitution in colonial India', *Environment and Planning D: Society and Space*, 28(1): 68–94.

Levine, P. 2007. *Gender and Empire*. Oxford: Oxford University Press.

Lewis, H. M. 1877. *Ancient Society or Researches in the Lines of Human Progress from Savagery through Barbarism to Civilization*. London: MacMillan and Company.

Lewis, R. 2014. '"Gay? Prove it": the politics of queer anti-deportation activism', *Sexualities*, 17(8): 958–975.

Lewis, H., Dwyer, P., Hodkinson, S. and Waite, L. 2014. *Precarious Lives. Forced Labour, Exploitation and Asylum*. Bristol: Policy Press.

Lock, F. 1879. 'Memo: Vagrant Ordinances', Brigadier General, Aden, Political Residence to Colonial Office London. British Library, IOR/V/10/553, File 1149/181–184.

Lockwood, A. 2013. 'Black Europe body politics: towards an Afropean decolonial aesthetics', *Social Text*, 15 July. Available at: https://socialtextjournal.org/periscope_article/black-europe-body-politics-towards-an-afropean-decolonial-aesthetics/ (accessed 23 July 2017).

London Safeguarding Children Board. 2018. 'Safeguarding children exposed to extremist ideology'. Available at: www.londoncp.co.uk/chapters/sg_ch_extremist.html (accessed 3 September 2019).

Lorde, A. 2007. *Sister Outsider: Essays and Speeches by Audre Lorde*. Berkeley: Crossing Press.

Lowe, L. 2015. *The Intimacies of Four Continents*. Durham, NC: Duke University Press.

Lowthorpe, P., dir. 2017. *Three Girls* [television miniseries]. London: Studio Lambert and BBC Studios.

Lugones, M. 2008. 'The coloniality of gender', *Worlds and Knowledges Otherwise*, 2: 1–17.

Lugones, M. 2011. 'Toward a decolonial feminism', *Hypatia*, 25(4): 742–759.

Luibhéid, E. and Cantú Jr., L., eds. 2005. *Queer Migrations: Sexuality, U.S. Citizenship, and Border Crossings*. Minneapolis: University of Minnesota Press.

MacDonald, A. 2012. 'The identity thieves of the Indian Ocean: forgery, fraud and the origins of South African immigration control, 1890s–1920s', *Proceedings of the British Academy*, 179(0): 253–276.

Mair, L. P. 1944. *Welfare in the British Colonies*. London: Royal Institute of International Affairs.

Madhwi. 2015. 'Recruiting indentured labour for overseas colonies, circa 1834–1910', *Social Scientist*, 43(9/10): 53–68.

Margulies, J. D. 2019. 'On coming into animal presence with photovoice', *Environment and Planning E: Nature and Space*, online first, 30 May. https://doi.org/10.1177/2514848619853060.

Martin, L. 2011. 'The geopolitics of vulnerability: children's legal subjectivity, immigrant family detention and US immigration law and enforcement policy', *Gender, Place and Culture*, 18(4): 477–498.

Martin, L. 2012. 'Governing through the family: struggles over US noncitizen family detention policy', *Environment and Planning A*, 44(4): 866–888.

Marx, K. 2008. *Capital: A New Abridgement*. Oxford: Oxford University Press.

Maxwell, A. 2000. *Colonial Photography and Exhibitions: Representations of the Native and the Making of European Identities*. London: Bloomsbury.

May, R., and Cohen, R. 1974. 'The interaction between race and colonialism: a case study of the Liverpool race riots of 1919', *Race and Class*, 16(2): 111–126.

Mayblin, L. 2017. *Asylum after Empire: Colonial Legacies in the Politics of Asylum Seeking*. London: Rowman and Littlefield International.

Mbembe, A. 2003. 'Necropolitics', *Public Culture*, 15(1): 11–40.

Mbembe, A. 2017. *Critique of Black Reason*. Durham, NC: Duke University Press.

McClintock, A. 1995. *Imperial Leather*. London: Routledge.

McCulloch, J. 2000. *Black Peril, White Virtue: Sexual Crime in Southern Rhodesia, 1902–1935*. Bloomington: Indiana University Press.

McGregor, W. 1873. 'Report of the Inspector of Liberated Africans to the Chief Civil Commissioner, Seychelles'. National Archives, CO 882/3/11. File 463–477.

McGuiness, T. and Gower, M. 2017. 'House of Commons briefing paper: Deprivation of British citizenship and withdrawal of passport facilities'. London: House of Commons Library.

McKee, P. 2009. 'Racial strategies in Jane Eyre', *Victorian Literature and Culture*, 37(1): 67–83.

McKendrick, M. and Finch, J. 2015. '"Under heavy manners?": social work, radicalisation, troubled families and non-linear war', *British Journal of Social Work*, 47(2): 308–324.

McKeon, M. 2005. *The Secret History of Domesticity*. Baltimore: Johns Hopkins University Press.

McLaughlin, C. 2018. '"They don't look like children": child asylum-seekers, the Dubs amendment and the politics of childhood', *Journal of Ethnic and Migration Studies*, 44(11): 1757–1773.

McLennan, J. F. 1865. *Primitive 'Marriage': An Inquiry into the Origin of the Form of Capture in 'Marriage' Ceremonies*. Edinburgh: A. and C. Black.

McLoughlin, P. 2016. *Easy Meat: Inside Britain's Grooming Scandal*. London: New English Review Press.

McWhorter, L. 2009. *Racism and Sexual Oppression in Anglo-America: A Genealogy*. Bloomington and Indianapolis: Indiana University Press.

Mead, M. 1964. *Coming of Age in Samoa*. London: Routledge and Keegan Paul.

Meek, A. 2016. *The Catastrophe of Images: Biopolitical Media: Catastrophe, Immunity and Bare Life*. Abingdon: Routledge.

Mendoza, V. 2016. *Metroimperial Intimacies: Fantasy, Racial-Sexual Governance, and the Philippines in U.S. Imperialism, 1899–1913*. Durham, NC: Duke University Press.

Menski W. 1999. 'South Asian women in Britain, family integrity and the primary purpose rule', in *Ethnicity, Gender and Social Change*, edited by R. Barot, H. Bradley and S. Fenton, pp. 81–96. Palgrave Macmillan, London.

Metcalfe, T. 1998. *Ideologies of the Raj*. Cambridge: Cambridge University Press.

Mezzadra, S. and Neilson, B. 2013. *Border as Method, or, the Multiplication of Labor*. Durham, NC: Duke University Press.

Mignolo, W. 2011. *The Darker Side of Western Modernity: Global Futures, Decolonial Options*. Durham, NC: Duke University Press.

Mignolo, W. and Vazquez, R. 2013. 'Decolonial aestheSis: colonial wounds/decolonial healings', *Social Text*, 15 July. Available at: https://socialtextjournal.org/periscope_article/decolonial-aesthesis-colonial-woundsdecolonial-healings/ (accessed 30 July 2018).

Mill, J. 1817. *The History of British India*, vol. 2. London: Baldwin, Craddock and Joy.

Mills, C. 2017. *Black Rights/White Wrongs: The Critique of Racial Liberalism*. Oxford: Oxford University Press.

Mills, R. 1995. 'The confession as a "practice of freedom": feminism, Foucault and "elsewhere" truths', *Law Text Culture*, 2:100–117.

Mills, S. 2008. *Gender and Colonial Space*. Manchester: Manchester University Press.

Mitchell, T. 2000. *Colonising Egypt*. Berkeley: University of California Press.

Mitchinson, T. 2015. 'Editors comments: 'Killed because he looked Muslim' – neo-Nazi fascist marchers have the blood of a lovely old man on all their hands', *Star*, 28 August. Available at: www.thestar.co.uk/news/editor-s-comment-killed-because-he-looked-muslim-neo-nazi-fascist-marchers-have-the-blood-of-a-lovely-old-man-on-all-their-hands-1-7432452 (accessed 6 September 2018).

Modood, T. 2007. *Multiculturalism*. Cambridge: Polity Press.

Mody, P. 2002. 'Love and the law: love-marriage in Delhi', *Modern Asian Studies*, 36(1): 223–256.

Moffette, D. and Walters, W. 2018. 'Flickering presence: theorizing race and racism in the governmentality of borders and migration', *Global Movement Assemblages*, 12(1): 92–110.

Mohanty, C. 1984. 'Under Western eyes: feminist scholarship and colonial discourses', *boundary 2*, 12(3): 333–358.

Mohapatra, P. P. 2004. 'Assam and the West Indies, 1860–1920, immobilizing plantation labour', in *Masters, Servants and Magistrates in Britain and the Empire, 1562–1955*, edited by D. Hay and P. Cravens, pp. 455–480. Chapel Hill: North Carolina University Press.

Mongia, R. 1999. 'Race, nationality, mobility: a history of the passport', *Public Culture*, 11(3): 527–555.

Mongia, R. 2018. *Indian Migration and Empire: A Colonial Genealogy of the Modern State*. Durham, NC: Duke University Press.

Morgan, L. H. 1877. *Ancient Society*. Tucson: University of Arizona Press.

Morrison, T. 2014. *Beloved*. London: Vintage.

Mountz, A. and Hyndman, J. 2006. 'Feminist approaches to the global intimate', *Women's Studies Quarterly*, 34(1/2): 446–463.

Murphy-Bates, S. 2018. 'Kurds pay their respects as bodies of two British men who died after going to Syria to fight against ISIS arrive back at Heathrow', *Daily Mail*, 10 January. Available at: www.dailymail.co.uk/news/article-5255855/Bodies-two-Brits-went-fight-ISIS-repatriated.html British citizens killed by drone strikes after passports revoked (accessed 8 November 2018).

Nahaboo, Z. 2018. 'Rémy Ollier and imperial citizenship', *Interventions*, 20(5): 717–733.

Nandy, A. 1988. *The Intimate Enemy: Loss and Recovery of Self under Colonialism*. Oxford: Oxford University Press.

Neocleous, M. 2008. 'The dream of pacification: accumulation, class war and the hunt', *Journal of the Society for Socialist Studies*, 9(2): 7–31.

Neocleous, M. 2011. 'War on waste: law, original accumulation and the violence of capital', *Science and Society*, 75(4): 506–552.

Neti, L. 2014. 'Imperial inheritances', *Interventions*, 16(2): 197–214.

Nishiyama, H. 2015. 'Towards a global genealogy of biopolitics: race, colonialism, and biometrics beyond Europe', *Environment and Planning D: Society and Space*, 32(2): 331–346.

Nittle, N. 2018. 'The Serena Williams catsuit ban shows that tennis can't get past its elitist roots', *Vox*, 28 August. Available at: www.vox.com/2018/8/28/17791518/serena-williams-catsuit-ban-french-open-tennis-racist-sexist-country-club-sport (accessed 17 September 2018).

Oswin, N. and Olund, E. 2010. 'Governing intimacy', *Environment and Planning D*, 28: 60–67.

Owens, P. 2015. *Economy of Force: Counterinsurgency and the Historical Rise of the Social.* Cambridge: Cambridge University Press.

Pagden, A. 2003. 'Human rights, natural rights, and Europe's imperial legacy', *Political Theory*, 31(2): 171–199.

Pain, R. 2015. 'Intimate war', *Political Geography*, 44: 64–73.

Pain, R. and Staeheli, L. 2014. 'Introduction: intimacy-geopolitics and violence', *Area*, 46(4): 344–347.

Papadopoulos, D, Stephenson, N. and Tsianos, V. 2008. *Escape Routes: Control and Subversion in the Twenty-First Century.* London: Pluto Press.

Papadopoulos, D. and Tsianos, V. 2008. 'The autonomy of migration: the animals of undocumented mobility', *Translate*, 15 September. Available at: http://translate.eipcp.net/strands/02/papadopoulostsianos-strands01en (4 April 2017).

Parashar, S., Tickner, A. and True, J. 2018. *Revisiting Gendered States: Feminist Imaginaries in International Relations.* Oxford: Oxford University Press.

Parker, N. and Vaughan-Williams, N., eds. 2009. *Critical Border Studies.* London and New York: Routledge.

Parl. Deb. (series 3). 1888. 'Debate on Australian Colonies: Admission of Chinese Immigrants', vol. 326, col. 1514, 8 June.

Patterson, O. 1982. *Slavery and Social Death.* Harvard: Harvard University Press.

Peach, D. *et al.* 2015 'Needs analysis report following the sexual exploitation of children in Rotherham'. Salford: University of Salford and Rotherham Borough Council.

Pegler-Gordon, A. 2009. *In Sight of America: Photography and the Development of U.S. Immigration Policy.* Berkeley: University of California Press.

Perera, J. 2019. *The London Clearances: Race, Housing and Policing.* London: Institute for Race Relations.

Peterson, V. S., ed. 1992. *Gendered States: Feminist (Re)visions of International Relations Theory.* London: Lynne Rienner Publishers.

Peterson, V. S. 1999. 'Sexing political identities/nationalism as heterosexism', *International Feminist Journal of Politics*, 1(1): 34–65.

Peterson, V. S. 2014a. 'Sex matters: a queer history of hierarchies', *International Feminist Journal of Politics*, 16(3): 389–409.

Peterson, V. S. 2014b. 'Family matters: how queering the intimate queers the international', *International Studies Review*, 16(4): 604–608.

Peterson, V. S. 2017. 'Towards queering the globally intimate', *Political Geography*, 56: 114–116.

Philo, G., Byrant, E. and Donald, P. 2013. *Bad News for Refugees*. London: Pluto Press.

Picture Capital. 2016. 'United Family and Friends Campaign (UFFC) Annual Procession 2016' [video], YouTube, published 29 October. Available at: www.youtube.com/watch?v=QA68DbaSYYQ (accessed 16 September 2019).

Plonski, S. 2018. 'Material footprints: the struggle for borders by Bedouin-Palestinians in Israel', *Antipode*, online first, 13 March. https://doi.org/10.1111/anti.12388.

Povinelli, E. 2006. *Empire of Love*. Durham, NC: Duke University Press.

Povinelli, E. 2011. *Economies of Abandonment: Social Belonging and Endurance in Late Liberalism*. Durham, NC: Duke University Press.

Puar, J. 2008. *Terrorists Assemblages: Homonationalism in Queer Times*. Durham, NC: Duke University Press.

Puar, J. and Rai, A. 2002. 'Monster, terrorist, fag: the war on terrorism and the production of docile patriots', *Social Text*, 20(3): 117–148.

Quijano, A. 2007. 'Coloniality and modernity/rationality', *Cultural Studies*, 21(2–3): 168–178.

Rao, R. 2014. 'Queer questions', *International Feminist Journal of Politics*, 16(2): 199–217.

Rajaram, P. K. 2018. 'Refugees as surplus population: race, migration and capitalist value regimes', *New Political Economy*, 23(5): 627–639.

Rajchman, J. 1988. 'Foucault's art of seeing', *October*, 44: 88–117.

Razack, S. 2004. *Dark Threats and White Knights: The Somalia Affair, Peacekeeping and the New Imperialism*. Toronto: University of Toronto Press.

Razack, S. 2007. 'Stealing the pain of others: reflections on Canadian humanitarian responses', *Review of Education, Pedagogy, and Cultural Studies*, 29(4): 375–394.

Razack, S. 2008. *Casting Out: The Eviction of Muslims from Western Law and Politics*. Toronto: University of Toronto Press.

Razack, S., Malinda, S. and Thobani, S., eds. 2010. *The States of Race*. Toronto: Between the Lines.

Reid, J. and Dillon, M. 2009. *The Liberal Way of War: Killing to Make Life Live*. Abingdon: Routledge.

Rhys, J. [1966] 2000. *Wide Sargasso Sea*. London: Penguin.

Richter-Montpetit, M. 2014. 'Beyond the erotics of Orientalism. Lawfare, torture and the racial-sexual grammars of legitimate suffering', *Security Dialogue*, 45(1): 43–62.

Rifkin, M. 2015. *When Did Indians Become Straight? Kinship, the History of Sexuality, and Native Sovereignty*. Oxford: Oxford University Press.

Roberts, D. 1997. *Killing the Black Body: Race, Reproduction, and the Meaning of Liberty.* New York. Pantheon Books.

Roberts, D. 2015. 'Complicating the triangle of race, class and state: the insights of black feminists', *Ethnic and Racial Studies*, 37(10): 1776–1782.

Robinson, C. 1983. *Black Marxism: The Making of a Radical Tradition.* Chapel Hill: University of North Carolina Press.

Rodney, W. 2018. *How Europe Underdeveloped Africa.* London: Verso.

Ross, A. 2014. 'Deprivation of citizenship: what do we know?', *Immigration, Asylum and Nationality Law*, 28(4): 316–325.

Ross A. and Galey, P. 2014. 'Making UK citizens non-persons', *openDemocracy*, 3 February. Available at: www.opendemocracy.net/opensecurity/alice-ross-patrick-galey/making-uk-citizens-non-persons (accessed 3 July 2017).

Royston, J. and Mills, J. 2016. 'Tell us the tooth', *Sun*, 18 October. Available at: www.thesun.co.uk/news/2003927/mps-demand-dental-tests-of-child-migrants-asconcerns-grow-over-ages-of-asylum-kids-arriving-in-britain-who-look-closer-to-40 (accessed 8 March 2018).

Repo, J. 2013. 'The life function: the biopolitics of sexuality and race revisited', *Theory and Event*, 16(3).

Rutazibwa, O. U. and Shilliam, R. 2018. *Routledge Handbook of Postcolonial Politics.* Abingdon: Routledge.

Sabaratnam, M. 2017. *Decolonising Intervention: International Statebuilding in Mozambique.* London: Rowman and Littlefield International.

Sabir, R. 2017. 'Blurred lines and false dichotomies: integrating counterinsurgency into the UK's domestic "War on Terror"', *Critical Social Policy*, 37: 1–27.

Said, E. 1978. *Orientalism.* London: Penguin.

Sancto, C. 2018. 'Visibility in crisis: configuring transparency and opacity in We Are Here's political activism', *Invisible Culture: An Electronic Journal of Visual Culture*, 28. Available at: https://ivc.lib.rochester.edu/visibility-in-crisis-configuring-transparency-and-opacity-in-we-are-heres-political-activism/ (accessed 16 September 2019).

Sassen, S. 2016. 'At the systemic edge: expulsions', *European Review*, 24(1): 89–104.

Saucier, P. K. and Woods, T. P. 2014. 'Ex aqua: the Mediterranean Basin, Africans on the move, and the politics of policing', *Theoria: A Journal of Social and Political Theory*, 61(141): 55–75.

Scheel, S. 2019. *Autonomy of Migration?: Appropriating Mobility within Biometric Border Regimes.* Abingdon: Routledge.

Scheerhout, J. 2017. 'Four of the Rochdale grooming gang are fighting deportation – and only two are still in jail', *Manchester Evening News*, 3 July.

Available at: www.manchestereveningnews.co.uk/news/greater-manchester-news/rochdale-grooming-gang-jail-deported-13057964 (accessed 8 November 2018).

Scott, J. 2013. 'The distance between death and marriage', *International Feminist Journal of Politics*, 15(4): 534–551.

Scott, J. 2017. *Against the Grain*. New Haven: Yale University Press.

Semple, R. A. 2013. 'Christian model, mission realities: the business of regularizing family in mission communities in late nineteenth-century north India', *Journal of Colonialism and Colonial History*, 14(1). https://doi.org/10.1353/cch.2013.0003.

Sewell, T. 2018. 'Let's talk about gang culture's elephant in the room: absent black fathers', *Telegraph*, 28 August. Available at: www.telegraph.co.uk/news/2018/08/29/talk-gang-cultures-elephant-room-absent-black-fathers/ (accessed 11 September 2019).

Sexton, J. 2011. 'The social life of social death: on Afro-pessimism and black optimism', *InTensions*, 5: 1–47.

Shah, N. 2012. *Stranger Intimacy Contesting Race, Sexuality and the Law in the North American West*. Durham, NC: Duke University Press.

Sharpe, C. 2010. *Monstrous Intimacies: Making Post-Slavery Subjects*. Durham, NC: Duke University Press.

Sharpe, C. 2016. *In the Wake: On Blackness and Being*. Durham, NC: Duke University Press.

Shephard, B. 1986. 'Showbiz imperialism: the case of Peter Lobengula', in *Imperialism and Popular Culture*, edited by J. MacKenzie, pp. 94–112. Manchester: Manchester University Press.

Sherwood, H. 2017. 'Muslim population in Europe could more than double', *Guardian*, 29 November. Available at: www.theguardian.com/world/2017/nov/29/muslim-population-in-europe-could-more-than-double (accessed 5 September 2019).

Shilliam, R. 2013. 'Be.Bop 2012. Black Europe body politics', *Social Text*, 15 July. Available at: https://socialtextjournal.org/periscope_article/be-bop-2012-black-europe-body-politics (accessed 30 September 2018).

Shilliam, R. 2014. *The Black Pacific*. London: Bloomsbury.

Shilliam, R. 2018. *Race and the Undeserving Poor*. London: Pluto.

Shukla, N., ed. 2016. *The Good Immigrant*. London: Unbound.

Singha, R. 2000. 'Settle, mobilize, verify: identification practices in colonial India', *Studies in History*, 16(2): 151–198.

Sirriyeh, A. 2015. "'All you need is love and £18,600": class and the new UK family migration rules', *Critical Social Policy*, 35(2): 228–247.

Sivanandan, A. 1989. 'New circuits of imperialism', *Race and Class*, 30(4): 1–19.

Sleeman, H. W. 1839. '*A report on the system of megpunnaism or the murder of indigent parents for their young children (who are then sold as slaves) as it prevails in the Delhi territory and the native states of Rajpootana, Ulwar and Bhurtpore*'. Delhi: Serampore Press.

Smale, A. 2016. 'As Germany welcomes migrants, sexual attacks in Cologne point to a new reality', *New York Times*, 14 January. Available at: www.nytimes.com/2016/01/15/world/europe/as-germany-welcomes-migrantssexual-attacks-in-cologne-point-to-a-new-reality.html (accessed 7 November 2018).

Smith, E. and Marmo, M. 2014. *Race, Gender and the Body in British Immigration Control: Subject to Examination*. London: Palgrave.

Smith, S. 2012. 'Intimate geopolitics: religion, marriage, and reproductive bodies in Leh, Ladakh', *Annals of the Association of American Geographers*, 102(6): 1511–1528.

Smitherson, R. and White, C. 2017. 'Prevent duty: early help and children's social care extremism guidance and assessment support'. Birmingham: Birmingham City Council.

Sousa Santos, B. de. 2007. 'Beyond abyssal thinking: from global lines to ecologies of knowledges', *Review (Fernand Braudel Center)*, 30(1): 45–89.

Southall Black Sisters, 2001. *Forced Marriage: An Abuse of Human Rights*. London: Southall Black Sisters.

Spence, P. T. 1887. 'Memo. First Assistant to Governor General of Baluchistan: Deterrence against fanatics', Colonial Record India, British Library, IOR/L/MIL/17/13/21.

Spillers, H. J. 1987. 'Mama's baby, Papa's maybe: an American grammar book', *Diacritics*, 17(2): 64–81.

Spivak, G. C. 1985. 'Three women's texts and a critique of imperialism', *Critical Inquiry*, 12(1): 243–261.

Spivak, G. C. 1988. 'Can the subaltern speak?', in *Marxism and the Interpretation of Culture*, edited by C. Nelson and L. Grossberg, pp. 271–316. London: Macmillan.

Starkey, D. 2011. 'UK riots: it's not about criminality and cuts, it's about culture… and this is only the beginning', *Telegraph*, 19 August. Available at:

www.telegraph.co.uk/news/uknews/law-and-order/8711621/UK-riots-Its-not-about-criminality-and-cuts-its-about-culture...-and-this-is-only-the-beginning.html (accessed 10 July 2019).

Stevens, J. 1999. *Reproducing the State*. Princeton: Princeton University Press.

Stierl, M. 2016. 'A sea of struggle: activist border interventions in the Mediterranean Sea', *Citizenship Studies*, 20(5): 561–578.

Stierl, M. 2019. *Migrant Resistance in Contemporary Europe*. Abingdon: Routledge.

Stoler, A. L. 1995. *Race and the Education of Desire: Foucault's 'History of Sexuality' and the Colonial Order of Things*. Durham, NC: Duke University Press.

Stoler, A. L. 2002. *Carnal Knowledge and Imperial Power: Race and the Intimate in Colonial Rule*. Berkeley: California University Press.

Stoler, A. L., ed. 2006. *Haunted by Empire: Geographies of Intimacy in North American History*. Durham, NC: Duke University Press.

Stoler, A. L. 2016. *Duress: Imperial Durabilities in Our Times*. Durham, NC: Duke University Press.

Sturge, G. 2018. 'House of Commons briefing paper: UK prison population statistics'. London: House of Commons Library.

Sykes, P. 2016. 'Denaturalisation and conceptions of citizenship in the "War on Terror"', *Citizenship Studies*, 20(6–7): 749–763.

Taylor, C. 2012. 'Foucault and familial power', *Hypatia*, 27(1): 201–218.

Taylor, D. 2018. 'Home Office broke its own rules on avoiding family separations', *Guardian*, 11 March. Available at: www.theguardian.com/uk-news/2018/mar/11/home-office-broke-own-rules-family-separations-children-taken-into-care-father-deportation (accessed 10 July 2019).

Tazzioli, M. 2014. *Spaces of Governmentality: Autonomous Migration and the Arab Uprisings*. London: Rowman and Littlefield.

Tazzioli, M. and Walters, W. 2016. 'The sight of migration: governmentality, visibility and Europe's contested borders', *Global Society*, 30(3): 445–464.

Tepe-Belfrage, D., and Montgomerie, J. 2016. 'Broken Britain: post-crisis austerity and the trouble with the Troubled Families programme', in *Scandalous Economics: Gender and the Politics of Financial Crises*, edited by J. True, pp. 79–91. Oxford: Oxford University Press.

Thapar, C. 2015. 'Frantz Fanon's psychology of race, in photographs', *British Journal of Photography*, 5 November. Available at: www.bjp-online.com/2015/11/bruno-boudjelal-frantz-fanon (accessed 6 November 2017).

Thatcher, M. 1982. 'TV Interview for BBC (Falklands)', Margaret Thatcher Foundation, 5 April. Available at: www.margaretthatcher.org/document/104782 (accessed 23 June 2019)

The Economist. 2017. 'Migrants with mobiles', 11 February. Available at: www.economist.com/international/2017/02/11/phones-are-now-indispensable-for-refugees (accessed 19 October 2018).

The Times, 2011. 'Revealed: conspiracy of silence on UK sex gangs', 5 January. Available at: www.thetimes.co.uk/article/revealed-conspiracy-of-silence-on-uk-sex-gangs-gpg5vqsqz9h (accessed 24 January 2018).

Thiara R. K., Roy, S. and Ng, P. 2015. 'Between the lines: lives of black and minority ethnic (BME) women: disclosure, help-seeking and professional responses', report by Imkaan and University of Warwick. Available at: https://drive.google.com/file/d/0B_MKSoEcCvQwM2tBZDJxV1R4LUk/view (accessed 28 July 2019).

Thomas, G. 2007. *The Sexual Demon of Colonial Power: Pan-African Embodiment and Erotic Schemes of Empire.* Bloomington: Indiana University Press.

Tichenor, D. 2002. *Dividing Lines: The Politics of Immigration Control in America.* Princeton: Princeton University Press.

Ticktin, M. 2016. 'What's wrong with innocence', Hot Spots, *Cultural Anthropology,* 28 June. Available at: https://culanth.org/fieldsights/whats-wrong-with-innocence (accessed 6 July 2017).

Torpey, J. 2009. *The Invention of the Passport: Surveillance, Citizenship and the State.* Cambridge: Cambridge University Press.

Tolia-Kelly, D. P. 2016. 'Feeling and being at the (postcolonial) museum: presencing the affective politics of "race" and culture', *Sociology,* 50(5): 896–912.

Townsend, M. 2018. 'UK admits only 20 unaccompanied child refugees in two years', *Guardian,* 3 November. Available at: www.theguardian.com/world/2018/nov/03/uk-admits-only-20-unaccompanied-child-refugees-in-two-years (accessed 7 March 2019).

Tozer, W. G. 1872. 'Letter to the Church Missionary Society', 16 October. National Archives, CO 882/3/11, File 471–472.

Trexler, R. 1995. *Sex and Conquest: Gendered Violence, Political Order and the European Conquest of the Americas.* Ithaca: Cornell University Press.

Tudor, A. 2018. 'Cross-fadings of racialisation and migratisation: the postcolonial turn in Western European gender and migration studies',

Gender, Place and Culture, online first, 27 February. https://doi.org/10.108 0/0966369X.2018.1441141.

Tufail, A. W. 2015. 'Rotherham, Rochdale, and the racialised threat of the "Muslim Grooming Gang"', *International Journal for Crime, Justice and Social Democracy*, 4(3): 30–43.

Turner, H. G. 1904. *A History of the Colony of Victoria*, vol. 2. London: Longmans Green.

Turner, J. 2014. 'The Family Migration Visa in the history of marriage restrictions: postcolonial relations and the UK border', *British Journal of Politics and International Relations*, 17(4): 623–643.

Turner, J. 2016. 'Governing the domestic space of the Traveller in the UK: family, home and the struggle over Dale Farm', *Citizenship Studies*, 20(2): 208–227.

Turner, J. 2017. 'Domesticating the 'troubled family': racialised sexuality and the postcolonial governance of family life in the UK', *Environment and Planning D: Society and Space*, 35(5): 933–950.

Turner, J. 2018. 'Internal colonisation: the intimate circulations of empire, race and liberal government', *European Journal of International Relations*, 24(4): 765–790.

Turner, J. and Vera Espinoza, M. 2019. 'The affective and intimate life of the Family Migration Visa: knowing, feeling and encountering the heter-onormative state', *Geopolitics*, online first, 25 April. https://doi.org/10.108 0/14650045.2019.1603994.

Tyler, I. 2010. 'Designed to fail: a biopolitics of British citizenship', *Citizenship Studies*, 14(1): 61–74.

Tyler, I. 2013. *Revolting Subjects: Social Abjection and Resistance in Neoliberal Britain*. London: Zed Books.

Vaughan-Williams, N. 2015. *Europe's Border Crisis: Biopolitical Security and Beyond*. Oxford: Oxford University Press.

Venn, C. 2009. 'Neoliberal political economy, biopolitics and colonialism: a transcolonial genealogy of inequality', *Theory, Culture and Society*, 26(6): 206–233.

Virdee, S. 2014. *Racism, Class and the Racialised Outsider*. London: Palgrave.

Virdee, S. 2019. 'Racialised capitalism: an account of its contested origins and consolidation', *Sociological Review*, 67(1): 3–27.

Virilio, P. 1989. *War and Cinema: The Logistics of Perception*. London: Verso.

Walia, H. 2014. *Undoing Border Imperialism*. Oakland: AK Press.

Wall, T. and Linnemann, T. 2014. 'Staring down the state: police power, visual economies, and the "war on cameras"', *Crime, Media, Culture*, 10(2): 133–149.

Walters, W. 2002. 'Deportation, expulsion, and the international police of aliens', *Citizenship Studies*, 6(3): 265–292.

Walters, W. 2004. 'Secure borders, safe haven, domopolitics', *Citizenship Studies*, 8(3): 237–260.

Walters, W. 2006. 'Border/control', *European Journal of Social Theory*, 9(2): 187–204.

Walters, W. 2012. *Governmentality: Critical Encounters*. Abingdon: Routledge.

Walters, W. 2016. 'The flight of the deported: aircraft, deportation and politics', *Geopolitics*, 21(2): 435–458.

Webb, A. 2017. '"Swanning back in"? Foreign fighters and the long arm of the state', *Citizenship Studies*, 21(3): 291–308.

Weber, C. 2016. *Queer International Relations: Sovereignty, Sexuality and the Will to Knowledge*. Oxford: Oxford University Press.

Webster, W. 1998. *Imagining Home: Gender, 'Race' and National Identity, 1945–1964*. London: University College London Press.

Weheliye, A. G. 2005. *Phonographies: Grooves in Sonic Afro-Modernity*. Durham, NC: Duke University Press.

Weheliye, A. G. 2014. *Habeas Viscus: Racialising Assemblages, Biopolitics and Black Feminist Theories of the Human*. Durham, NC: Duke University Press.

Wekker, G. 2016. *White Innocence: Paradoxes of Colonialism and Race*. Durham, NC: Duke University Press.

Welland, J. 2015. 'Liberal warriors and the violent colonial logics of "partnering and advising"', *International Feminist Journal of Politics*, 17(2): 289–307.

Wemyss, G. 2009. *The Invisible Empire: White Discourse, Tolerance and Belonging*. London: Ashgate.

Wemyss, G, Yuval-Davis, N. and Cassidy, K, 2018. '"Beauty and the beast": everyday bordering and sham marriage discourse', *Political Geography*, 66: 151–160.

Wexler, L. 2000. *Tender Violence: Domestic Vision in the Age of U.S. Imperialism*. Chapel Hill: University of North Carolina Press.

White, M. A. 2014. 'Archives of intimacy and trauma: queer migration documents as technologies of affect', *Radical History Review*, 120: 75–93.

Wilderson, F. 2010. *Red, White and Black: Cinema and the Structure of U.S. Antagonisms*. Durham, NC: Duke University Press.

Wilson, A. 2007. 'The forced marriage debate and the British state', *Race and Class*, 49(1): 25–38.

Wilson, A. 2014. 'Criminalising forced marriage in the UK: why it will not help women', *Open Democracy*, 13 January. Available at: www.opendemocracy.net/en/5050/criminalising-forced-marriage-in-uk-why-it-will-not-help-women/ (accessed 3 September 2019).

Wilson, A. 2018. 'Rotherham: the silencing of Muslim voices', *Open Democracy*, 23 August. Available at: www.opendemocracy.net/uk/amrit-wilson/rotherham-silencing-of-muslim-voices (accessed 6 September 2018).

Wilson, S. 2015. *Violated: A Shocking and Harrowing Survival Story from the Notorious Rotherham Abuse Scandal*. London: HarperCollins.

Wolfe, P. 2006. 'Settler colonialism and the elimination of the native', *Journal of Genocide Research*, 8(4): 387–409.

Woods, C. and Ross, A. 2013. 'Former British citizens killed by drone strike after having their passports cancelled', *Bureau of Investigative Journalism*, 22 February. Available at: www.thebureauinvestigates.com/stories/2013-02-27/former-british-citizens-killed-by-drone-strikes-after-passports-revoked (accessed 7 November 2018).

Wray, H. 2015. 'The "pure" relationship, sham marriages and immigration control', in *Marriage Rites and Rights*, edited by J. Miles, P. Mody and R. Probert, pp. 141–165. Oxford: Hart.

Wray, H. 2016. *Regulating Marriage Migration into the UK: A Stranger in the Home*. Abingdon: Routledge.

Wray, H., Kofman, E., Grant, S. and Peel, C. 2015. 'Family friendly? The impact on children of the family migration rules: a review of the financial requirements', project report. London: Children's Commissioner. Available at: www.barrowcadbury.org.uk/wp-content/uploads/2015/09/Childrens-Commissioner-and-JCWI-report-on-family-immigration-rules.pdf (accessed 23 September 2019).

Wright, S. and Drury, I. 2017. 'How old are they really? Damning verdict of face recognition software on "child" migrants as town hall chief say they'll take away benefits from any who fail age tests', *Daily Mail*, 20 October. Available at: www.dailymail.co.uk/news/article-3853816/Verdict-face-recognition-software-child-migrants.html (accessed 7 September 2018).

Wynter, S. 2003. 'Unsettling the coloniality of being/power/truth/freedom: towards the human, after man, its overrepresentation – an argument', *New Centennial Review*, 3(3): 257–337.

Young, A. 2017. 'When Britain can deport EU citizens – according to the law', *The Conversation*, 23 November. Available at: https://theconversation.com/when-britain-can-deport-eu-citizens-according-to-the-law-86896 (accessed 8 March 2019).

Yuval-Davis, N. 1997. *Gender and Nation*. London: Sage.

Yuval-Davis, N., Wemyss, G. and Cassidy, K. 2018. 'Everyday bordering, belonging and the reorientation of British immigration legislation', *Sociology*, 52(2): 228–244.

Index

EU authorised representative for GPSR:
Easy Access System Europe, Mustamäe tee 50,
10621 Tallinn, Estonia
gpsr.requests@easproject.com